The Legacy of the Holocaust

Psychohistorical Themes in the Second Generation

by
Robert M. Prince

OTHER

Other Press
New York

First softcover printing 1999

Copyright © 1985 by Robert Maurice Prince

10 9 8 7 6 5 4 3 2

Library of Congress Cataloging-in-Publication Data

Prince, Robert M., 1948–
    The legacy of the Holocaust : psychohistorical themes in the
  second generation / by Robert M. Prince.
       p.   cm.
    Originally published: Ann Arbor, Mich. : UMI Research Press,
  c1985. (Research in clinical psychology : no. 12). With new preface.
  Includes bibliographical references and index.
    ISBN 1-892746-26-3 (softcover)
    1. Children of Holocaust survivors—Psychology. 2. Holocaust,
Jewish (1939–1945)—Psychological aspects. I. Title. II. Series:
Research in clinical psychology ; no. 12.
D810.J4P699 1999
940.53'18—dc21

                           99-25641

For the Generations of the Holocaust

Contents

And I only am escaped alone to tell thee.

[Job 1:19]

Preface

I am very grateful to Other Press and Michael Moskowitz in particular for rediscovering *The Legacy of the Holocaust*, an almost thirty-year-old work. Holocaust studies, perhaps more than any others, acquire a provenance that significantly informs the subject. T*he Legacy of the Holocaust* began in 1971, intended as a doctoral dissertation in clinical psychology. At that time, the subject of survivorhood was an unexplored country and children of survivors were rumored but essentially unknown. After the completion of the doctoral dissertation at the end of 1974, I set out to publish it. The efforts of an agent who specialized in psychology as well as my own direct solicitation of interest among academic and trade publishers proved very disappointing. The typical response, when there was one, was that the editor could not foresee appreciable interest or a readership that would justify publication.

On the other hand, over the next ten years I was rewarded by letters and phone calls from dozens of graduate students who had managed to find the original doctoral dissertation and used it, to a greater or lesser degree, as a jumping-off point for their own work. *The Legacy of the Holocaust* was the first attempt to look at children of survivors in an in-depth way, exploring them in the context of their family relationships, their current cultural context, but above all, in relation to their connection to the Holocaust as a historical event of such magnitude that it can be termed a "historical *novum*." It was also the first attempt to use a "shared themes" approach that explored children of survivors in their individuality. I saw as its most significant contribution its attempt to look not only at the influence of family relations and the transmission of trauma across generations, but also at the impact of history, writ large, on the person's identity. I experienced special resistance in my attempt to generalize findings about children of survivors to demonstrate the impact of the Holocaust on the twentieth century. Nevertheless, during this period of time, the corpus of literature was expanding, first slowly, then exponentially. Despite the failure of the dissertation to become a book, I was extremely proud that, based on the feedback I was receiving, it was having a significant methodological and conceptual influence on the emerging work.

In 1984, after giving up any thought of seeing *The Legacy of the Holocaust* in print, UMI Research Press contacted me about its desire to issue it as Number 12 in its Research in Clinical Psychology Series edited by Peter Nathan. After some revisions, it was published in 1985. By this time, I was speaking at various university colloquia and medical center grand rounds. One recurring criticism directly challenged what I considered to be among the major findings of the study. I had concluded that there is tremendous diversity among children of survivors along most of the major dimensions of personhood—in personality styles; in preferred modes of interpersonal relationships; in relationships to parents; in attitudes, ideas, and beliefs; in Jewish identification; and in conscious identification and self-attribution of the importance of having been a child of survivors. I felt that I had demonstrated through the in-depth analysis of shared themes that the Holocaust had an overwhelmingly powerful impact on each individual, providing a basic cornerstone of identity, but in an entirely unique way on each individual. These critics insisted that the lack of *consistent* or *uniform* effects meant no effects. I see this response as but one derivative of "psychic numbing," a response to trauma based on a desymbolizing attack on meaning in the service of cutting off feelings, which, if allowed into existence, would be overwhelming. I see all of the Holocaust studies as entailing a struggle against psychic numbing.

As *The Legacy of the Holocaust* took its place in the growing corpus of literature, belying the attribution ten years earlier of insufficient interest, a new dismissal was in the air having to do with what was now being derisively called "The Holocaust industry," of which it was now presumably a part. It seems to me that both these attributions are important as examples of resistances to knowing about the Holocaust. As I have tried to show lately, one of the great myths about the Holocaust is that survivors didn't want to talk. Indeed, there has been a "conspiracy of silence," but from the outside in. Over and over it can be demonstrated that where survivors have a need to tell their story, the rest of the world is motivated to avoid what the survivor has to say. It might then be asked: How have Holocaust studies come so far?

At least one answer is suggested by simultaneously looking at a time line of Holocaust studies and of survivor families as they reconstituted. Modest arithmetic calculations disclose that the trickle of investigations of survivor families and their children began just as children born in the period 1946 to 1950 reached their early twenties, the earliest possible age that would put them in the position of conducting serious research. This observation speaks to one of the few discrete traits that this study found children of survivors to have in common: children of survivors universally want to pass on knowledge of the Holocaust to their own children. Thus, in the face of psychic numbing, Holocaust studies had to wait for the children of survivors of the Holocaust to come of age and promote its study.

The data in this book was collected thirty years ago. Even then I argued, to the consternation of many who wanted a more definitive statement, that it was embedded in time and culture. Why then be interested in it? I would like to think the answer is because all trauma, and especially what I have termed historical trauma, is about the struggle between meaning and numbing. The meaning of trauma is not fixed but expands and evolves; eventually the impact of trauma is determined as much by what comes after it as by the original circumstances. Thus the news of today, the newer genocides, the resurgence of anti-Semitism in Germany, the stonewalling of the Swiss banks as they hoard plundered treasures, provide a new lens through which to view the lives of young adult children of survivors. And the reason for viewing their lives should be that the legacy of the Holocaust is not reserved for survivors and their families. Try to refuse it or not, it is bequeathed to us all.

Robert Prince, Ph.D.
Great Neck, N. Y.
March 1, 1998

Acknowledgments

This study was originally conceived at a time just before research interest in children of Holocaust survivors became apparent. The magnet that drew me to the subject resides in my personal history. Because of my closeness to the subject, the work was often painful. The work was often a lonely enterprise as well: I did not come across other children of survivors who, like myself, were becoming or about to become investigators. For these reasons, I am especially and deeply grateful to those who provided me with both emotional and substantive support.

First, I wish to express my gratitude to Beatrice Beebe, who reviewed each chapter as it was written and provided suggestions and encouragement throughout. I want to thank Arnold Rachman, for helping me understand the meaning of portions of the data, and most of all, for helping guide me to an understanding of my personal relationship to what I was writing.

I also wish to thank a number of people whom I met as I pursued this work and whose interest and spontaneous offers of encouragement and assistance are appreciated. Robert Liebert went out of his way to make time to discuss the psychohistorical perspective of the Holocaust with me. DeWitt Crandell similarly gave generously of his time and support. During the pursuit of this work, teachers, clinical supervisors, and colleagues responded with interest and encouragement. I would like to thank Morton Deutsch, Paul Byers, Leah Lapidus, and Rosalea Schonbar.

Similarly I would like to thank Rita Frankiel, Joanne Medalie, and Robert Berk, who discussed and encouraged the work. Gail Albert and Harry Albert provided a critical reading of the first draft.

In the years between the completion of the original research and its revisions for publication, the interest of a number of people was important in helping me revise and develop concepts. In particular, Dori Laub provided inspiration through the development of the Video Archive for Holocaust Testimony Project at Yale. His dedication and sensitivity continue to be a model for me. Similarly, Judith Kestenberg has been a model through her blend of the compassionate and scientific spirit. Martin Wangh went out of his way to read and comment on this manuscript and I was touched by his courtesy and interest. Nanette Auerhan helped me refine some ideas and themes, both through her direct comments and through the example of her own fine work. I wish also to thank Sylvia Axelrod for her helpful comments about parts of this work.

Most personally, I thank members of my family. It was the European experience of my parents that inspired me. My mother, Magda Prince, escaped from rural Hungary just before anti-Semitism reached its crescendo there. My father, Alex Prince, survived a Nazi slave labor camp. This book is implicitly dedicated to them in gratitude for what they taught me.

I wish to thank Ivan and Evan who have, through letting me participate in their adolescence, shared the realities of their world and have thus given me an additional perspective, one three generations removed.

Finally, I deeply thank my wife Andrea and my son, Aaron, for it is they who finally enable me to have knowledge of the Holocaust. It is in becoming a husband and father that I came to understand all that it means to have—and thus to appreciate—the awful possibility of loss. Before I had this understanding, I could not understand the Holocaust.

1

Introduction

I tell you what I know! My brothers died here—but my brothers built this place; our hearts have cut these stones.

[A. Miller, 1965, p. 162]

The exact numbers are not known and are probably not important, but it is estimated that in the 30-odd principal Nazi concentration camps, 7,125,000 out of 7,820,000 inmates, most of them Jews, died between the years 1939 and 1945 (Kogan, 1971). Lifton's (1971) comments on another milestone of this century, the atomic destruction of Hiroshima, are appropriate here as well: historical man's encounter with the concentration camps must surely represent a tragic turning point in his experience of himself. The survivor of the holocausts of the twentieth century is "thrust into special prominence, and imposes upon us all a series of immersions into death which mark our existence" [Lifton, 1969, p. 479]. At the same time, the experience of the survivor mobilizes in us all a "psychic numbing" [Lifton, 1967, p.509] to defend against our vicarious participation in it, because the drama that takes place in the deepest recesses of our individual and collective unconscious occurred for him in reality. The image of the survivor, mediated through the universal symbols of dreams and fantasies, confronts the dark side of human nature and transcends the boundaries of historical time and geographical space. We all, in our psychic representations of self and other, participate in the experiences of both the victims and perpetrators of the Holocaust.

The experience of the survivor was to be uprooted from his home and robbed of all his possessions. The survivor's love objects were taken from him, brutalized, and murdered, sometimes in front of him. He was starved, beaten, and tortured. Sometimes his life was saved at the price of the death of another, sometimes at the price of debasing and prostituting himself. Even when this was not the reality, it was often the concentration camp survivor's fantasy (Krystal, 1968). But, as Niederland (Krystal, 1968) wrote, "The trauma of being outlawed, outcast, and reduced to the state of unwelcome vermin has to be considered in addition to the actual cruelties suffered by the victims . . . " [pp.

20-21]. The concentration camp survivor experienced nothing less than the destruction of all the actual and psychological pillars on which one's identity normally is based. As Bychowski (Krystal, 1968) wrote, "we see a picture characterized by the destruction of his world, the destruction of the basic landmarks on which the world of human beings in our civilization is based, i.e., basic trust in human worth, basic confidence, basic hope" [p. 81]

As might be expected, the concentration camp experience did not end for the survivors with their liberation. The post-traumatic sequelae have been well documented (Eitinger, 1973; Herz, 1967; Hoppe, 1968; Krystal, 1968; Tuteur, 1970). One common pattern, called "post concentration camp syndrome" was described by Niederland (1968):

> a pervasive depressive mood and morose behavior and a tendency to withdrawal, general apathy, alternating with occasional short-lived angry outbursts, feelings of helplessness and insecurity, lack of initiative and interest, and the prevalence of self-deprecatory attitudes and expressions [p. 12].

Niederland went on to describe other common features of the syndrome: "anxiety and agitation resulting in insomnia and nightmares, motor unrest, inner tension, tremulousness, fear of renewed persecution, often culminating in paranoid ideation and reactions" [p. 12]. Krystal (1968) described prevalent permanent characterological changes. These included the "development of a passive aggressive personality, the permanent inhibition in ability for sexual initiative and potency, severe inhibition of intellectual functioning, memory, and interest in anything outside work and home routine" [p.3]. Niederland (Krystal, 1968) summarized the "survivor syndrome" as including the three features of reactive depression, anxiety syndrome, and survival guilt. He also noted that there were often paranoid elements and feelings that life began with the trauma. According to him, other symptoms resulting from the concentration camp experience were "propitiatory and expiatory tendencies, denial of aggression with masochistic features, brooding absorption in past and present events, obsessive compulsive ruminations, permanent feelings of loss and sadness, partial and complete somatization of complaints" [p.66].

The symptoms included in the survivor syndrome encompass virtually the entirety of the diagnostic manual, suggesting that this syndrome is more than just another category in the psychiatric nomenclature. It has a special relationship to our history and culture, defined by our continuing identification with the survivor as the symbol of both our own unconscious experiences and the events of our time. To tolerate our own vicarious experience of the images of Dachau, Hiroshima, My Lai, Bangladesh, and the poverty on the streets around us, we must all engage in some degree of the same "psychic closing off"—defined as simply ceasing to feel (Lifton, 1967)—that the survivor used to defend himself against total psychological destruction. Our basic response to the survivor, who embodies our worst fantasies of both the consequences of our own aggression and our own vulnerability, is to try to blind ourselves to him. (This is seen in the refusal for many years of the German reparation agencies to consider psychiatric impairment resulting from massive trauma as a basis for financial restitution.)

The difficulties psychotherapists have found in dealing with the survivor is one measure of the emotional difficulties with which the survivor confronts us. Winnik (1966) perceived an "inner hesitation and embarrassment" to approach the "emotionally charged" issues of survivorhood in a "scientific spirit" [p.3]. Krystal (1968) wrote that the concentration camp survivor provokes "a variety of emotional responses, such as guilt and anxiety or disgust, because of the threat implied to our own denial of death or cowardice" [p.29] Klein (Krystal, 1968) wrote of survivors:

> Such a patient presents a problem of counter-transference for the therapist. The therapist who faces suffering and life experiences of such magnitude is liable to have impulses to act out his own guilt feelings because he himself didn't suffer or didn't do enough during the holocaust to fight the 'evil.' He may have to deal with nurturing impulses to turn into a good mother, one who gives and receives. . . . A frequent reaction to such counter-transference is the use of isolation mechanisms. . . . [p. 240].

Finally, Kestenberg (1972) observed that psychoanalysts resisted "the unearthing of the frightening impact of Nazi persecution on children of survivors" [p. 315]. She reported that many of the psychoanalysts who had treated children of survivors were, when surveyed by her, startled by her inquiry "because it never occurred to them to link their patients' dynamics to the history of their parents' persecution" [p. 315].

Focus of the Study and Review of the Literature

If the survivors of Nazi persecution directly confront our consciousness within historical, psychological, and moral contexts, then their children are the legacy of that confrontation. The present study concerns itself with the exploration of the lives of a group of children of survivors who are now approaching or are at the age at which their parents became victims and survivors of the Holocaust.

The literature through 1976 on children of survivors was comprised of passing references to them in the survivor literature itself, a number of case reports, and a scattering of formal investigations. The emphasis of the literature is the exploration of the effect of the survivors' past traumatization on their relationship with their children and the consequences for the latter's evolving personalities. To a lesser extent, the literature emphasizes the impact on their own functioning of survivors' children's knowledge of their parents' past experiences.

The Dynamics of Survivor Families

One pervasive theme of the survivor literature involves the difficulties they experienced in reinvesting in life (Krystal, 1968). Sometimes, as Tanay (Krystal, 1968) pointed out, the survivor needed to maintain the experience of living in a concentration camp. Krystal (1968) suggested that the survivor was deeply ambivalent about engaging in a new family. He described the survivor's conflict as follows:

> As a result of such experience [of persecution] the attitudes toward the world are permanently modified. There is a fear of bringing another generation into being.... The survivors of Nazi persecution, after consciously rejecting the idea of having children, had an extremely high rate of miscarriages and a low birth rate. The median in survivor families falls considerably below two children per family. The only reason that the survivors had any children at all was a need (working in the opposite direction) to try to undo the destruction magically by creating a family as soon as possible... [p. 192]

The observation of the role of survivors as parents which dominates the literature is that the relationships of survivor parents to their children "are too strongly determined by the past and not adequately by the children's needs" [Sigal, 1971, p.57]. On the one hand, they were observed to have tremendous difficulties meeting their children's needs; on the other hand there was much that they needed from their children.

Krystal (1968) wrote that survivor mothers frequently found themselves "bewildered about their role as mothers." He observed that they had lost access to "the introjected prototype of the good mother." He continued:

> As a result, we see, in increasing numbers, children of survivors suffering from problems of depression and inhibition of their own functioning. The survivor mothers tended to need a symbiotic relationship with their children and the dread of their own aggression interfered with their children's accomplishment of successful individuation and separation. Hence we see pathological symbiotic relationships between mothers and their children.... This is a clear example of social pathology being transmitted to the next generation [p. 193].

Similarly, Sonnenberg (1974) reported that a workshop held during the fall, 1971 meeting of the American Psychoanalytic Association in in New York City had concluded that, in survivor parents, "there is a disruption of 'integration for parenthood.' Ego functions necessary for child rearing are lost, to some degree, in each survivor. Capacity to reintegrate varies" [p. 202].

One constellation that Aleksandrowicz (1973) observed in an unspecified proportion of the survivor families he studied was what he called the "Affective Deficiency Syndrome," which was characterized by flatness and void attributable to massive repression of traumatic memories. Klein (1973) saw as the central feature of parent-survivors a continued mourning while raising their children. Lipkowitz (1973) saw three consequences of the "chronically depressed and withdrawn" state of survivor mothers: the inability to assist the child in the task of separation; the inability to inspire basic trust; and the "cueing" of the child for symbiosis.

For Rakoff et al. (1966), the central failure of survivor families was a "lack of true emotional engagement" between parents and children as a consequence both of the parents' lack of resources for the child and of their needs from the child. She attributed parents' lack of resources to their "total preoccupation with tormenting memories and with an unending re-living of their traumatic past" [p. 211]. To this, Sigal and Rakoff (1971) added that the parents' preoccupation resulted in a lack of energy to control their children. Sigal (1971) added that parents lacked the necessary "flexibility" to cope with their children.

Sigal observed that survivor parents had expectations of their children that were rooted in the past. Sigal and Rakoff (1971) wrote that survivors' children "were seen as the overvalued representation of all the relatives lost in the holocaust of European Jewry" [p. 393]. Rosenberger (1973) specified two types of survivor parents. The first type disregarded "the children's emotional needs and are obsessed instead with the need to provide food and goods in order to prevent hunger and material deprivation as they had experienced in Europe" [p. 375]. The second type identified "almost totally with the growing child, reliving their childhood through him or believing in identification with their own deceased parents" [p. 375]. In addition, Sonnenberg (1974) reported that survivor parents identified their children with their own murdered siblings. Parents often forced their offspring "into a mold reflecting parental expectations for the dead child" [p. 202].

Both Trossman (1968) and Barocas and Barocas (1973) observed that survivors' children became the object of parents' savior fantasies. Barocas and Barocas wrote: "The child is frequently forced to take on the burden of having to fulfill not only his own developmental needs but also his parents' unrealistic expectations in that he must compensate for the parents' sense of worthlessness" [p. 821]. Trossman (1968) wrote: "Perhaps the most deleterious parental attitude is . . . that this child must provide meaning for the parents' empty lives, that he must vindicate all the suffering they must have endured" [p. 122].

Another dimension of the parent-child relationship which appeared to have its roots in the past is parental concern for their children's safety. Trossman (1968) reported that parents were "excessively overprotective, constantly warning their children of impending danger" [p. 122]. Sonnenberg (1974) reported the consensus of a workshop held during the fall, 1971 meeting of the American Psychoanalytic Association that survivor parents experienced profound anxiety about their children. Klein (1971) observed that survivor parents in the kibbutz displayed an "inappropriate emotional and physical response" to their first-born children. He wrote: "These parents have lived in fear that something terrible would happen to the children, especially in infancy: this has continued for many years" [p. 73].

Another dynamic attributed to survivors' families involves issues of parental control. Rakoff et al. (1966) wrote: "Limit-setting may be either rigid or chaotically ineffectual, but rarely related to the needs of the child . . . "[p. 24].

Sigal and Rakoff (1971) found that, when compared to the clinic records of a control group, the records of survivor families showed greater difficulties around issues of control. Aleksandrowicz (1973) also observed that parents' attitudes toward their children in 21 out of 25 families were characterized by "a combination of pampering with inconsistent discipline because of unresolved guilt and/or overcompensated aggression" [p. 387].

A number of investigators have called attention to the rule of aggression in survivor families. Krystal (1968) wrote:

> The aggression in the survivor family, as well as the delayed work of mourning and adolescence, produce a syndrome of explosion in the families of survivors. The adults may completely suppress their aggression, but their children, born in this country, develop aggressive and delinquent behavior. In this way, the aftermath of Nazi persecution is already affecting the next generation [p. 60]

Kestenberg (1973) raised the possibility that "the pathology of parents who have been exposed to Nazi persecution can produce bizarre sadomasochistic interchanges between parent and child as a result of 'identification with the aggressor' " [p. 360]. Trossman (1968) reported that one survivor's child he treated was addressed by his parents by some derogatory name, such as "Stupid" or "Fool" rather than his given name. Both Sigal (1971) and Barocas and Barocas (1973) speculate that survivor parents may have communicated subtle cues for their children to act out aggression and thus provide vicarious gratification for themselves.

In evaluating the above characterizations of survivor families, it must be emphasized that, for the most part, they are the product of impressions. One danger in drawing definitive conclusions from them is that the nature of the material is such that there is a natural tendency to generalize from a few dramatic examples. Thus it is not surprising that one finds contradictions both between and within studies. For example, Aleksandrowicz (1973) wrote of the survivor families he observed: "In some cases there were also excessive expectations, a wish for the child to compensate the parent for his or her loss of opportunities" [p. 387]. At the same time, three pages later (pp. 390-91), Aleksandrowicz specifically noted that he could not replicate Trossman's (1968) or Rakoff's (1966) observations of excessive parental expectations, particularly that "the children be a continuation of the parents' tragic lives." He also noted that he could not replicate their observation that parents were overprotective of their children. Aleksandrowicz attributed the differences between his and Trossman's and Rakoff's observations to the fact that the latter investigators had studied "lonely aliens" while he studied Israeli families. He also felt that the constellations of behavior reported by them were typical of Jewish families in general.

Klein (1971), who studied Israeli families living on kibbutzim, did find that overprotectiveness was a characteristic of survivor families. However, he specifically noted that "inhibition of affectivity or emotional ability for nurturing in the mothers was not observed" [p. 86]. One may attribute Klein's negative findings to the fact that he was the only investigator to study a nonclinic population. At the same time, Sigal and Rakoff (1971) reported the finding, based on the comparison of clinic records of survivor and control families, that there was no greater "dysphoria" in the survivor families. They did find, however, that in survivor families there was more overvaluing of the identified patient. They were also the only investigators to report more sibling fighting in survivor families than in control families.

Characteristics of Children of Survivors

The emphasis of the literature describing the children of survivors has been on the psychopathological consequences of family dynamics. For example, Aleksandrowicz (1973) introduced his study by asking the question, "Do the psychic scars carried by people who survived such an ordeal affect the mental health of their children?" [p. 385]. Barocas and Barocas (1973) believed that the survivor syndrome characterized the second generation as well as the first. They wrote:

> Based on clinical experience with such patients [children of survivors] our impression is that these individuals present symptomatology and psychiatric features that bear a striking resemblance to the concentration camp survival syndrome described in the international literature [p. 820].

Several investigators concluded that common symptomatology characterized children of survivors. Rustin and Lipsig (1972), on the basis of conducting psychotherapy with late adolescent children of concentration camp survivors, reported finding "a cluster of common clinical characteristics." Specifically, they reported: "Consistent evidence of depression and guilt as well as confusion attendant to the subject's identity both as a Jew and an American appears in each and every record" [p. 87]. Sigal and Rakoff (1971) observed that children brought to their clinic "appeared to have a range of psychopathology but a core of one or more of the following: depressive features leading to suicidal attempts in some cases, a variety of school problems and excessive quarreling among the children" [p. 393]. Rakoff et al. (1966) also described the following characteristics: "Lack of appropriate involvement in the world; often apathy, depression, and emptiness appear. . . . There may be an agitated hyperactivity reflecting great dissatisfaction with parents, themselves, and society at large"[p. 24]. Sigal (1971) characterized children of survivors, in their teen years, by a "sense of anomie and a lack of sense of identity"[p. 57].

The attribution of specific symptomatology, or behavioral traits, to children of survivors has not, however, been completely supported. Sigal et al. (1973), working on the assumption that "homogeneity of parental experience may lead to a particular homogeneity of behavior in their children," obtained 25 survivor families and 20 control families from the files of their clinic. They administered a Child Behavior Inventory (CBI) and a Behavior Problem Check List (BPC) to parents of children between the ages of 8 and 14 years and 15 and 17 years. They also administered a Brief Mental Health Questionnaire (BMHQ) to the children in the 8- to 14-year-old group. They administered the BMHQ and two additional measures of alienation and anomie to the 15- to 17-year-old group. In the 8- to 14-year-old group they found no significant differences between the survivor and control groups. In the 15- to 17-year-old group, the survivors' children were scored significantly higher than the controls on all three subtests of the BPC. These were "conduct problem (unsocialized aggression, psychopathy)," "personality problem (neurotic-disturbed)," and "inadequacy-immaturity." On the CBI the survivors' children scored significantly higher on the following subtests: "Child shows excessive dependence" and "Child tests limits." They showed significantly lower scores on the subtest "Child shows good coping behavior." There were no significant differences on "Child shows healthy independence," "Child curbs aggression," and "Child does not curb aggression." It must be pointed out that both the BPC and the CBI were scored by parents about their children and may therefore reflect only the style of survivor parents' perceptions of their children. Although the 15- to 17-year-old survivors' children scored significantly higher on the BMHQ, one may wonder about the validity of a 22-item mental health questionnaire. On what would seem the most important instrument, the measures of alienation and anomie, the survivors' children tended to score higher than the controls but not significantly so.

Rustin (1971) hypothesized that children of survivors, when compared to children from similar socioeconomic backgrounds, would show differences in guilt, hostility, and Jewish identification. Using standardized, paper-and-pencil measures of each variable, he was forced to conclude:

> The findings of this study tend not to support the widely held clinical belief that the effects of traumatic experiences upon one generation are transmitted to their offspring. In the areas investigated, the similarities between the groups were greater than the differences [p. 95]

Klein (1971) reported that none of the 25 children studied by him showed any "conspicuous disturbance." He also found that survivors' children's relationships with their peers were characterized by "warmth and feelings of security and belongingness." At the same time, he reported that the survivors' children tended to stay as much as possible with their parents and to dislike even short separations. Difficulties with aggression were also manifested. Klein (1971) wrote:

> When confronted with open aggression (from children and adults as well) or with danger of war, the children's tendency is to react passively, to escape, to hide, to cry, to stick to the group of children, and not to respond by active aggression [p. 83].

Another approach to the study of children of survivors has been to examine their psychodynamics in the context of their awareness of their parents' experiences. For example, Lipkowitz (1973) felt that, if the patient he treated was representative of children of survivors, "It is the awareness of the parents' previous horrors, denied and personalized, which leads to psychiatric illness in their children" [p. 141].

Several investigators have called attention to the patterns of identification of children of survivors. For example, Klein (1973) wrote:

> In some cases, identification with the fantasy image of the parent is at the expense of libidinal investment. Interpersonal relationships within the family are characterized by awe, respect, and an affirmation of solidarity rather than intimacy [p. 401].

Sonnenberg (1974) reported a "trend to psychopathy," that is, a need "to get away with things," on the part of survivors' children, based on their identification with a parent who "got away." Kestenberg (1972) cited Blos (1968) who repeatedly found in survivors' children an identification with relatives who had died during the Holocaust. Kestenberg (1972) reported a patient of her own who behaved in a "bizarre way, starving himself in woods and treating me in transference as a hostile persecutor" [p. 311]. She reported that his symptoms abated when she connected them to the real experience of his parents in Europe. Sonnenberg (1974) reported that children of survivors "acted out parental experiences as they either knew or fantasized them" [p. 203] In some cases, they experienced paranoid, psychotic feelings of persecution.

Sonnenberg also reported that survivors' children, in addition to identification with the victim, also experienced contradictory identifications with Nazis which led to "ego-splitting." Lipkowitz (1973) found that guilt had been produced in his patient both by identification with his guilt-ridden parent and identification with Nazi aggression. Lipkowitz believed that the identification with the Nazis was fostered by, first, attempts to separate from the mother, and, second, by the Oedipal conflict. He also pointed out that the

Oedipal conflict was intensified by the fact that the father had been overpowered and imprisoned.

In contrast, Klein (1973) felt that survivors' children's identifications with images of the parents' past, while they had a telling effect on the resolution of the Oedipus complex, was not necessarily deleterious. He wrote:

> The 'experienced fairy tales' of the children of survivors, with their recurring themes of danger, death, and salvation, as well as their emotional content have a telling effect on the resolution of the oedipal conflicts in their sons. The internalization of the father-image as victim of aggression and as hero who was miraculously saved for the sake of the children results in the diminishing of castration fears derived from the original oedipal constellation. Instead of perceiving the father as a threatening aggressor who metes out punishment for libidinal fantasies, the sons tended to identify with the fathers and project their fears onto fantasized external aggressors [p. 401].

Klein also questioned the assertion that the child's knowledge of the past was necessarily traumatic. He observed that the children he studied responded to such knowledge by emphasizing its triumphant and heroic aspects. He found that knowledge of the past contributed to the children's identity formation by providing a sense of historical continuity. Klein also found that the fantasies that were generated in the children provided them with "a sense of security and cathartic relief from their anxieties. In some cases, the children believed that their parents' triumph over extreme danger left them invulnerable to present or future dangers" [p. 401]. Klein (1971) also noted: "The children in the kibbutzim do not identify fully with the victims in their parents; they view the traumatic past somehow as a lost battle, compensated for by more recent victorious ones leading to the rebirth of Israel" [p. 73].

Furman (1973) observed that a survivor's child she treated from childhood, during his early adolescence became deeply interested in the events of World War II. She felt that he utilized the imagery of the past, which found its way into his fantasy life as he "struggled with pregenital and homosexual impulses as well as with attempting to develop an independent identity" [p. 383]. During the patient's prepuberty years, Furman helped his parents explain to him "phenomena he observed and found confusing, e.g., the numbers branded on his mother's arm, her panic at police dogs, her reaction to certain topics" [p. 383]. Furman's feelings were that such information "reassured him more than upset him as it strengthened his reality testing" [p. 383].

Some reports emphasized the special resources of children of survivors. For example, Kestenberg (1972) quoted Brody's observations of the two children of survivors she had treated: "Behavior of both patients not typical. Both impress all observers as having better ego strength than their overt behavior would suggest. Both show a kind of perversity in surrender to irrational impulses, and in disrupting object relationships" [p. 315]. Williams

(1973) also focused on strengths in children of survivors. She challenged Laufer's (1973) interpretation that his patient's normal infantile omnipotence had been damaged by "the atmosphere of vulnerability and death within which he grew up" [p. 383]. Williams felt that a good deal of omnipotence had survived. She also dealt with the question: "How was it possible for this boy, who appeared to be a very disturbed young adolescent and whose life had been cruelly disrupted so many times, to emerge as a comparatively well-functioning human being?" [p. 368]. Williams concluded that he must have "felt like a very loved child." She wrote: "From a negative point of view one could look at the mother's influence . . . in terms of her grief and depression. But this assumption omits the influence of her drive and determination which are outstanding features of courage" [p. 369]. Williams felt that the mother's strength supplied her child with "the ego strength and the ego ideal of a continuous thrust toward life and achievement" [p. 369].

The Definition of Survivorhood

An implicit question raised by the literature involves the definition of survivorhood. Sonnenberg (1964) writes, "Should a definition of survivorhood reflect experiences, specific psychological states, or some combination of both?" [p. 202]. His question emphasizes confusion about the specificity of experiences that define survivorhood. Thus, for example, Sigal and Rakoff studied a group of children whose parents had been in concentration camps and a group whose parents, though not in the camps, had immediate family members who had been killed by the Nazis. When compared, there were no differences between these subgroups. Sigal and Rakoff concluded that "it is the affective consequences of these losses [i.e., of family members] which are responsible for problems in the family" [p. 395]. Their findings highlight the difficulties of categorizing traumatic experience and outcome. In considering the experiences which led to the survivor syndrome, Krystal (1968) wrote:

> We have little correlation between measurable severity of persecution (e.g. length or kind of camp) and the severity of post-persecution pathology. To expect this simple cause-and-effect relationship would be to lose sight of the fact that the person has to interpret and live his experience in terms of his psychic reality [p. 2]

Similarly, Aleksandrowicz (1973) wrote of his attempt to compare four groups of families with different Holocaust experiences:

> It became apparent at an early stage of the study that a statistical analysis of the impact of concentration camp traumatization was both impractical and unreliable. There were too many individual variables, some of them not susceptible to measurement [p. 385].

It may be that an event of the enormity of the Holocaust makes survivorhood an encompassing concept. Minimally, when comparisons are made between having endured the physical brutality of a concentration camp or having hidden from persecutors under conditions of fear and starvation or having been a partisan who lost family members, fine discriminations between degrees of trauma may miss the point.

A contrasting approach to the question of the definition of survivorhood was suggested by Sigal (1971). He compared clinical observations of survivor families with observations of families, the parents of which had suffered disorder and deprivation in their childhoods. He felt that the only difference between them was that the survivor family's dynamics could be attributed to the effects of massive psychic trauma, while the dynamics of the nonsurvivor families could be attributed to the cumulative psychic trauma of the parents. Sigal concluded that the consequences for the second generation of each kind of parental trauma were identical.

If Sigal is correct, then the particular context in which trauma occurs is, for clinical purposes, unimportant. Survivorhood becomes defined by the fact of trauma, not the nature of it. The questions here are: Did Sigal fail to consider the possibility that similar clinical presentations have different significance?; and: Are the consequences of trauma and second-generation trauma specifically colored by a historical context?

Problems in the Literature

The most definitive conclusion emerging from the literature on children of survivors is that they present the investigator with a complex problem. Sigal (1973) pointed to the difficulty of finding a common denominator in the families of survivors. Aleksandrowicz (1973), Furman (1973), and Laufer (1973), all called attention to the difficulty of isolating the "essential problem connected with being a survivor's child" [Laufer, 1973, p. 363], and in making meaningful comparisons among children of survivors. Sonnenberg (1974) reported the conclusion drawn by the workshop held during the fall, 1971 meeting of the American Psychoanalytic Association in New York: "Clinical evidence supported the position that every child of a survivor is unique and responds to his life experiences uniquely. Generalizations did not seem justified" [p. 203]. At the same time, he reported that many symposium contributors "voiced the view that further metapsychological assessment in psychoanalysis might reveal common denominators. Although not enough is known to formulate generalizations, this should not stifle further efforts" [p. 203].

Although the collective literature is limited in the conclusions that can be drawn from it, one strength is that it provides data from clinical contexts

(Kestenberg, 1972; Lipkowitz, 1973), nonclinical contexts (Rustin, 1971), North American settings (Sigal, 1971; Trossman, 1968), and Israeli settings (Aleksandrowicz, 1973; Klein, 1971, 1973). This diversity raises important issues concerning the roles of different mediating factors in the lives of children of survivors. For example, Klein (1971, 1973) attributed the divergence between his and others' observations of survivors' children to the fact that Israel's culture provides institutionalized expressions of mourning and other coping mechanisms as well as a sense of belonging to survivor families. Similarly, contrasts between clinic and nonclinic populations raise the issue of the inevitability of the family survivor syndrome as a consequence of the survivorhood of one of its members.

The major criticism of the body of literature on children of survivors is that it too often investigated the relationship between children of survivors and their parents' experiences via what Spiegel (1971) termed a "linear analysis." That is, it attempts to define a causal relationship between an antecedent condition (survivorhood of parents) and a presumed effect of that condition (i.e., behavior of children of survivors). The resulting simplification tends to exclude from consideration the complex, reciprocal relationship between people and events, as well as the factors which mediate between them. Spiegel insisted on an approach which emphasizes the complexity of relationships in order to understand them. The linear methodology which characterizes the literature limits the investigation of children of survivors to attempts to ascribe specific traits to them. The alternative is a transactional approach, described by Spiegel, which emphasizes dynamic processes in the context of many influences. The transactional approach frees the investigator of children of survivors to consider the change and evolution of their individual lives and the meaning of the differences as well as of the similarities between them.

The Problem

The literature raises many challenging questions. Among these are: Are children of survivors unique in any way? Are they characterized by distinctive psychopathology? Do they have any special strengths? Do they manifest any specificity of psychodynamics, character structure, personality traits, or symptomatology?

One difficulty in answering these questions is that each presumes that the network of influences in the lives of children of survivors has been defined. At least three sources of influence in the lives of children of survivors have been suggested.

The first source of influence involves the alteration of parents' character by the trauma of persecution and the consequent effect of the parents' relationship with their children. However, it is not clear to what extent, and in what ways, the dynamics of different survivor families resemble each other. Indeed, the range of symptomatology defined by the survivor syndrome is sufficiently broad to allow one to suppose that, at least in some ways, survivors are very different from one another. Further, one must wonder about the validity of the general premise that children with the same background of family dynamics will have similar psychodynamics because, while psychodynamics can be understood in terms of family background, there is a broad range of possible adaptations to family background. Finally, in comparing two groups of families, one of which is comprised of survivors, one might expect to find as many similarities as differences.

The second source of influence involves the participation of children of survivors in imagery from their parents' past. However, there is reason to believe that, in some circumstances, children of survivors experience such imagery as traumatic, while in other circumstances they experience it as a source of meaning. Further, it is not clear to what extent and in what ways children of survivors share the images from their parents' past. In some cases, the imagery of the past which influences children of survivors may be based on actual stories and tales, while in other cases it may be fantasized reconstruction of events on the basis of minimal data. Each would be likely to have a different effect. Finally, it is not clear how the images of the Holocaust influence children of survivors differently from other people who have been raised during the post-Holocaust era.

The third suggested source of influence in the lives of children of survivors involves the cultural context in which children of survivors have been raised. The role of being the first generation in a new culture with values which conflict with the values of a world that has been lost (but which has nevertheless been remembered) needs to be explored. Variables such as the nature of the community in which a child of a survivor is raised, whether it is predominantly Jewish or not, whether it is homogeneous or heterogeneous, and the vicissitudes of peer socialization—all these need to be explicated.

The first aim of this study will be to explore the role of these and whatever other influences can be discovered in the lives of children of survivors. A context for understanding these influences needs to be defined. The emphasis of the literature has been to treat each as an independent "cause" producing a hypothesized "effect." An alternative context is that of a "transactional field" (Spiegel, 1971). Within this context, the role of any one of these influences in the lives of children of survivors cannot be understood without simultaneously considering the others, because they are interdependent. The relationship of the child of the survivor to this transactional field is not linear. Rather, it is a reciprocal relationship within which the child of the survivor is affected by and in turn affects each of these influences.

At the same time that the questions raised by the literature are important, the emphasis on discovering the differences of children of survivors from other children is not necessarily the most fruitful one. The central significance of the study of children of survivors may very well be discovering what they can teach us about ourselves and especially about the relationship of our inner lives to the events that have defined our times. Erikson (1969) suggested the importance of the study of the psychohistorical figure when he wrote the following about the study of the life of Ghandi:

> I therefore will come back to the fact which provided one rationale for this book, namely, that Freud, when he listened to the 'free associations' of his confused and yet intelligent and searching patients, heard *himself* and heard *man* in and through their revelations [p. 438].

Thus, the second aim of this study is to examine the thread of images and associations to the past that run through the lives of a group of individuals who are now approaching the age their parents were when they entered one of the most overwhelming and nightmarish events of our, or possibly any, time. This thread of imagery will be investigated in terms of the relationship that can be discovered between it and the present identity and future expectations of the child of survivor parents. From this perspective, the study of children of survivors from Nazi persecution becomes a study of the relationship between the lives of individuals and the events of history, involving observation of their adaptation to history and anticipation of their effect on it.

2

Method

The fear of error is already an error, and if it is analyzed there will be revealed in its depths a fear of the truth.

[Hegel, cited by Ortega y Gasset, 1960, p. 90]

Because of the complexity of the subject, it did not seem desirable to approach the psychological issues raised by children of concentration camp survivors by traditional research methods. Rather, a study was designed which would generate data by means of a depth interview. Light would thus be shed on both the unique influences in the lives of children of survivors and on their possible adaptations to these influences.

Given that the development of personality is so complex, there was no good reason to assume that the experience of being a child of a survivor would always have its impact on the same areas or in the same way. Neither was there any reason to assume that its impact would always be immediately obvious. For this reason, a methodology was required that would allow for the greatest flexibility and psychological depth in the investigation of the lives of children of survivors.

At the same time, the focus of the study was not on individuals, but on a group whose membership is defined by their relationship to one of the most traumatic and formative historical events of this century. Thus, the thrust of the study was to identify themes which were characteristic of that group and which also differentiated individuals within that group.

The data generated by interviews with children of survivors are clearly within the realm of psychology. At the same time, the emphasis of the study is on understanding psychology within the context of history. As such, the approach used included the contribution of both disciplines to the understanding of the development of character. Examples of such an approach are Lifton's (1967) study of atom bomb survivors, Liebert's (1967) study of radical and militant youth, and Keniston's (1960) study of uncommitted youth. A description of this approach that has influenced the investigator was provided by Lifton (1971), who described "psychohistory" as the emphasis on:

seeking out groups of men and women whose own history illuminates our era. The focus is therefore upon themes, forms and images that are in significant ways shared, rather than upon the life of a single person as such. . . . I retain a psychoanalytically derived emphasis upon what goes on inside people, upon interviews which encourage the widest range of associations, and also upon the reporting of dreams. But all this is done in a manner departing greatly from ordinary psychiatric protocol, through something close to a free dialogue emerging from the specific situation in which interviewer and interviewee find themselves. The relationship we develop . . . is more one of shared exploration. . . . The method is therefore partly empirical (in its continuing stress upon specific data derived from interviews); partly phenomenological or, as I prefer, formative (in its stress upon forms and images that are simultaneously individual and collective); and partly speculative (in its use of those and other observations to posit relationships between man and his history, or to suggest concepts which eliminate the artificial separation of the two) [pp. 7-8]

The Sample

The 20 subjects who comprised the sample were those who, of an original pool of 28 volunteers, completed the interviews.

Method of Obtaining Subjects

The investigator contacted colleagues, personal acquaintances, rabbis, and instructors of courses on the Holocaust to facilitate obtaining subjects. Each was told that an interview study of children of concentration camp survivors was being conducted by the investigator. Each was given the following criteria for the selection of subjects: individuals between the ages of 18 and 26 who had at least one parent who was a survivor of either a Nazi concentration or slave labor camp. In addition, subjects either had to have been born in the United States or to have emigrated to the United States before puberty. Referral sources were asked to obtain the names and telephone numbers of volunteers and to inform them to expect a telephone call from an investigator. Ultimately, subjects were obtained from a number of different sources, as shown in Table 1.

Table 1.   Sources of Subjects (N = 20)

Source of Referral	Number of Subjects
Colleague of investigator	6 (3)*
Other participant in study	6
Instructor of course on Holocaust	3 (5)
Printed announcement	2
Personal acquaintance of investigator	2
"Heard about study"	2

*Numbers in parentheses indicate volunteers who did not complete the procedures.

Description of Sample

The sample consisted of 20 subjects, 10 male and 10 female. The subjects ranged in age from 18 to 26 years. The mean age of males was 21.6 years and of females was 22.4 years. Fourteen subjects were born in the United States, the remaining six subjects in Europe. Four of these had immigrated to the United States in infancy and early childhood, two at puberty.

The range of the parents' age was 44 to 73 years old. Two subjects did not know their parents' ages. Three subjects had one parent who had died during the subjects' adolescence. Three subjects were only children. Two had older half-siblings from whom they had been distant throughout their lives. Eleven of the other 15 subjects had at least one younger sibling.

The parents of all but two subjects came from Eastern Europe. The exceptions had one parent who was American-born. Both parents of 16 subjects were survivors. One subject knew only that his mother had been in a concentration camp and did not know his father's experience. The remaining three subjects had one survivor parent. Nineteen subjects reported that at least one parent had been in a concentration camp. Many did not know names of either the camp or camps their parents were in. The camps parents were in included Auschwitz, Buchenwald, Belsen, Dachau, Mauthausen, and Treblinka. Seven subjects reported that at least one parent had been in a slave labor camp, not a concentration camp. Several subjects did not know whether their parents had been in concentration or slave labor camps. A number of subjects reported that their parents had had additional experiences of persecution such as having to hide for prolonged periods.

The socioeconomic status of parents ranged from quite poor to comfortably middle class. Some of those families which were now comfortable had been impoverished in the years following emigration to the United States. Parents' socioeconomic status in Europe, before the war, ranged from poor to wealthy landholders.

Both parents of all subjects were Jewish. Nine families were Orthodox Jewish. Nine families observed Jewish religious ritual only on major holidays. Two families observed no Jewish rituals or holidays. At least one of the parents of five families was affiliated with a survivor organization. Most of the families of subjects lived in predominantly Jewish neighborhoods.

All subjects had had some Jewish education. Five subjects had attended a yeshiva or Hebrew school throughout high school. All others had attended Hebrew school classes after public school for a minimum of three years before the age of 13. All but one male subject had been Bar Mitzvahed, the exception being one subject who had defied his parents' wishes and refused to go through with the ritual.

All but one subject were either college students or college graduates. The one exception had dropped out of college in her second year. Eight subjects were in college at the time of the study. Of these, four were about to enter their sophomore year, two their junior year, and two their senior year. Five subjects were in graduate or professional school, and, in addition, two were about to enter professional schools to which they had been accepted. The remaining five subjects were out of school and were working. All but three subjects had clearly defined ambitions and interests. These are summarized in Table 2.

Table 2.   Subject's Ambitions and Career Choices (N = 20)

Ambition or Career Choice	Number of Subjects
Medicine and biological science	3
Behavioral sciences	8
Business and Commerce	3
Law	2
Writing	1
Uncommitted	3

At the time of the study, 11 subjects were living in their parents' homes, while nine lived away. Of these nine, two had moved out of their parents' homes to be married.

Description of Volunteers Not Included in the Sample

Eight potential subjects did not complete the interview after having volunteered to participate in the study. Three of these were initially very enthusiastic and expressed considerable interest in participating. Each of these cancelled or broke a number of appointments and then gave circumstantial excuses for not being able to participate. A fourth expressed intense ambivalence about participating, including fear that her parents might find out. After deciding that it might be valuable for her, she found it impossible to schedule a meeting. A fifth decided that he could not participate if the study involved "being open about myself." The remaining three explained that they had become very busy since the time they had originally volunteered and could not spare the time to meet with the interviewer.

The Interview

Design of the Interview

A semistructured interview (see Appendix) was designed as the chief instrument of the study. The interview was designed to generate data by focusing on certain broad areas which, on the basis of the existing literature and the investigator's own speculation, were thought likely to be especially pertinent to the problem Those areas were:

1. Parents' life histories and subjects' reports of their influence on them.
2. Parents' character and family relationships.
3. Subjects' developmental histories with special attention to the evolution of their interaction with the world.
4. General characterological assessment of subjects with particular attention to modes of adaptation to issues of separation, aggression, and mistrust.
5. Unconscious themes with special attention to Holocaust symbolism.
6. Identity, with special attention to the possible influence of the Holocaust.

Also included in the study were requests that subjects generate fantasies which might shed light on their unconscious experience of the Holocaust. It was expected that important data about unconscious experience would be revealed by careful clinical observation of such interview behavior as relationship with the interviewer, tone of voice and associated affect, self-contradictions, and defensive style.

In spite of the extensive schedule of questions, the interview strategy was to foster mutual exploration by subject and interviewer. Subjects were encouraged to raise issues as the issues occurred to them. The plan was, whenever possible, to follow subjects' associations rather than to present interview questions in successive order. In order to adapt the interview clinically in this way, the interviewer had to familiarize himself in great detail with interview questions. With such familiarity, the interviewer was able to cover the interview topics in whatever order was most productive for each particular subject. The interviewer's preference throughout was to facilitate the spontaneous generation of relevant material rather than to direct and elicit material on a question-and-answer basis.

Administration of the Interview

Instructions to subjects. Subjects were told that the interview was designed to help provide an understanding of the lives of people whose parents were survivors of Nazi persecution. They were told that the schedule of questions which the interviewer kept with him throughout the interview was aimed at facilitating this goal. They were asked to share whatever associations or feelings they had as the interview progressed, and to feel free to bring up any issue that occurred to them. In some cases, the interview would begin with a theme spontaneously generated by the subject and pursued by the interviewer. In most cases, subjects seemed to prefer that the interviewer provide structure with the schedule of questions. All questions raised by the subjects about the study were treated as vehicles for engaging them in the interview. Although the interviewer sought out associations, he did not press or confront subjects when they seemed resistant or anxious. All subjects were told that the interviewer would provide them with a summary of the results of the study once it was completed. Permission was asked to tape-record all interviews.

Place of interview. The interviewer originally intended to meet with all subjects in his office at a college counseling service. Four subjects, however, consented to meet with the interviewer only if he met in their homes, which he did. Two of these interviews were conducted with the parents present in the home at the time of the interview. Two other subjects asked that the second interview be conducted in their homes, to which the interviewer also agreed.

All other interviews were conducted in the interviewer's office. Subject and interviewer sat in identical swivel chairs. Whenever possible, the interviewer attempted to provide coffee and other refreshments for subjects.

Length of interview. All subjects were told to expect one or two interview sessions that would last a total of between two and three hours. The time required for the interview was dependent on the subject's productivity and spontaneous elaboration of issues. The absolute minimum time was whatever was necessary for discussion of all interviews in the interview schedule.

The actual range of interview time reflects the wide range of differences between subjects. The shortest interview lasted approximately 70 minutes. The longest interview lasted approximately four hours. The average length of an interview was approximately two and one-half hours.

After having gone through approximately half of the interview, the interviewer would typically suggest a break. The interviewer would also estimate the remaining time and offer the subject the choice of continuing or scheduling another appointment. The interviewer met with 10 subjects for one session, nine subjects for two sessions, and one subject for three sessions.

Time and context of interviews. Interviews were scheduled at the subjects' convenience between May and September, 1973. During this period, news reports concerning the Watergate scandal and spiraling inflation formed the social background of the interviews. In addition, some subjects were aware of news reports which concerned Nazi war criminals. In particular, subjects mentioned reports of deportation hearings of a housewife accused of being a former concentration camp guard and reports that Martin Bormann had been discovered hiding in South America. The "Yom Kippur War" had not yet taken place, and the Arab-Israeli conflict was not predominantly featured in news reports. It is important to note that these interviews took place prior to public interest in children of survivors as manifested through popular magazine articles or books, prior to conferences organized by and for children of survivors, and prior to widespread "consciousness raising" groups for these children.

Interview Behavior

Behavior on First Contact

The subjects' behavior when initially contacted by the interviewer may be divided into three somewhat overlapping categories. The first category represents nine subjects who were generally cooperative and helpful. Scheduling an appointment was accomplished without undue difficulty. The telephone interaction was brief and cordial. Some of these subjects expressed a desire to help the investigator with his work. Otherwise the interaction was not remarkable.

The second category represents seven subjects who manifested a high degree of personal interest in the study. About four of these wanted to participate in the study because they thought it would be helpful to them. For example, one said, "Like to do it would get a lot of things off my chest." Others of these seven subjects indicated a sense of personal obligation to participate. For example, one of these subjects said, "I want to help if somebody has the guts to write about it."

The third category represents four subjects who, although they had volunteered, seemed hesitant about participating. They were not responsive during the phone contact; and it was difficult to set up an initial appointment with them.

Behavior During the Interview

Subjects' behavior during interviews can also be divided into three somewhat overlapping categories. The first included seven subjects who were cooperative with the interviewer and seemed to use the interview for self-exploration and personal growth. These subjects were productive and spontaneous, and seemed able to discuss the feelings generated in them by particular issues.

A second category included eight subjects who can best be described as appearing highly invested in communicating their feelings and beliefs to the interviewer. They also seemed to be invested in convincing the interviewer of a particular image of themselves.

A third category included five subjects who were either unwilling or unable to provide information about themselves. They seemed either constricted or guarded. One of these repeatedly gave tangential responses to the interviewer's questions. None of these subjects was spontaneous.

Reactions to the Interview

Subjects were asked, at the end of the interview, about their reactions to having participated in the study. Their responses can be divided into four categories. The first category includes six subjects who felt that their participation had been helpful to them in some way. They felt that the interview had provoked thought, added insight, and enabled them to express some of their innermost feelings. Several subjects compared their participation in the study with consulting a therapist. One subject said that the interview "made me feel I'm not so different." Two subjects left the interview with the resolve that they would ask their parents questions that they had always been afraid to ask. All of these subjects indicated that, although the interview had raised painful feelings in them, they had enjoyed participating.

A second category includes five subjects who indicated that they enjoyed talking about themselves. They added that they found the subject interesting.

A third category includes four subjects whose response was neutral. They did not find the study rewarding beyond providing a chance to help someone else. For example, one of these said, "My pleasure, I just answered your questions."

A fourth category includes five subjects whose response seemed to be somewhat negative. One of these struck the interviewer as being extremely disappointed and having the feeling that she had come expecting something she did not get. She subsequently wrote the interviewer a letter asking him not to take the things she revealed too seriously. Other subjects seemed diffusely anxious. For example, one said:

> I don't know, I felt funny on a number of questions and I don't know . . . I'll remember this because it's like a very personal interview. Things that I really haven't related to myself, I'm relating for the first time and situations which I didn't think about are coming up right now. [Is that good or bad?] Neither, it's like a funny feeling. [Mr. A.]

Analysis of the Interview

Once verbatim transcripts were obtained, the major task of the study was to organize the mass of data into the areas the interview was designed to investigate. In the process, the themes within each area became elaborated and further defined.

Different types of data were generated. For example, subjects provided some self-descriptions which were consistent and which seemed reliable. They also provided some descriptions which were belied by other material. Other data were reports of incidents, dreams, and memories; descriptions of others; and observable feelings—all of which were amenable to clinical interpretation.

Clinical judgement was often employed to determine the areas and themes for which data was relevant. The data was extremely complex and rich in meaning, and often one statement made by a subject simultaneously illustrated several different areas and themes. In addition, a subject's response to a question which was intended to elicit data relevant to one area often produced data relevant solely to an entirely different area. For example, a question about a subject's parent's character might produce little data about the parent and provide a great deal of insight into the subject's defensive structure. Throughout the report of themes in subjects' lives, the kinds of data used to document the dimensions of a particular theme will be noted. This was done to provide the investigator with a method of not only illustrating the theme, but also indicating his level of confidence in the data used as evidence for the importance of that theme in the subjects' lives.

Although examples of data used to support a theme will be provided, the actual number of subjects who generated such data will not. Rather, adjectives of number, such as "a few" (to denote at least three subjects), "some" (to denote at least one-quarter of the sample), "many" (to denote at least two-fifths of the sample) and "most" (to denote more than one-half of the sample) will be used. It was felt that reports of the actual numbers would be misleading and distracting because:

1. The selection of the sample could be neither controlled nor large enough to insure that it would be representative of the population.
2. Since subjects' responsiveness to the study determined the length of the interview, some subjects generated a great deal more data than others.
3. The data produced by different subjects was qualitatively different. For example, some subjects were quite guarded while others were quite open. Some subjects were unable or unwilling to retrieve memories while others were able to describe their lives more fully. Some subjects were vague and diffuse while others were precise and articulate.
4. The nature of the study required that the generation and elaboration of themes (rather than the specification of the distribution of themes among subjects) be of primary importance.

Because of the type of data generated, the results are presented in such a way as to allow the reader to make his own independent judgments.

Investigator Bias

A basically clinical investigation of highly emotionally charged events cannot be kept entirely free of the investigator's biases and private concerns. The problem is compounded when the exploratory nature of the study requires that the investigator rely on subjective inference and intuition. For these reasons, the investigator must be aware of the sources of his biases and the means by which they interfere with the pursuit of the study. In doing so, it is hoped that he will be able to conduct an investigation which results in objective conclusions based on accurate observation. At the very least, the possible sources of bias must be stated so that readers are free to make their own judgments.

In the present study, the foci of investigator contamination involved, first, the investigator's prior expectations of what he hoped to find; and second, the interference of the investigator's personal reaction (both to the subjects and the subject matter) with objective observation. The investigator's investment in certain of his expectations as well as the intensity of some of his reactions were in part due to the fact that he, himself, met all of the criteria he established for subjects.

During the course of this study, the investigator often found himself struggling to distinguish that which he observed from that which he had expected and/or wished to observe. For example, perhaps naively, the interviewer had expected (and hoped) that children of survivors would have looked upon the Holocaust as a kind of existential lesson which produced an abhorrence of racial prejudice and a commitment to social justice. He found difficulty in accepting a somewhat different conclusion based on his observations. Two other expectations required special concentration and attention to the data. The first was the anticipation that subjects would be far more explicit about the effects of their parents' survivorhood on their own lives than they actually were. As a result, he had to compensate for his emphasis on those subjects who met his expectation and his tendency to minimize those who did not. The second was expectation of less diversity than actually emerged. As a result, the investigator had to compensate for a tendency to "level" distinction among subjects.

The interviewer experienced a wide range of emotional reactions to each subject and during different segments of each interview. He felt especially close and warm toward some subjects. Often he responded to a perceived or imagined similarity between himself and particular subjects. At these times he felt able to pursue interview themes more sensitively on the basis of his own experience. He also felt he had to be more careful in order not to confuse his own experiences with the subjects' reports.

With other subjects, the interviewer experienced anger or dislike, accompanied by a controlled desire to complete the interview as quickly as possible. This reaction was often to those subjects who expressed ego-syntonically some of his own ego-alien thoughts.

The interviewer also responded to unconscious material he felt he shared with subjects by feeling comforted and reassured by a feeling of community with others. This most often occurred in reference to material he had investigated in his own psychoanalysis. At other times he had to deal with his own anxiety in order to pursue the material.

Though the interviewer had a general feeling that he was intruding into a very private and difficult area of subjects' lives, this feeling was especially acute with particular subjects. At times, he became hesitant about pursuing questions that he felt would pain or raise anxiety in the subject. In listening to and transcribing tape recordings of interviews, he sometimes felt that this feeling was accurate and at other times a projection.

The interviewer felt himself as much, if not more, threatened as the subjects, as they described some of the cruelties their parents had endured. He also, as he pursued the study, found himself becoming victim to the same "psychic numbing" described so aptly in the literature of survivorhood.

3

Consciousness of the Holocaust and of Parents' Suffering as a Source of Influence in the Lives of Children of Survivors

And in this harsh world draw thy breath in pain,
To tell my story.

Shakespeare's *Hamlet*

This chapter will present a description of the psychohistorical background of the lives of survivors' children by investigating the parameters of the child's knowledge of and immediate responses to his parents' experiences of persecution.

The Child's Sense of Knowing that His Parents are Survivors

Of the few characteristics that all subjects shared, one was the sense of always having known that their parents were survivors. Typical answers to the question, "When did you find out your parents were in a concentration camp?" were:

> As long as I can remember, I feel like she's always been telling them [referring to her mother's communications to her about her experiences in the concentration camps]. When I could understand, that's when she started telling them. [Miss G.]

> I couldn't really say, I guess it's something that I've always known, five or six I would say . . . I couldn't remember the first time I heard about it. [Miss D.]

While none of the subjects could remember the first time they found out that their parents had been so brutally persecuted, some of them had childhood memories, perhaps combinations of memories, that gave some point of reference to their sense of "always having known." The following quotations give some sense of the process of the child's discovery:

Even before, I was aware, because of my Hebrew school. Also, it would be mentioned. People would come over, I'd say, 'Where do you know them?' They'd say, 'I know them from the concentration camp.' So I had an awareness that my parents had been in this place, a concentration camp, whatever it was. [Mr. E.]

You're sort of born with it, it's always around. You somehow, something that you've lived with. I knew it, I felt it by the year I said candles. And I'd ask 'em, 'Why are there candles there?' 'One's after your grandmother,' and 'Where's my grandmother?' 'She died, she was killed.' I was a kid. 'Why was she killed, Mommy?' 'Because she was Jewish.' And that's how it started. [Miss C.]

I remember being seven when I found out I had a brother or maybe had a brother. There was some talk of some guy who was my father's son. I'd say it was before that, I'd say it was very early. [Miss A.]

I don't think it was till later, I don't remember. I think I do just because I remember my aunt has a number on her arm and I remember asking about it. [Do you remember what you were told?] Just something about during World War II, we were in concentration camp and it didn't mean anything until I was older. I mean it was a process, um, you never, if you keep telling a child he was adopted from the time he was young, then he never remembers the first time you told him he was adopted. I guess it was like that. [Miss B.]

I must have been young, I don't remember. I would guess, and this is really guessing, I might have asked them, 'How come she [his mother] doesn't have a family. How come I don't have grandparents?' [Mr. J.]

Implicit in each of the above quotations is the child's sense of some otherwise unexplainable detail, like the absence of grandparents, a missing brother, a tattoo, that is the key to an important mystery. Thus, attendant to the clear indication of the pervasive quality of the knowledge that their parents had been in a concentration camp is another, more vague, elusive quality. It is almost as if the child had been given an elaborate jigsaw puzzle which had most of the pieces missing. For example, few children of survivors knew any of the details of their parents' incarceration. They tended not to know how long their parents had been in the camp or even the name of the camp. Often critical information about their parents' history was learned by accident. For example, one young man who was born in a displaced persons' camp learned only during late adolescence that his real mother had died in childbirth, and that the woman he had experienced as his mother was, in fact, his stepmother. Other subjects discovered, by accident, that their parents had been previously married.

Most children of survivors, even if they were not content with it, chose to live without discovering the mysteries of the past. In contrast, some have made a point of learning the exact chronology of their parents' past. These were able to cite the exact dates of the major events in their parents' lives.

Parents' Style of Communication about Their Past

General Range of Parents' Descriptions

The range of different parents' styles of communication about their experiences of persecution mirrors the dual aspect of the child's sense of knowing that his parents are survivors described above. At one extreme are those parents who have communicated very extensively to their children about their experiences. Such parents were described as follows:

> They've always talked about it. I've always known. [Miss F.]

> My father said I could never really be happy unless I knew what happened. Really, as soon as I was able to talk or understand, he'd tell me. [Mr. B.]

At the other extreme are parents who were extremely reticent about talking about anything related to the past. For example, one subject said:

> My mother talked about it very little, it was like pulling teeth, when I was younger, I'd ask. The answer would be, 'Oh, you have time to know about such things, it's not nice.' [Miss C.]

Often, when both parents were survivors, their styles of communication were complementary. For example, a subject said:

> My mother does, my father doesn't, never has. He won't talk about the concentration camps at all whereas my mother has told me of many, many experiences she had. [Miss I.]

In the extreme, one parent may raise the subject, and the other parent may respond by walking out of the room or chastising the first by admonishing him not to upset the child.

Qualitative Aspects of Parents' Communications

As one listens to survivors' children describe their parents' mode of communicating their experiences of persecution, one gets the sense of a wide variety of nuances and subtleties characterizing those communications.

One very distinct impression emerging from subjects' reports is that parents are extremely ambivalent about communicating their experiences to them. On the one hand, the parents seem terribly in need of unburdening themselves. On the other hand, they seem equally in need of closely guarding disclosures that might tend to portray themselves in a bad light or which might re-evoke memories of pain and vulnerability.

The ambivalence may have set the context for the fragmentary nature of many parents' disclosures to their children. Subjects described such fragmentary reports as follows:

It just keeps being added, sentence by sentence. [Mr. H.]

They didn't hide it from us, they would just talk about it in bits and pieces. [Miss J.]

Another aspect of this fragmentary style of communicating involved the parents sharing some event at the same time he withheld the context of the event. For example, a parent might vaguely mention that a relative had been "taken away," without revealing either who that relative was or the circumstances and details around the event.

Another mode of communicating was through the vehicle of denial. In this mode, a parent communicated what he did not suffer rather than what he did. Two examples of such a style were described in response to the interviewer's question, "What kinds of things do they say about what they went through?":

Nothing he says, he just tells how, what they did. Not really, they didn't do anything to him like they did to, he was like strong, he was a young boy, so he was able to work, so they didn't do anything to him . . . [Miss E.]

They talk about it very infrequently and when they do talk about it, it's in the most romantic glorified version. [What do you mean?] Oh, how 'daddy saved me here and how daddy saved me there and how we were always in good straits and how I was always a lady in concentration camp, even.' That kind of thing. [Miss D.]

Even among parents who seemed to talk about the concentration camps a great deal, the actual amount of information that was exchanged was often minimal. In such cases, the parent essentially repeated the same event or story many times. For example, subjects state:

She just tells the same ones. [Miss F.]

The same ones over and over again, the cruelty of it, nothing to eat, no food, you know I can't, there's no story. [Mr. H.]

One has the sense that many parents wanted to let their children know about their experiences but were unable to communicate to them directly. These parents often took advantage of circumstances that allowed indirect communication. For example, they talked about the concentration camps with visitors and allowed their children to overhear details that they had heretofore suppressed. In one family, parents "accidentally" left photographs of concentration camp inmates in an album which contained baby pictures of the child. In other cases, parent and child might be watching television, and an association to whatever program was on would be the means through which the parent communicated to the child. In one family, the parent suggested that the child read a particular novel, the theme of which was survival in and after the concentration camp, saying, "It's my life."

Emotional Aspects of Communication of Holocaust Experiences

One has the impression that in most instances survivor parents repressed and denied feelings when they recounted their experiences to their children. Children, in turn, tended to perceive this as defensive. At the same time, parents intermittently did communicate the emotional dimensions of their experiences. For example, some subjects reported having heard a parent screaming in terror during the night and understood that the parent was having a nightmare about the Holocaust. A number of subjects reported that their parents would tell them the content of such nightmares. In at least one of these, a parent told her son that she had dreamt that the Germans were "taking you away." Children also reported that at times parents became either sad or agitated when they spontaneously recalled or were reminded of the past.

In other cases, the communication of feelings was disguised. For example, a parent might abruptly cut off the other parent's description of some incident out of the past, thus indicating a powerful emotional experience but not making its nature clear. One parent was described as never having discussed any aspect of her experience, while at the same time admonishing her son, "You should remember these things." Here, one might surmise, she was making a very personal statement about her feelings, the exact definition of which is ambiguous.

In at least one case, the interviewer had the sense that the style of communication adopted by the parent betrayed powerfully angry feelings which were displaced onto his daughter. She described her father's typical mode of communication:

> For example, my father goes, 'Today July 19th, 25 years ago, we were taken away. Today, July 26th, 25 year ago, this and this. Today, 25 years ago, my grandmother was taken away and my uncle buried her,' whatever. [Miss H.]

She went on to describe a typical interaction she had with him:

> To me it seems unreal how somebody can come into your home, take you away. I mean, say, 'Come on, let's go.' I can't believe that so I'd ask, 'How did they come in?' and he'd say, 'What do you mean! How did they come in! They'd say, "pick up," and tomorrow you were dead.' [Miss H.]

The above incident suggested to the interviewer that the father, still in a rage at the brutalities inflicted on him (and possibly also experiencing "survivor guilt") needed to constantly remind himself and those around him of the real crimes of which he had been victim. However, as obvious as this might seem to one listening to his daughter's report, he nevertheless had to disguise these feelings of fury. In the brittleness of his attempts to do so, his family perceived his anger as directed towards them. Though supported by little concrete evidence, it was the interviewer's impression that this was true in other families as well.

Modes of Communication Emphasizing that the Parent has Mastered Trauma

In spite of the picture presented above—that survivor parents, as they communicated their experiences to their children, continued to struggle with the unresolved emotions generated by the unprecedented brutality they had endured—at least two subjects portrayed their parents' communication about the past in such a way that suggested the parents had resolved their emotion. In both cases there is no evidence that contradicts the following reports:

> I think they're able to tell it in a way that it happened and it's over and that they made it through. [Mr. E.]

> His approach to it was very casual and it wasn't full of anxiety, pain, and regret. It was, it was coping, and it was a situation he had to cope with, and he had to feed himself, and the feeling I've always gotten from him was that he wasn't a very different human being there than he was his whole life. . . . [Mr. F.]

Specific Information Communicated by Parents to Their Children

Description of Life before the Holocaust

Descriptions of the parents' life before the Holocaust were either of a perfect world—a Garden of Eden, populated by mythic beings that have been lost forever—or of a harsh world in which life was defined by poverty and a constant, difficult struggle. Often, one parent would provide the former image while the other would provide the latter.

Those parents who idealized their past presented a world of sophisticated leisure and ease. They emphasized the tradition and culture of the *shtetl* and the grace of the cities. If they came from rich families, they presented a benign world of aristocratic privilege. If not, they emphasized the respect people had for each other and their responsibilities and successes as they earned the good life for themselves and their families. In both cases, stories are told of the pleasures of old-world Europe and the warmth and intimacy of the family.

The people of that world assume a larger-than-life aspect. For example, one young man recalled his father's image of his grandfather's strength: "The last thing he did was he hit the bed with his fist and then he died."Other parents described their own parents as people who had ruled their large families with patrician generosity. Still others described the sparkling qualities of lost relatives which had earned them respect and stature in their communities. Some had been Talmudic scholars whose lives were devoted to study and wisdom. Others had been men and women imbued with a creative spirit, or rebels with visions of a new world. Some of these had been patrons of the arts, while others had been active Socialists and Zionists.

Survivor-parents portrayed themselves in romantic terms which sharply contrasted with their contemporary reality. One subject describes her impressions of her mother's life in Europe as "equivalent of an old Southern plantation." She went on to say, "My mother, I've always pictured very much like Scarlett O'Hara...except a Jewish Scarlett O'Hara." Another subject's parent described "the happy-go-lucky, wonderful life he had."

Other parents who described their life in Europe emphasized the many hardships they endured, even before the Holocaust. They cited the early loss of a parent to illness, anti-Semitism, lack of opportunity, the unavailability of education, poverty, and the necessity of backbreaking labor as some of the conditions of their lives. One subject summarized this view of Europe as she described her understanding of her mother's background: "A very poor, suffering feeling that I get...."

Stories of the Holocaust

While parents' descriptions of their experiences of persecution vary in detail and vividness, there is one common feature: none of the fragments parents communicated to their children approached the overwhelming horror of the descriptions made available in documentaries, movies, and books about the concentration camps. Nevertheless, the parents' descriptions were simultaneously evocative and numbing. The interviewer, for one, had tremendous difficulty asking subjects to elaborate descriptions of their parents' experiences. While transcribing tapes, he often would find himself turning off the tape-recorder just as subjects began such a description. The main themes that can be identified in parents' accounts to their children follow.

Denial of culpability and affirmation of personal virtue and sacrifice. The themes of personal virtue and denial of personal guilt emerged concomitantly. During the interview one was aware of an unstated but nevertheless denied accusation that some parents may have survived at the expense of someone else's death. During more abstract discussion about the Holocaust in general, most subjects spontaneously remarked that one of the most destructive aspects of the concentration camp experience was that people were forced to fight each other for food and commit other "crimes" in order to survive. Some subjects reported parents having described other inmates as having engaged in such behavior. Other subjects, all women, recalled stories of their mothers having been aided in some way by German officers. The implication seemed to be that the motivation of the officers was sexual. However, there was no indication that these subjects had consciously entertained the thought that their mothers had been compromised in any way. On the other hand, several male subjects wondered if their fathers had been "sexually abused." Nevertheless, the focus of subjects' reports of their parents' descriptions remained the risks and sacrifices parents had made for others. For example, the only subject who reported that his father had been a *Capo* stated that his father had used the position to smuggle prayerbooks, at the risk of his own life, to other prisoners. Other subjects recalled that their parents had told them of giving their meager rations, or of stealing items from the Germans, to give to inmates who were worse off than they. Other stories of personal sacrifice involved parents nursing other sick and dying inmates back to health, and taking the blame (and hence the life-threatening punishment) for minor infractions of rules committed by other prisoners. For example, one father told of knowing that another man was so weak that he would have been killed by a beating that was about to be inflicted upon him. The subject's father assumed the man's identity and was beaten so badly that he was left for dead on top of a pile of corpses.

Themes of suffering, loss, and deprivation. Most parents described their experiences of suffering, loss, and deprivation in only the barest outline form. Many denied that they had suffered, either in comparison to others or at all. Others only implied that certain "things were done" to them. In no case did a parent describe the actual conditions so nightmarishly detailed in literature on the concentration camps.

The experience of loss of loved ones—parents, siblings, husbands, wives, and children—is most often described by the parent with the terse comment, "They took him away." Occasionally, a survivor-parent may tell his children of the efforts he made to communicate with a loved one from within the camp. Rarely did a survivor-parent say that he saw a loved one killed or die. In some cases, a parent referred, with no accompanying details, to having seen a loved one shot or marched to a gas chamber. Often, the parent would not identify the loved one.

A somewhat wider range of details accompanied descriptions of suffering and deprivation. Sometimes parents condensed their entire experience into one symbolic fragment. For example, a mother, once a musician, expressed the horrors she had endured by stating that she had not felt afraid until the moment she entered the camp and the guard smashed her one possession, a violin. Other parents described the brutalization, not of themselves, but of some other person. For example, parents described assaults on other inmates that were motivated by some whimsy of S.S. officers or guards. Such descriptions, though brief, are painfully vivid. One parent described a woman, who had accidentally spilled water in front of a guard, being kicked in the spine and permanently crippled. Another parent described common camp tortures to his 8-year-old son. One of these was the submerging of inmates in vats filled with ice water.

Some parents did tell their children of at least some of the brutalities they had personally endured. One parent described how he had had to stand in formation, on one leg, for hours at a time with the "sun beating down on his bald head." Another described having been beaten so badly that many of his bones were broken. He had been saved from death only because other inmates had hidden him while they nursed him back to life.

Most of the descriptions of camp conditions had to do with the hard work parents were forced to do at the same time that they were starving. Some parents described themselves as so hungry that they would eat leaves off trees and search through piles of garbage for scraps of food. Some parents also described the conditions of filth that existed. For example, one described how he and others would sit for hours killing the lice on their bodies "because they had nothing better to do with their time."

Themes of the capriciousness of life and death. A dominant theme of parents' accounts involves the portrayal of chance as the prime determinant of life and death. Parents described a number of accidental circumstances that had resulted in their survivorhood. For example, several parents mentioned that a kindly-disposed guard had instructed them to lie—for example, to say that they were older than they were or that they possessed a certain skill. With this information, the parent was able to have himself sent to work rather than to a gas chamber. Others describe "selections" during which they had managed to guess which of two lines was destined for life and which was destined for death. If chance then provided the right circumstances, they were then able to sneak onto the correct line. However, chance could still have resulted in their being caught, and the choice had not always been obvious. At least three parents described having met chance in the guise of the infamous Dr. Mengele of Auschwitz. In these confrontations, which had lasted no more than a minute, he had decided their fate. One is struck that children, recounting their parents' descriptions, used the title "Doctor."

Other parents ascribed their survival to the chance appearance of a savior. For example, a subject told the following:

> When my mother was in concentration camp she was dying, very skinny, no food, and they were taking all of her friends to be killed and they called her name and she thought she was going into the chambers and she was petrified, and it turned out that one of her aunts had come and had brought her bread and water...and she saved her life just with a piece of bread, she was emaciated. [Miss H.]

Still other parents described having escaped death by a hair's breadth. For example, one subject, whose father had been in a slave labor camp, described the following:

> there was a period of typhoid, and they put them all in a barn and burned them. My father had typhoid also and he said he just missed being burned, the night before he moved out of that barn....[Mr. I.]

Parents also described the death of relatives as a consequence of some otherwise more or less innocuous event. For example, parents described relatives as having suffered a minor injury, such as a hurt foot, which could have been treated easily. However, such an injury would mean not being able to work as effectively, and death had resulted from causes the parents did not describe, presumably murder.

Themes of escape and survival. To many of the children interviewed, the least understood element of their parents' experiences is the miracle of their having survived. Some of these subjects, particularly those whose parents had been in slave labor camps, seemed to have had the impression that the conditions their parents lived in may have been harsh but not life-threatening. Others had the impression that their parents were strong enough to perform work for the Germans, and were thus spared from being murdered.

Parents sometimes portrayed the cunning that they used to stay alive. For example, one parent told of "smuggling a gold coin in his ass" into the concentration camp in order to bribe a guard into having him transferred into a labor camp. Another parent told of having passed for a Catholic. A third parent recalled having been given the choice of either marching or taking a train to a concentration camp. He shrewdly chose to march and ended up in a factory, while all those on the train perished in the gas chambers.

Perhaps the most common type of account related to children involves escape. Many parents told of having taken every opportunity to escape either a life-threatening circumstance or the camp itself. For example, one parent told of having managed to hide each time she was "chosen." Rarely were the details made explicit. However, a parent's simply mentioning his feat of having escaped from Treblinka, Belsen, and Dachau is suggestive of rare courage.

Another "explanation" of their survivorhood that parents gave was allying themselves with others for collective support and survival. Finally, one father communicated to his son that he had survived because he had mastered the Nazis with dignity and courage.

Responses to Parents' Accounts

In examining the more immediate and specific responses of the children the parents' accounts of the past and to images conveyed through those accounts, the investigator often found it difficult to differentiate between such specific responses and more generalized ones. He finally settled on an approximation of his intent to differentiate the two.

Defenses Against the Imagery of the Holocaust

The intensity of the subjects' responses to images of their parents' persecution is portrayed by the qualitative aspects of the defenses they mobilize to guard themselves from the impact of such imagery. These defenses often have a brittle quality, as suggested by the following exchange:

> Interviewer: How much do you know about what your father went through?
> Miss E.: Well, my father talks about it a lot but I don't want to listen to it.
> Interviewer: What goes on in your mind when—
> Miss E.: I don't like to listen to it, I said.

The same subject, who was an A-student throughout high school and her first year of college, also asked, "What year did the war end, 1948?" In this way, she communicated the extent and intensity of her need to deny recognition of her father's experiences. Similarly, another subject who was asked to describe accounts told him by his father said, "For some reason, I just don't recollect them."

Another kind of defense is isolation of affect, which is illustrated by one subject who says, "My mother used to tell me these stories, unbelievable stories, a fairy tale, I don't believe it." The defensive aim of treating her mother's stories "like fairy tales" is suggested as she continued, "and then I don't know, I hit a certain age and then I just started drinking it in." By "drinking it in" she was referring to a full-blown obsession with thoughts about the Holocaust which, in her words, "possesses her." Subjects provided other examples of the use of isolation affect, which in some cases may also be considered to be "psychic numbing." What follow are some of these examples:

> I've pretty much closed my mind to it. . . . I just close my mind to things that are repeated over and over. [Miss F.]
>
> I distance myself from it. . . . [Miss D.]
>
> I don't think it was a true feeling, I'd listen to him and it would stay in my mind and I'd walk away. [Mr. C.]

Another subject described his struggle against "psychic numbing" by trying to "picture" relatives that died in concentration camps:

> You know, trying to make a really strong connection to those people, that they just weren't a statistic, that they just weren't somebody else killed because when you hear that, somebody's always killed, and, uh, I try to make, you know, these people more meaningful for me....[Mr. H.]

Prominent Affects Emerging through Subjects' Defenses

A number of prominent affects emerge through subjects' defenses against Holocaust imagery communicated to them by their parents. These were horror, guilt, anger at the world, and anger at parents.

Horror. One feeling that emerged as subjects described their reactions to accounts communicated to them by their parents may best be described by the word "horror." For example, one subject described his experience when his mother told him the actual details of her experiences for the first time when he was 22 years old. He described it as "an excruciating experience for me, it was too vivid and alive...after that I never wanted to ask again."

This same subject reported being "very upset" around the age of seven or eight when he saw documentaries about the concentration camps. One must assume that his reaction and interest in these, even as a child, involved issues directly related to his parents. The pattern of ascribing feelings or reactions to documentaries or movies, and denying the connection of such feelings to information communicated by parents, was a common one. For example, another subject recalled childhood memories of having responded to such documentaries but no memory of having responded to information from his parents:

> I read books and saw TV documentaries which made me feel very ill...a lot of scenes in the movie first of all disgusted me, I was very sad after watching them. [Mr. J.]

Other subjects describe reactions which they characterize with such words as "horror" and "terror." Some of these describe having had nightmares as children in response to information communicated to them by their parents. For example, one subject said:

> I used to have my own nightmares and be upset, she [her mother] would upset me a great deal. She said it was important that I know. [Miss I.]

It is often not clear if subjects had responded to specific content communicated to them, or to some emotional communication. For example, one subject describes "a nightmarish occasion" in the household when his mother began reading a popular novel about the concentration camps. It is not clear whether he had responded to anything beyond his mother's emotional state. Another subject described his own "terror" in response to his mother's nightmares:

> One of the scariest things is that sometimes she'll wake up screaming at night, sometimes it'll be directly related to an experience there [in the concentration camp] and sometimes it won't be. I'll hear her scream and run into the bedroom. [Mr. H.]

When asked to describe further his reaction, he said:

> Well, it happens very rarely, maybe once a month. [And how do you feel?] Terror. [Your own terror?] Yeah, it's happening, that experience is happening right there. [Mr. H.]

Reactions of guilt. Guilt is often an implicit dimension in subjects' responses to their parents' communications. However, in only a very few cases does this dimension emerge clearly. For example, the following exchange took place during one interview:

> Miss D.: I'm sort of grateful that they pick out the glamorous aspects of it instead of dwelling on the horrible aspects of it.
> Interviewer: What do you mean, grateful?
> Miss D.: Well, I really don't want to hear about that, I would feel guilty.
> Interviewer: Can you tell me more about that?
> Miss D.: It would make me feel uncomfortable because they never talked about it in that way.

In the above exchange, the subject's experience of guilt, given without any clue to the mediating factors between it and hearing her parents talk about their experiences, emerged and was then quickly suppressed. Clues to the mediating factors between the experience of guilt and parents' communications are provided by other subjects. In one case, a subject said that although she realizes it is irrational, nevertheless she "feels somehow responsible" for her parents' past suffering. Another subject remembered thoughts he had had around the age of ten:

> I really didn't realize what they went through, and maybe a lot of the time I thought I should be nicer, maybe a little more understanding, maybe not as selfish. At times, I think I was. [Mr. E.]

Implicit in his statement is a feeling of obligation to his parents in response to his knowledge of their suffering, and a feeling of guilt for not meeting this obligation through his own good behavior. Still another subject describes the following:

> I really can't feel as much as I should, the depth of emotion maybe that I should feel. [What do you think you should feel?] Well, sometimes I think I'm sort of blasé about it, the whole thing, and I don't think that's right. [Mr. J.]

Implicit in this statement is a feeling of guilt for not responding sufficiently to his parents' pain. In part, he experienced guilt for his own defenses against feelings generated by his parents' accounts. One might even speculate that he feels guilty for defending himself against feeling guilty.

Anger at the world. Another response was to experience a general rage at the outside world. For example, one subject described her evolving response to her parents' communication as follows:

> First it was wonder...then you feel anger.... It wasn't fair that it happened and you go around hating the world for a while, at least I did....[Miss C.]

The above statement gives the sense that the process of integrating the response to knowledge of the parents' experiences is one that evolves over time. In those cases in which a resolution was not achieved which allowed the survivor's child to affiliate himself with the outside world, he used the fact of his parents' persecution to rationalize his alienation. For example, one subject manifested a generalized contempt for her peers, insisting, among other things, that they were not capable of caring about the sufferings of others and that they were unmoved by the historical image of the concentration camp. When she asked the interviewer to validate her perception, he gave an equivocal answer. Her response was "Where were their parents when mine were in a concentration camp?"

This response, however, was not always so dramatically portrayed. Often it was taken outside of the context of personal interaction and represented as a general rejection of the idea of the worth of others and the feeling that one must look out for one's own interests.

Anger at parents. A response given by some subjects whose parents often raised the issue of their past suffering at the hands of the Nazis was anger and annoyance. However, only one subject clearly indicated that she expressed this feeling directly to her parents. Others indicated that they did become angry, but made a point of keeping these feelings to themselves. These may add that they listen politely, "to be nice." Still others denied any such response to their parents while, at the same time, communicating feelings of rage to the interviewer. One such subject responded to the question, "How do you feel when your father talks about it?" by saying, in an indignant tone of voice, "What do you mean! How do I respond! I'm used to it. That's history." On further questioning it became apparent that this subject was unaware of any of the feelings of anger that the interviewer sensed.

Those who explicitly indicated a response of anger explained that they became annoyed with the repetitious quality of their parents' communications. For example, one subject said:

> She seems, she's always telling me about it after she's had a dream about it or after she's spoken to someone or is reminded of it, and I just feel pity, and I feel, I feel annoyed. At times now, stories that she tells me, maybe she doesn't realize, and I don't want to tell her that she's repeated them, yeah, annoyed would be a good word. [Miss F.]

Another subject explained:

> A couple of years ago, I didn't like it because I didn't want to be bothered with it ... it just kind of struck me, Why does she have to tell me about what happened 25 years ago? It happened to her, it won't happen to me. You know, it was really sad, but why should, later I resented it because I felt that it, you know, why does she have to tell me that people are so bad, that was like in ninth and tenth grade, maybe even earlier. I was trying to see people the way they really are, and here she's trying to convince me that they're really mean and rotten.... [Miss B.]

The comments of this subject are important because other subjects, though perhaps unable to articulate them, may have shared angry feelings that their parents' communications about the past inhibited their own growth.

Fantasies Generated by Parents' Accounts

Some subjects reported that fantasies were generated by their parents' accounts of their experiences. These are to be differentiated from fantasies, daydreams, and dreams, the manifest content of which directly involves Holocaust imagery.

Among the kinds of fantasies generated were those having to do with specific details of the information received from parents. For example, one young man learned that his uncle had been his mother's first husband and had been killed in a concentration camp. He would very often wish that this uncle, who had been an educated professional, had been his father rather than his real father, whom he perceived as inadequate. Similarly, subjects reported imagining that their grandparents had not been killed, and elaborating the relationship they might have had with them.

Other fantasies which were generated have to do with unknown aspects of the parents' past life. Occasionally the interviewer had the suspicion that an incident reported as fact involved the subject's own construction of events based on minimal information. In other cases, subjects wondered if parents had committed some crime in the concentration camp and imagined what that crime would be.

Yet another kind of fantasy was generated, not directly by the information communicated by parents, but by a stimulus from the outside world that was experienced in relationship to information communicated by parents. For example, one subject described his reaction to seeing an image of a "pile of bones" during a television documentary on the concentration camps. He reported:

> You just think that your mother could have been one of those, her brothers and sisters were one of those and sometimes I think it would have been so easy for me to have been one of those. If I had been just 25 years older, you know, in a different time period, I would have been one of those. [Mr. H.]

Other subjects reported the identification with the victim that is involved in the above statement. These often imagined themselves in a concentration camp. Examples of their reports are:

> You put yourself in the situation, how would have acted and would you have become a normal person again. [Miss C.]

> I feel sad for her, I very often try to picture that happening to me and if I could make it through, you know, I don't know if I would be as strong a person. . . . [Mr. E.]

Positive Feelings Generated by Parents' Accounts

A number of subjects reported predominantly pleasurable or favorable responses to one of their parents' accounts of their experiences before or during the Holocaust. Others reported some positive component in their overall reaction to their parents' accounts.

One aspect of the positive responses reported was a feeling described by one subject who said, "I've always had just this extreme awe that my parents went through what they did and just lived through it." In this way, this subject, along with others, indicated that his parents' communications produced in him a sense of pride in the possibilities of human strength.

Another kind of positive response is a feeling of trust and closeness insofar as the child experienced his parents' disclosures as a sharing of a private and painful part of his life. One subject described his father as telling him his concentration camp experiences "in moments of special closeness." This kind of response extended to the parent's description of his life before the war and was taken as a gift by the parent to the child. Often, this sense of the parents' account as a gift was implicitly accompanied by the child's sense of having been able to give the parent a gift in return:

I love hearing my mother's stories because I like to hear about her family, and I always ask, and the next day she'll say, well, I dreamt about it last night. [Miss H.]

In addition, many subjects reported that they experienced their parents' descriptions of the past as enriching their own lives by providing them with an affiliation to a world which no longer exists.

The Desire to Learn More about the Past

Almost all of the subjects interviewed indicated a desire, of greater or lesser intensity, to learn more either about their parents' specific history or the more general conditions in the concentration camps. The one exception was a subject who expressly stated a desire to avoid any information about either. However, as will be seen, other subjects also portrayed their ambivalence about learning the dark secrets of the past.

Subjects gave two rationales for their interest. The first was involvement in discovering the nature of the concentration camps accompanied by an explicit or implicit curiosity about the parents' specific psychological experiences in them. An example of such an interest, explicitly stated, was given by a subject who wanted to know:

How does it feel to be 14 years old, and, and, and just locked up? And how does it feel to be a slave to, to these people who can just kill you any time they feel like it, and to have your life in doubt, you know, What's going to happen to you tomorrow? And particularly, you know, Do you lose hope in a situation like that? I guess more or less the psychological things about it rather than the physical things. . . . [Mr. J.]

The second rationale involved a desire to learn more about or understand better some aspects of their own lives. Some of the subjects, who described having asked their parents questions during their childhood, explained that they were confused about their being different from other children. The particular concern that most often emerged as the focus of this sense of being different was expressed in the question, Why don't I have grandparents like other children? Subjects indicated that their present motivation to ask their parents questions involved a desire to understand better their own identity through understanding the forces that had affected their parents and, indirectly, themselves. For example, subjects explained:

Lately I would ask some questions in terms of what my own place in the world is, trying to find that, what my background is, what about people who lived at the time, sort of a historical curiosity. [Mr. H.]

I don't know, it's important for me to know what happened in their lives . . . something like to get their histories, also they're living with it every day, and I'm living with them. [Mr. I.]

Specific Information Survivors' Children were Interested in Discovering

While most subjects indicated only a general interest in learning about their parents' experiences of persecution, some had specific questions they wanted to ask. In some cases, the subject was more interested in learning about one parent than he was in learning about the other. This was particularly true when the subject had clearly identified with one parent and had rejected an identification with the other. Often the subject's curiosity about the experiences that were hidden by one parent was matched by his annoyance at the repetitious revelations of the other.

The specific questions children had in mind invariably involved some particular aspect of the parents' concentration camp experience. Several subjects wanted to know if their parents had ever stolen food or killed someone. Two subjects wanted to know if their parents had been sexually abused. One of these had noticed "two brown marks on his [his father's] ass" and had wondered, ever since childhood, if these were a result of such abuse. Another subject very much wanted to ask, and finally did ask, if it had been his father's experience that camp inmates "followed Bettleheim's analogies." He was referring to reports in the literature that camp inmates had become childlike and had identified with guards.

Hesitation to Ask Parents

All subjects expressed some degree of reticence about approaching their parents with questions about the concentration camp experience. Some of these indicated that they had already satisfied their interest in the details of their parents' past, and explained that any more information would produce an unspecified unpleasant feeling in them. Others, who at the same time professed a deep interest in learning about their parents' past, and who had studied the Holocaust in detail on their own, could not give an explanation of this reticence. One such subject said that, in spite of his interest, he had never "really sat down and talked to them." When asked, "Why not?" he answered "I really don't know." Another, who had earlier talked about his intellectual interest in the Holocaust, explained, "Because I don't know what to ask them." Still another subject, one who had tape-recorded an interview with his mother under the guise of having to do an assignment for a class he had taken on the Holocaust, said of his never having asked his father about his experiences:

> I don't know too much about my father because he doesn't bother telling and I don't bother asking. Nobody had it easy." [Mr. A.]

The most prevalent reason subjects gave for not asking questions of their parents was the desire to protect them from painful reminders of the past. Subjects said:

> I just feel that it would hurt him so much that I don't want to ask him. [Miss F.]

> Primarily because I can see, well, she doesn't like to watch war movies, she doesn't like to read books about things like that, therefore I've, like seen her get upset like once in a while, I know that she's a nervous person, I don't want to like inflict any pain. [Mr. J.]

> I'm just sort of fearful it might bring out some emotionalism or it might trigger, it might make them unhappy to have to recall some of these things. [Miss D.]

Other subjects described a feeling that it would be "cruel" to ask parents questions and make their wounds "bleed again."

It is important to note that few of the above subjects expressed the thought that it would be painful to them to have their parents answer their questions. Thus, for example, one subject learned that her father had had a wife and family before World War II. She expressed both a curiosity to learn more and a reticence to satisfy that curiosity ostensibly because of her parents' vulnerability rather than because of any vulnerability of her own.

Modes of Satisfying Curiosity

Many children of survivors were confronted with a dilemma. On the one hand they needed to avoid confronting their parents with their questions about the past while, on the other hand, they needed to learn about the past. They solved this dilemma in a variety of ways. Several subjects reported that they had surreptitiously gone through their parents' papers. Others reported relying on other people to ask the questions they were afraid to ask. For example, they would allow a friend or girl friend to enter into a conversation with their parents about the past while they sat back and listened. Some subjects also asked friends of their parents to tell them about their parents' experiences. For example, two subjects, who were distantly related to each other and whose parents had gone through a concentration camp together, reported asking the other's parents about their own parents' experiences. Two other subjects described relying on a pretext to ask their parents questions. One, taking a college course in European history, told his father that he needed to talk to him in order to write a required paper for the course. Another used the pretext of the requirements of a course on the Holocaust to question his mother.

Other subjects reported having studied the Holocaust extensively. Some of these said that they did so as a way of avoiding asking their parents about it. One may infer that others, perhaps without themselves being conscious of it, also displaced their interest from their parents' lives to a general interest in the historical events of World War II. However, even such an approach did not fully resolve subjects' conflicts about learning about the past. For example, one subject reported that she had always wanted to learn about the Holocaust, and in particular the concentration camps, but had never fulfilled her desire. She said:

> There was a morbid fascination with the concentration camps.... I think there was an ambivalence, I wanted to, but not enough to do it.... I was comfortable with wanting it and not doing it. [Miss A.]

The Child's Relationship with His Parents in the Context of Their Survivorhood

Subjects either implicitly portrayed or explicitly described their relationships with their parents as existing within the context of their parents' survivorhood. One subject said:

> I feel it's been part of me, it's been part of the whole relationship with them, and it's always something that I take into consideration in judging them, when I think of them.... [Miss I.]

The context of survivorhood altered both children's perceptions of their parents and their behavior toward them.

In discussing their perception of the effect on their parents of having been survivors, subjects often contradicted themselves. When asked directly, many denied any perception of damage, while during another part of the interview, they spontaneously described major areas in which their parents were affected by these experiences. Subjects ranged from seeing their parents as minimally affected by the persecution they endured to seeing their parents as massively affected.

Some subjects, who can be described as hesitant to attribute aspects of their parents' character to their survivorhood, attributed their perception of their parents' anxieties and vulnerabilities to their parents being immigrants. Others, who have only one survivor parent, compared their parents, and concluded that since both parents had difficulties in living, the impact of the concentration camp on the survivor parent must have been minimal. Still others insisted that their parents' "nature," not the fact of persecution, was responsible for their character. These insisted that their parents "would have turned out the same way" if they had not been in a concentration camp.

The majority of subjects, however, perceived their parents as affected by their experiences during the Holocaust. Some of these saw the effect as positive, or at least neutral. For example, some of these subjects attributed their parents' valuing and maintaining Jewish traditions as a consequence of having been persecuted for being Jewish. Other saw their parents as being more invested in their families because of their earlier losses. Some subjects described their parents as "being proud" that they had the strength to endure. Others saw their parents as having developed positive virtues, such as strength, endurance, and responsibility in the crucible of the concentration camp.

Most subjects, however, perceived the long-term effects of the concentration camps as damaging. Some attributed the negative aspects of their relationship with their parents to the impact of the past. Others described their parents as having specific scars. Some of these were continuing nightmares, difficulty trusting people, being easily intimidated by people, having a violent temper, racial prejudice, and guilt for having survived.

It was often difficult to make the distinction between subjects who perceived their parents as seriously scarred by their experiences and those who perceived their parents as irrevocably damaged. One subject clearly expressed the latter view. She said, "They just live from day to day, it's not living, their life was just taken away."

Defending against Experiencing Parents' Suffering

In a way similar to their descriptions of defending themselves against specific information communicated to them by their parents, subjects referred to a need to "distance" themselves from the feelings produced by their general knowledge of their parents' suffering. These gave the impression that the knowledge of their parents' experiences created in them an almost overwhelming feeling of obligation. They described feelings of guilt and pity when these defenses were eased. One subject said:

> I think something awful might happen to me if I let myself experience or have the full weight of those years. I just don't want to think about my parents suffering in that way. [Miss D.]

This subject had previously described herself as somewhat resentfully visiting her parents once every week. When asked to describe what might happen to her if she allowed herself to think about her parents' suffering, she said, "I might go home twice a week, I don't know." Another subject described her knowledge of her father's experiences as making her "feel sorry" for him and also making her feel that "I owed it to him, um, to make his life." She knew that this was an impossible task, and felt that her only possible defense, in her words, was to "distance myself" from these feelings.

Although a relatively small proportion of the sample explicitly reported having been affected in the above ways, it seemed quite likely that many were so affected. Indeed, the distance and lack of expressed feelings that was evident as many subjects described their understanding of their parents' past tended to support this speculation.

Admiration for Parents

A feeling of profound admiration and respect was produced in survivors' children when they considered the circumstances their parents had endured. For example, one subject said that, as a consequence of his parents having been in a concentration camp, "I always see them as being able to do anything, any place." Another subject described her perception of her mother in response to the question, "How does her being a survivor affect how you see her?":

> My mother I see as extremely strong, I really admire her for going through what she did, just being hidden underground for such a long time. Yeah, I see her as an incredibly strong woman with this amazing will to live. This drive to live under incredible circumstances. [Miss G.]

It is sometimes difficult for subjects to reconcile the images of strength they associated with their parents' survival with their images of their parents in contemporary reality. For example, one subject said:

> . . . one thing that amazes me is that my mother is just like any old middle-class lady, and my father, he's just like anybody else, that sometimes you wonder how they could have gone through that. . . . [Mr. I.]

Many subjects experienced their parents' survivorhood as having fed their own self-esteem; while others communicated a sense of their own weakness and inferiority in contrast to images of their parents' strength. These felt that they would not have been strong enough to survive. One of these, who is now at the same age as his father was at the time of the Holocaust, compared his own sense of being a "weakling" and "coward" with images of his father's strength. After discussing his father's escape from a slave labor battalion, he concluded:

> My father had experiences where everyone was killed except for him. . . . At the age of 21, my father was a captain in the Red Army, had been wounded three times, had been decorated five times, had been in———and———and some of the hardest fights the Red Army had at the time, and had been taken out of the front lines because he had been wounded so many times and had no one left in the world; and at the age of 23, essentially his formative years, they were almost over. These were the experiences that formed him and he came out of it, resiliant, tough, um, he had absolutely nothing, his former experiences had been wiped away. He had to make his, do everything for himself after that, and I think that had a lot to do with it, I don't know what he was like before, if he was like me or not. . . . [Mr. G.]

Negative Feelings

Although sometimes elusive, a sense emerged that subjects' knowledge of their parents' experiences sometimes produced negative feelings. Perhaps it would be more accurate to say that subjects produced evidence which suggested that they defended against such feelings. One finds such evidence in the following spontaneous denial:

> It doesn't really matter to me, you know, their experiences in Europe because I don't really think it's going to affect my respect for them, because you know, I respect them both, you know. . . . [Mr. A.]

Another subject gave the following description of the reactions of others to her parents as survivors:

> Survivors are looked upon as mutations. 'Oh, you went through it, you got those funny numbers on your arms,' instead of being respected, 'There must be something wrong with them, they went through it.' It's a sensitive thing. . . . A lot of people are afraid of survivors, they don't even want to know about it. . . . They either don't believe it or give sympathy, 'Poor thing.' [Miss C.]

This statement (though certainly a valid one) may gain its force through a defensive use of projection. Still other subjects described their parents' concentration camp experiences as having resulted in an impairment of their ability to relate to their children. These said that having been survivors made it impossible for their parents to understand them or respond to them in a way that would be helpful.

Another veiled area was the negative feeling produced by fantasies of parents' having committed some kind of crime in order to stay alive. One may wonder if these have to do with the child's experience of the parent as an aggressor against him. One subject supported his contempt and rage at his father's behavior toward him and his family with the following image of his father's behavior in the concentration camp:

> As a matter of fact, I have images of my old man doing all right in a camp. I sort of see him as a party guy, going around with the crowd, getting favors from the Germans, I don't know, I don't think he had that rough a time. [Mr. C.]

One may also speculate that images of parents' degradation in the past represent assaults on the child's idealized image of his parents. No concrete evidence exists, and one would not necessarily expect to find such evidence outside of the course of a depth-psychoanalytic treatment. However, in considering this possibility, one might consider the following description of his father provided by one subject:

> When the Russians came and liberated the camp he was in, he was just so dirty and filthy and so strung-out that he broke into a German supply room, and the first thing he did, I guess he must have been in a work camp and eating a little bit, and I guess he knew well enough not to eat too much because you could die after something like that, but the first thing he did, he was so dirty, that he saw a German air-force uniform, he ripped off everything that he was

> wearing, and he put it on, and he went outside, and the only thing that was going on in his mind was that it was clean clothes, and he almost got killed because he was wearing a German uniform, and I guess he just started yelling, because they didn't shoot him.... [Mr. E.]

Involved in this image is a tragic representation which might also be taken for a gruesome black comedy. One must wonder how such an image touches the object representations of the survivor's child.

Altered Reactions to Parents

The context of survivorhood affected subjects' reactions to parents. One such effect was for survivors' children to report feeling "sympathetic," "tolerant," and "understanding" of their parents. This reaction extended to making sacrifices, sometimes major ones, for parents. For example, one subject took a job because he felt a need to "make things easier for them." Another subject, who described herself as wanting to move out of her parents' home, has continued to live with them out of consideration for their past hardships. Still another subject described going to synagogue every Saturday, even though he despised doing so, out of a similar consideration.

Other subjects described trying to restrain anger at their parents. One such subject said, "What my parents went through makes me more careful not to hurt them." Another subject, who resented his parents' negative comments about his non-Jewish girlfriend, also excused them:

> ... but something like that I can understand because of what they went through due to their religion and what they've lost, and it's not that easy to let go you know Judaism to them is something they can't let go of because they've lost so much because of that. [Mr. E.]

Another subject, who otherwise was in an intense, constant rage at her parents, said:

> Yeah, I suppose if they were American parents I could never forgive them for what they did to me, but I take that into consideration that they did go through the nightmare and that in part makes them the way they are. [Miss D.]

Another aspect of this response to parents was to be more "understanding" of them. Often when parents were behaving overly intrusively or overly protectively, the child "understood" and excused this behavior on the basis of its having roots in the experience of persecution. This understanding extended to the pathology that subjects perceived. For example, one subject said of his mother that he was "more tolerant of her worries and when she gets depressed" because of her experiences. Another subject said that he "understood" his mother was a "sick woman" and was "willing to attribute it to her experiences in Europe."

4

The Relationship between Survivor Parents and Their Children

*'Joy, happiness, treasure, my prince, may I suffer your
every pain, my sweet little Mochele,' she cooed and
pressed the boy's head to her bosom.*

*Little Georg tried to tear loose from her arms and
kicked his legs against his mother's lap, 'Let me go,
Mutti, I must go to my horse.'*

[I. J. Singer, 1973, p. 8]

This chapter will describe aspects of the relationship between children of
concentration camp survivors and their parents. The descriptions that follow
are based on three sources of data: first, the subjects' conscious representations
of their relationships with their parents; second, subjects' portrayal of events
that have occurred in their families; third, subjects' styles of describing their
parents. The aim of describing the relationship between parents and their
children is to provide the psychodynamic background necessary for
understanding children of survivors.

Patterns of Subjects' Descriptions of Their Parents

In considering descriptions of parents and parent-child relationships, one must
remember that these often emerge from the background of the child's distorted
perceptions of his parents as well as from his defenses against thoughts and
feelings about his parents. An understanding of these distortions and defenses
is as important as the actual descriptions which emerge, both because they
contribute to the total picture of the survivor family and because they provide
an insight into the typical ego defenses used by children of survivors.

Perhaps the most striking feature of survivors' children's descriptions of
their parents was that many portrayed an extraordinary sensitivity to negative
thoughts and feelings about their parents. On first inquiry, subjects tended to
provide only superficial or idealized descriptions. It was only as the interview

progressed that negative feelings and perceptions, or reports of incidents that might cast parents in a bad light, emerged. At times, the interviewer had the sense that subjects responded to either the interviewer's nonverbal cues which may have suggested his doubts about the subject's idealized portrayal, or to their own internal sense that another person might question the veracity of their portrayal. For example, one subject interrupted her description of her relationship to her parents to say, "It's an odd relationship." By this she meant that other people did not care about their parents as much as she did, and that, in fact, her parents were so special that other children chose them to confide in. Another subject who presented an idealized picture of his parents, and who had not made a single critical remark about them, seemed uncomfortable about the possibility that some negative feeling might have emerged. Toward the end of a glowing description of his parents, he said, in reference to what he wanted his own children to know about them:

> I want them to know what kind of person that my mother, that my parents are, and to respect them for being that, and to accept them for all their faults. I don't want to say they're saints, but I understand them so they don't bother me and I don't know if that came out or not. [Mr. G.]

Another striking feature of some subjects' descriptions was that they adopted a global, undifferentiated mode of perception on which vague, elusive descriptions were based. Often they seemed to experience a momentary panic when asked to be more specific in their descriptions. For example, one subject responded to the interview's request that he describe his mother by saying, "Oh God, what can I say, she's my mother, she does everything, you know, that's required of her, you know, no complaints, well, what do you mean?" In such cases, a possibly negative description sometimes seemed to "sneak out" despite the subjects' caution when confronted by a specific question. For example, the following exchange took place:

> Interviewer: Can you describe your parents' relationship?
> Miss E.: Oh, they're o.k.
> Interviewer: Do they do a lot of things together?
> Miss E.: Oh, they do everything together. My mother's totally dependent on my father.

Subjects who had more precise and detailed descriptions of their parents readily available to themselves often defended against these by isolation of affect. For example, during one interview, the interviewer reflected his understanding of an extremely unstable condition that the subject described as existing in his family. The subject responded that the interviewer's comment "hurt." When asked why, the subject said, "Because it's a reality and someone else referring to it makes it real." He went on to describe himself as tending to "forget" about problems in his family and "pretending" that his family did not have more problems than others.

Four distinct patterns of subjects' descriptions of their parents, none of them mutually exclusive, emerged during the course of interviews. The first pattern involved subjects who provided a portrait of their parents that involved either complete idealizations or a distinctly idealized component. These subjects described their parents as possessing all possible human virtues. They used superlative comments such as "great," "very warm," "a great listener," "interested in everything," "loved by everybody," to describe their parents. An example of such an idealized description follows:

> She's [his mother] an incredibly strong person, she loves her family very much, and she's had punishment after punishment in life. She's an excellent mother and a good wife.... He's [his father] also very strong, takes very good care of my mother, he's very, very independent minded, somewhat of a cynic, he also loves his family very much. He's a very good person, incredibly honest... [Mr.G.]

A small number of subjects provided descriptions of their parents that were as extremely negative as the above subjects' descriptions were idealized. Subjects who provided such descriptions seemed to be as sensitive to and as defensive against providing positive descriptions as other subjects were about providing negative descriptions. For example, one subject summarized her view of her parents by saying:

> I would say that my father is depressed and my mother is just overly anxious, she's just a hysterical Jewish mother, I mean. She called up my shrink one day and my shrink said other people are anxious, your mother is terrified, that's how I describe her, a terrified woman. [Miss D.]

A third mode of describing parents involved the presentation of one parent in very positive terms and the other in very negative terms. The following is an example of this pattern:

> My mother doesn't have a very strong mind, like she's easily swayed in any direction... I mean she's my mother and I love her, but if I were her neighbor, I don't think I'd like her.... I have great respect for my father as a person, he's a very good person, just an unbelievably good person.... [Miss J.]

A fourth pattern of description is represented by a few subjects who were able to provide full, balanced portraits of their parents. These descriptions were typically characterized by unusually sharp and psychologically sophisticated insights. Often these subjects were able to describe the weakness and impairment of their parents' character at the same time they showed a profound appreciation of their parents' resiliency and strength.

The Personality Features of Survivor Parents and Characteristics of the Relationship between Them

Although subjects' descriptions of their parents were influenced by their own defenses, the characteristics that did emerge from their descriptions tended to confirm studies of survivors found in the literature. The following is a summary of subjects' portrayals of their parents as individuals and of the relationships between them.

Personality Features of Survivor Parents

Psychiatric symptomatology was either directly described or could easily be inferred to be a characteristic of all survivor parents. However, a wide range of such symptomatology and severity was evident. Some parents were described as emotionally labile and beset by anxiety that in the extreme resulted in constant agitation. Other symptoms that were reported included profound distrust of others, depression, severe obsessions (particularly in the areas of food, cleanliness, and money), and lack of interest in anything outside of work and home. The only notable discrepancy between the literature and subjects' descriptions was that "survivor guilt" was not a prominent overt theme in most subjects' descriptions.

Subjects also described outstanding positive characteristics of their parents. Included in these were a quality of personal strength and resourcefulness, ambition, a high degree of personal honesty and integrity, and forcefulness in dealings with others. Some survivor parents were also described as extremely commited to their synagogues, in which several took a leadership role, and to Zionist organizations. Many parents were described as being extremely attractive to other people even when they themselves were simultaneously described as not desiring friendships. Perhaps most importantly, survivor parents were described as intensely devoted to their families.

Characteristics of the Relationship between Parents

Although there was a wide range of variety in the quality of parents' relationships with each other, certain distinctive features did appear. Although subjects were able to provide no more than a sketchy chronology, the general impression of the interviewer was that parents had hurried into marriage with the first person who provided them a link to their past. Surivors typically married either immediately after their liberation or immediately after emigration to the United States. Almost all husbands and wives (18 out of 20 couples) were European in origin. In addition, survivors chose spouses who not only came from the same country but also the same area of the country as they. In a number of cases, marriages occurred between relatives, such as cousins and former in-laws. Courtships tended to be extremely brief. Many marriages occurred between people who came from different social classes. In such families, parents often joked that they would never have considered the other as a prospective mate in the period of their lives that preceded the Holocaust.

Survivor families tended to be characterized by isolation. This was true even of those families who lived in predominantly Jewish neighborhoods. The only exceptions to this were affiliations to synagogues, survivor and Zionist organizations, and extensive contact with members of either parent's extended family. Very few friendships with others were described. Those that were described were almost always with other European Jews.

Subjects' descriptions suggested that the parents' relationship with each other was a symbiotic one in which for each parent the spouse was the only person, besides the children, who existed in his or her world. Parents were often described as "needing" each other or "lost" without the other. At the same time, however, parents were described as rarely sharing emotions or responding empathically to each other. They did not seem to be able to relate to each other far beyond performing services for each other and simply occupying the same physical space. This they seemed to need desperately.

The interviewer often had the sense that the children were central to the survivor parents' relationships with each other. One subject described her parents' relationship by saying, "The emphasis was me, I was the center of things." Other subjects described the main issue concerning their parents as negotiating about matters directly related to the children.

While subjects at first denied arguments or fights between their parents, on further inquiry many described their parents as constantly squabbling about "petty" matters. In addition, parents were described as constantly complaining to each other about their individual hardships. Some parents were extremely critical of each other. For example, in a number of cases, one parent's mismanagement of money was the source of seemingly never-ending strife. Subjects reported that on rare occasions explosions of anger occurred and that in such cases either parent might threaten to walk out of the house. However, these incidents were regarded by parents and children alike as aberrations and were not, at least overtly, taken seriously.

The family structure tended to be static, and there was little tolerance for any member deviating from established patterns. Only two conditions were reported that seemed to disrupt the family equilibrium. The first occurred when the family experienced a financial setback. The second occurred with a child's departure from the home. One subject described the disequlibrium caused by her departure by saying, "They [her parents] were faced with each other for the first time." At such times, parents seemed to attempt to maintain the status quo by making demands on their children to phone every day and visit often.

Although the relationship between parents, as one subject described it, was "not great," its strength and endurance was never questioned. None of the 20 subjects' parents had been separated or divorced. In only one case was there even a hint of marital infidelity. Even those few cases of relationships which were dramatically strained by hostility and mistrust had maintained themselves for more than 25 years. The devotion of parents to each other became most evident in times of real stress, such as a devastating illness on the part of one parent.

Dominant Themes in the Parent-Child Relationship

Although each subject's relationship with his parents had unique elements, certain characteristic themes can be identified. For clarity, these will be presented in three sections: the first section will include the aspects of the unavailability of parents for their children's needs, control, guilt, and aggression; the second will include characteristics of the parent-child relationship which inhibited separation; the third will include positive elements in the parent-child relationship. Although every effort was made to define these themes as those patterns of behavior which represented superordinate, dynamic categories, considerable overlap between them exists. For example, the theme of control may be, in part, derivative of aggression and also of the parents' need to inhibit separation. In addition, any specific behavior may be overdetermined and be included under descriptions of any number of themes. For example, parents' overprotective behavior described below as especially pertinent to the problem of the parents' inhibition of separation is also relevant to: unavailability insofar as overprotectiveness may represent counterfeit nurturance and the parents' unavailability for the real needs of the child; control, insofar as overprotectiveness serves to limit the child; aggression, insofar as overprotectiveness may be a reaction formation to the parents' destructive wishes toward their children; guilt, insofar as the child is made to feel badly that he has caused his parents worry; and also a positive element in the parent-child relationship insofar as it reflects the parents' genuine concern for their children.

Unavailability, Control, Guilt, and Aggression

Some combination of unavailability, control, guilt, and aggression were described by all subjects as characteristics of their relationship with their parents.

Unavailability. In spite of the fact that their children were, in many cases, the center of their emotional lives, a huge emotional gap was portrayed in the relationship between parent and child. This gap was most evident as parents failed to satisfy the emotional needs of their children.

At the simplest level, parents were either physically absent or unable to organize their lives in a way that would provide for their children's needs. Some parents, for example, devoted incredibly long hours, sometimes more than 70 hours a week, to their work. In cases in which both parents worked, the child was left alone or with caretakers for a great deal of the time. In other cases, parents moved to remote areas where it was physically difficult, if not impossible, for the child to socialize with peers.

Other evidence of parents' unavailability to their children included descriptions of parents who were unable to share feelings with their children . For example, one subject described his father as having "difficulty expressing warmth and concern for me except by slaving and money." Parents' unavailability may also be inferred from descriptions by children of their own inability to communicate with their parents. For example, one subject said, "I could never share feelings and emotions with them." Another described the following:

> I don't think it was an intimate 'Leave it to Beaver' relationship. I don't remember ever going and pouring out all my problems to them. In part, what it was, that my father would be sort of friendly-sarcastic about perfectly, normal, healthy kinds of things and I became sort of shy....[Mr. G.]

This unavailability often extended to the lack of simple communication between parent and child. For example, one subject said, "They're not conversationalists, it's very hard to sit down with either of them and have a conversation." In some cases, a feeling of having come out of an emotional void became evident. For example, some subjects described the following:

> Sometimes I needed them and they weren't there. [Miss. I.]

> They use to take me places when I was a kid, like the park on Sunday, but talking, I could never really talk to them, on no level could they comprehend what I was talking about... I had no one to communicate with for most of my childhood. [Miss D.]

> I had to learn about things myself, there was no one to teach me. [Mr. H.]

> I never did anything wrong so I never had to talk to them. [Miss E.]

Needless to say, many parents had difficulty helping their children deal with the normal issues of development. One subject, explaining his parents' inability to help him master his difficulties entering the world outside his family, said, "It was hard for my parents to understand this world because of where they came from.... " Many subjects described not having sufficient confidence in their parents to approach them with problems. For example, one subject said:

> Always a kind of superficial relationship with my father, lots of love and affection, you know, warmth and his willingness to do anything for me. I never discussed my problems with him because I always felt that it makes him uncomfortable, which it does. It makes him want to run; he likes everything nice and pleasant, he's always soothing things over.... [Miss G.]

Another said:

> I'd never come to her [her mother] with anything I didn't think she could handle.... If something was really bothering me, she wouldn't be able to handle it because she'd get upset for me. [Miss I.]

Two elements characterize both the above examples. First, the parents' unavailability for the child's needs seemed to derive more from inability than unwillingness. Second, the parents' failure to provide genuine nurturance was camouflaged by the provisions of counterfeit nurturance.

In extreme cases of parental unavailability, the child was left feeling unappreciated and unvalued. The following statements, in response to the question "What about you are your parents pleased with?" portrayed this feeling:

> About me, I don't know, I wish you could ask my parents. [Mr. A.]

> It's a very hard question, like they're not very good with praise. [Miss F.]

> I guess I don't get that much praise or criticism. [Mr. I.]

Control. Survivor parents exerted an extraordinary degree of control over their children's behavior. At some times the interviewer had the sense that the parent was highly invested in the child's behaving in specifically prescribed ways. At other times he had the sense that the parent's investment in the child's specific behavior was secondary to investment in being able to control the child for the sake of control. Although parental control was described or inferred to be a characteristic of all families, in some families overt control, through discipline, was extremely rigid while in others it was extremely lax. Children in the latter type of family seemed to be as constrained in their behavior as children in the former. One subject described her nearly total freedom as quite stressful. After she described her freedom "to do anything" and her parents' inability to set limits, she was asked if she enjoyed it. She responded:

> No, no. Many times I wish they would say 'No, don't do that.' I always felt that it was me who would have to decide what I was going to do, and sometimes I needed them. [Miss I.]

Another subject described his parents' permissiveness as follows:

I never had any of the problems that a fair percentage of other kids had. If I wanted to wear my hair long, I could wear it long; if I wanted to wear dungarees, I could wear dungarees; if I wanted to go to school, 'Go to school'; don't want to go to school, 'don't go to school, it's your life not mine.' [Mr. G.]

One may infer that the apparent permissiveness constituted a double bind insofar as it was accompanied by subtle messages not to take advantage of it. For example, although Mr. G. said that his parents allowed him anything he ever wanted, he said, "I never wanted anything."

In such cases, the degree of control exerted by parents could be overwhelming. For example, Mr. G., described above, indicated his own feeling of being controlled by his parents as follows:

I may have been on a leash, but I never knew it. . . . Somebody once told me that the reason I became a ——— was that my parents worked it out so cleverly. You know, whereas most parents actively laid down guidelines to follow, my parents by giving me the freedom that they did and by giving me hints whenever I moved from side to side, in actuality directed me into what they, I wanted. [Mr. G.]

Whether or not parents exerted strict control through overt discipline, they exhibited a behavior that may best be described as intrusive. One subject described this mildly as "They give me their advice." Another described this as follows:

During one period in my life, I was reading, my mother would say, 'What are you hanging around the house for?' O.K., I'd go out and play. Then she said, 'You play too much, you don't read enough.' They were always after me, you know. [Mr. C.]

In the transcript of the above subject's interview, the phrase "Leave me alone," in the context of something he would often tell his parents, appears frequently. Another subject also described going through "Leave me alone" phases.

In some cases, parents were reported to have made massive attempts to determine every aspect of their children's behavior. Often, it seems, they attempted to raise their children according to the European codes under which they themselves were raised. For example, one subject described his parents attitudes:

They want us to grow up so we should be right, you know. They don't want us to stay out late, you know. They still treat us like old European children, you know, in 1970. They're basically in that kind of attitude. [Mr. A.]

In these cases, parents do not take into account either contemporary American values which are different from their own or the growing age of their children. For example, the above-quoted subject was asked if his parents had changed as he grew older. He said:

I don't think they've changed at all, they still hold their rigid policies. They're not changing because we're growing older. Whatever their policies were when we were young, I see that because I see my younger brother. They treat him in the same way they treat me. [Mr. A.]

Not only did parents attempt to control how their children behaved, but they also attempted to control their children's beliefs and attitudes. This was often evident as subjects described their parents attempts to discourage their emergent humanistic beliefs. For example, a number of subjects reported their parents criticizing them for trusting people. Other subjects reported that they and their parents would have quite heated arguments about political issues.

Some subjects gave evidence of their parents' strict control of them not by actual descriptions (as often tended to be the case among those subjects who had struggled against their parents' control) but by portraying themselves as living their lives in absolute compliance with their parents' demands. Some of these subjects indicated that they adhered to their parents' values merely in an effort to please them. Others adopted their parents' values as if they were their own.

Guilt. That guilt is a characteristic of the survivors' children's relationship with their parents is suggested both by reported feelings from which parent-child interactions can be reconstructed, and also by specific incidents. Subjects' feelings of guilt can be located in three sometimes overlapping contexts: first, guilt for not being "a good enough" child; second, guilt for having grown up in "too easy" circumstances which, in the extreme, meant guilt for not having been in a concentration camp; and third, guilt for expressions of anger toward parents.

An example of guilt for not having been a "good enough" child was given by a subject who said, "I feel very suffocated by my own feelings of guilt for not helping out more." While he denied that his parents provoked this feeling in him in any way, one must wonder if his parents did not subtly express their disappointment to him, perhaps at the very same time that they were expressing gratitude for his feelings of concern for them. In another case, the parents' role of provoking guilt is clearer, although the subject denied feeling guilty. She reported that her father had told her that "he thought he should have another child." She explained that he made this statement "because he feels that I'm not affectionate enough, I'm not giving enough. 'Some children are one way and some children are the other way and you're the other way.' " In survivor families, one behavior which clearly resulted in the explicit or implicit accusation that the child was "not good enough" was the child's attempt to separate from the family. A great many subjects reported feeling guilty as they prepared to move out of their parents' homes, particularly since their parents made massive demands for them to stay.

The second context for children's guilt involved parents' telling their children that they "had it too good." Parents would often compare their own lives to those of their children and present the conclusion that the child "has everything" while they had suffered. For example, one father told his child, who had just been bought a new pair of shoes, "You think we had shoes!" Another subject reported that when, as a child, he was unhappy, his mother would say, "You have food in your mouth, don't you?" While subjects did not always report that such communications made them feel guilty, a number portrayed guilt by being scrupulously careful not to waste anything or unnecessarily indulge themselves in material things. Closely connected, was that, in spite of their past hardships, parents were still willing to "sacrifice themselves" for their children. As has been noted, many parents did work long and difficult hours. As a consequence of knowledge of this fact alone, many subjects described a desire to work in order to ease their parents' burdens. One subject reported that, in spite of this desire, her parents accused her of not being "grateful enough." They also would not let her work. She explained:

> It was more for them, really, reassuring themselves that I'm getting better than the neighbor's kid is getting. In a way, they wanted me to have it better than they ever had, ever will have. [Miss C.]

Her explanation leads to the conclusion that besides her parents' need to provide everything they could for her, they also needed to be able to accuse her of not being sufficiently grateful to them. The parents thus needed to interfere with her working, both to save her from the "burden" of work and to prevent her from showing her appreciation. Parents, as they insisted that their sacrifices be recognized, in fact, insisted that something be given in return. The following quotation illustrates the link between parents' sacrifices, children's guilt, and obligation to satisfy the demands implicit in the parents' sacrifice. Beginning by describing his parents, the subject said:

> I don't know, constantly bothering with the son to see that he's going to grow up to be somebody. That's an important thing that I got, I don't know ... the idea that I have to be somebody, my brother has to be somebody, that they sacrificed their lives. That's another reason you [subject substitutes "you" for "I"] want to know about their lives, because you get the idea that they sacrificed their lives for you, basically that you, if there's anything that they live for, it's my brother and I, you can't be a bum, you can't do this, you can't do that, you have to make something out of yourself. [How does that feel?] I really think I understand it, some people think, I, I mean I went out with this woman one time, and she said I'm too understanding of that and I should be more independent of them and do whatever I want, but I talked to my cousin about that fact that our parents want us to be something and that they're constantly emphasizing the fact that they worked for us. He had the feeling too and a feeling of responsibility to them more so than, sometimes, a feeling of responsibility to himself. I'm not saying himself, but a heavy responsibility to them. He has that same feeling, what they've gone through for us, it's our duty, to give something back to them. I really have that

feeling that they sacrificed for me. I don't know, maybe it's because they keep reinforcing it. [How do you mean?] You know, and you don't have to give them anything when you become something. You know, that if we do give them something, they'll really be surprised. Something like that is a one-sentence occurrence in a day, maybe every two or three days, they'll throw in a sentence like that. [Mr. I.]

A third context of guilt occurred with the child's expressions of aggressive and negative feelings toward parents. Parents seemed to be sensitive to such expressions even when the actual evidence for them was tenuous. For example, one subject said to his father, "He's always said that I've somehow tried to be intellectually above him." The subject's own sensitivity to the possible validity of this accusation was such that he said, "And maybe I have, trying to tell him about my field, but he really is, he is, I regret having done that if I did do that." Generalization of this sensitivity became evident as he presented his own academic career to the interviewer as if it were mediocre. On closer examination, however, it turned out that he had a brilliant record. When confronted, he said that he had withheld description of his successes because he did not want the interviewer to think that he was "bragging." In other cases, subjects portrayed guilt in response to arguments that they had with their parents. A stereotyped system, defined by three stages, emerged. The first involved provocation by parents. The second involved angry expressions by the child, sometimes including cursing with obscene language. The third involved the child's feeling guilty and penitent, often to an extreme degree.

Aggression. While the characteristics of unavailability, control, and guilt may be understood, in part, as defensive transformation of the parents' aggression, more direct evidence of parental rage exists.

The clearest evidence of the free-floating rage evident in many survivor families was provided by some subjects who described their parents as often hitting them. One such subject described his mother as "nervous and free with her hands." Another described his mother as losing her temper when he would do something that displeased her, for example, not eating or having bad school marks. At such times she would strike whatever portion of his body she could reach. Still another subject described his father hitting him until he reached adolescence and was as big as his father. On one occasion, he hit his father back with sufficient force to knock him down. Still another subject described the following:

I used to get hit a lot for anything because I was the bad sheep compared to my sisters who were very good. My father used to hit me with a strap; I used to hate him for it. I used to lock myself in the bathroom and my father once plastered up the lock so I couldn't lock myself in the bathroom so he could hit me. All my life I just really hated him and I started hitting him and cursing him back. [How old were you?] Pretty young, about 12. Curses would be 'Get the fuck off," "Fuck you,' and he'd hit me more. I always felt bad after I said it . . . I always would feel bad but I'd just get so upset. [Mr. E.]

Additional evidence for the free-floating rage characterizing survivor families was provided by subjects' descriptions of the frequent and violent verbal arguments between themselves and their parents and their parents' unpredictable temper tantrums.

Less extreme examples of parents' aggression was provided by many subjects' descriptions of parents' harsh and critical attitudes toward the children. For example, one survivor couple, whose son worked for a social welfare agency, wanted to know, "What I'm doing with these lousy people." His father complained about him "in relation to what some of my cousins are doing." The cumulative result of their attitude was expressed in response to the question, "What are your parents pleased with about you?" He said, "I don't know what they have to praise me about, really, just that I don't take drugs." Another subject summarized his parents' positive expressions about him by saying, "I don't think they have many faults against me." At times, parents' criticism could be quite brutal. For example, one subject described the following:

> I remember in sixth grade, I brought my first non-Jewish friend home. My old man went crazy, not when he was in the house, after he left the house. He was yelling, 'What are you hanging around with him for! Look at him! He's dirty and he's filthy!'

Another subject reported that her father "is not very subtle" and that his comments "often come down like a ton of bricks." She gave the example of approaching him, feeling badly, to tell him that she had just broken her engagement to her fiance. He responded, "Thank God."

One may speculate that the parents' critical attitudes had the joint aim of withholding positive emotional supplies and of actively humiliating the child in order to express aggression. One subject described her father as follows: "My father is the type, he's the type of person who'll criticize an awful lot, but he'll rarely compliment because he wouldn't want it to go to my head." [Miss B.] Another subject described his parents as "surprised" when he earned a university scholarship. Still another subject described her father as always complaining that she was "too skinny" and that he was "ashamed" to be seen on the street with her.

On the one hand, massive denial occurred as subjects minimized the importance of the expressions of anger, described above, in their families. For example, subjects tended to describe many of the incidents and feelings above as if they represented a temporary aberration. On the other hand, anger and aggression were also characterized by the idea that the child, having provoked it, could not mollify it. That is, aggression was presented as if it had run its natural course and could not be interrupted. For example, one subject described his father's attitude as "nothing is forgotten or forgiven." He gave the example of being in the car when his father went through a red light. A policeman stopped his father to give him a ticket, and his father explained that he hadn't seen the light. This satisified the policeman until the child blurted out that he had. Although the subject was only eight years old at the time, his father continues to tell him that "it was a stupid thing to do." Another subject described her father as chasing her around the house when she said something "disrespectful." There was no way for her to mollify her father's anger. She said,"it would slip out, you'd barely said it before you'd regret it. But you know, there was no such thing as an apology. You'd get a smack first" [Miss. C.].

Characteristics of the Parent-Child Relationship Inhibiting Separation

Perhaps the most outstanding theme which emerged as subjects described their families was that of inhibition of separation from parents. Many of the characteristics described in the preceding section can be understood as either causing or symptomatic of the inhibition of separation. For example, parental unavailability may, in part, reflect a symbiotic realtionship insofar as the parents' external distance represented the parents' internal failure to maintain a self-object differentiation. Similarly, the parents' extraordinarily controlling behavior may have represented the parents' attempt to exert control as if their children were extensions of themselves.

In many families of survivors, an undercurrent existed, often running parallel to the previously described rage, defined by the idea that the only value remaining in each parent's life was the children. One subject described her parents' life as:

> This life here isn't living for them, it's just as if they were uprooted and they died, and now they just have to exist because they died . . . they can't really attach meaning to life. [Miss J.]

In this context, children were constantly admonished to create for themselves lives better than their parents' lives. Children were given the idea, implicitly or explicitly, that their parents' total orientation was toward their welfare: "They never said it, but it was my life and whatever I had to do came first. Everything was done to make things easier for me." [Mr. G.]. This concern that the child have things easier than his parents, and the parents' willingness to sacrifice everything for the child's welfare, paradoxically produced in the child a feeling of responsibility not only for his own life but also for his parents':

> I feel my life is not only my responsibility but two other people are going to pieces if anything happens to me, they're just completely, their whole life revolves around me. [Miss D.]

The feelings generated by the contradiction between the parents' ostensible sacrifice for the child and the burdens placed on the child to live life for his parents were intensified in situations where, though the parents were so needy, they could not openly accept what was offered. Or, if they did, they had to appear to return what they received, with interest: "They're sort of dependent on us [the subject and her husband] but, uh, at the same time, they want to do ten times over for us if we do for them" [Miss I]. It was critical to survivor parents that their children accept what they had to offer, even if it was only a meal: "Oh, food was so important, if you like my food, then you like me, that was her attitude. [And if you don't eat?] Then you don't like me, after four portions, 'You don't like it?' " [Miss I.].

Children were forced by their parents' stated willingness to give them everything, to set their own limits, based on the estimation of what their parents could afford. For example, one subject, after telling how her parents provided her with everything she wanted, explained that she never became spoiled because "I didn't need more than I had and I never asked them for more." Sometimes the result of parental overindulgence was the child's deprivation. One subject described the following:

Before, you know, I really looked upon them, you know, as people who I actually depended on for money for everything, now, I try to make it easier for them, because I know my two younger brothers, I try to work, I don't try to ask my father for money or anything like that, you know, I'm thankful I've got a place to sleep and that they're both, that everybody's healthy, that's all. [Mr. A.]

The confusion between the parents' apparent self-sacrifice, overt unwillingness to receive, and covert demands on the child find expression in the following train of obsessive concern:

I wonder...how I'll treat my parents when they're old....[What thoughts come to your mind about it?] It's very difficult to say, very, very difficult. It will be very difficult for me, for instance, to take care of my mother because all my mother will be able to do without my father, say, I know I would be the one to take care of my mother. There would be nothing I could do, for example, try and be nice, but I can be cold when I want to be, I can be impatient, I can be nasty, and try as I can, I can curb myself but essentially I would be neglectful. You can't spend all your time, you know, with your mother, or with an older person, and try as you can, you cannot fulfill her needs like my father could; and uh, my father will not take anything from me, that I know. [Mr. G.]

The dynamic source of this confusion is that parents lived either vicariously or symbiotically through their children's lives. One subject said, "She [his mother] can't distinguish between herself and her children." Subjects provided clues that their parents expected them both to live out the dreams and aspirations that they had had for themselves before their lives were crushed by the Holocaust, and also to re-create, in their own lives, the loved ones who were lost. Several subjects were pursuing the professions that their parents had intended to follow. These typically denied that their choices were determined by their parents. One said, "Essentially, quite by accident, I turned into exactly what they wanted." Almost all of the subjects were named after relatives lost by parents during the Holocaust. In one family of two children, each was told that he reminded the parent of the relative whose name he bore. Another subject reported that he had recently learned some of the details of his grandfather's life and that, to his surprise, many of the things he has done in his life paralleled his grandfather's involvements. In a number of cases, the child had not only become a representation of lost relatives but also to take on the function of one of his parents. For example, one subject described his mother's expectation of him:

> She's very ambivalent about me and treats me as a husband and a father and a son at the same time, and it reflects in trying to treat me as a child and relate to me as a husband, or father, at the same time, so it's a difficult situation. [Mr. F.]

The parents' living through their children was not always as specifically manifested as in the requirement that the children isomorphically recreate the parents' lost objects and aspirations. Often, it was sufficient that the children simply become successful. One subject, embarked on a professional career, said, "They had plans for me, very ambitious plans." Another subject described the things her parents liked as "*naches* [i.e., comfort, gratification, or joy] from their children." Still another subject said of her parents, "They live off my successes." The children's accomplishments were regarded as antidotes to the parents' sense of their own failure in living. Thus, many parents were extremely overt about their demands that the child surpass them. For example, one subject, whose father considered himself a "failure," described the following:

> My parents were puzzled by my being an abysmal student, and I was spanked for bad report cards, and once I did do well, it was like a narcotic. They expected me to go on to do well. [Mr. F.]

Another described the following:

> Well, they want me to have things they couldn't have, you know . . . they want me to take advantage of the schooling, the things they wanted for themselves but could never get. . . . They want me to make something of myself, they don't want me, in their eyes, to just waste my life away, being a bum, because they just, the prime of their life was plucked away. [Mr. E.]

The importance of the child's being a success was expressed by one parent who would typically say, in response to any positive event in her son's life, "It's good that this happened to you, it gives me the strength to go on."

In addition, it seemed that it was extremely important for parents to present their children as successful to others. Often, for example, parents who were very critical about their children, were described as also boasting about them to neighbors. One subject, who is married but lives in the same neighborhood as her parents, explained, "I represent them in a way, in a very strong way, especially in this community."

At the same time, parents became distraught at events in the children's lives that they regarded as less than successful but about which the children were quite content. For example, one subject reported that his sister was planning to marry a man with some vaguely defined motor impairment:

> They're just so upset about it, totally upset, because they want the best for their children and I guess it's sort of selfish because they can't understand my sister's in love with him and that's all that counts. All they can see is the headaches she's going to have with this guy with the bad leg. 'The cripple' they call him. [Mr. E.]

Another subject described his mother as follows:

> She has almost sympathetic pains, if her children had pains, she would too. If my brother decides to take a year off from school, she would experience it as a mortal blow, as if she can't differentiate what makes her happy and what makes us happy. [Mr. D.]

In addition to insisting that their children be a success, parents also insisted that their children maintain their ideas and beliefs. For example, many parents put tremendous pressure on their children to maintain Jewish traditions. Parents disliked and discouraged their children's developing their own views of the world. For example, one subject, describing what his parents did not like about him, said:

> I could be stubborn, I used to be a lot more suggestible to their wishes and ideas and I guess a very great change, well not a great change, but I have changed due to being outside of their influence and so, by not being around them, I feel that I don't need them as much, uh, listen to everything they say to me, I more or less do what I think I should do even though I take into account their advice. I do think that might bug them on occasion, I might have been like overstating my case, I don't see any major things they dislike. [Mr. J.]

The interviewer's impression was that the more compliant a subject was to his parents' attitudes and beliefs, the less insistent he was that his parents had pressured him about them. Thus, it seemed that the man cited above understated rather than overstated his case.

In themselves, the specific views and attitudes that the parents insisted their children adopt seemed to pose a formidable barrier to the emergence of the child from a symbiotic relationship with his parents to a participation in the affairs of the world outside his family. Only two subjects included in their description of their parents' world view any affectively positive or prosocial element. In general, parents stressed a massively distrustful view of the world in which personal survival was always threatened. Such views were communicated directly or indirectly, from childhood. For example, one subject, describing her mother's image of the world as negative, said, "I can't remember a specific instance where my mother told me anything. . . . I just sort of got an overall impression." An example of an early communication of the dangers of the outside world was provided as one subject described a fairy tale that her mother often told her: "It would start out with, when little children were bad, they'd take them out to the forest, and the boogie men would come, and I would always get very scared" [Miss F.]. A less metaphorical description was provided by another subject who said the following:

> They were constantly telling me not to trust people, that the world was a vicious place and you have to watch out and, uh, not as often in religious terms but just in terms of life. I should watch out because I'm Jewish, some of that was involved, but, uh, principally that I had a much too idealistic conception of things. I was much too honest, particularly my father but also my mother, they were always concerned that I was much too honest and that I'd never get anywhere in life being that honest. . . . These lessons were consistently from childhood, I remember being overwhelmed by a constant derogatory approach to life and people, particularly my mother, my father began to reiterate them as I became assertive about what I believed. [Mr. F.]

Often parents' communications seemed to be directed against relationships the child formed or might form with someone outside the family. For example, whenever one subject was upset about a spat with a school chum, her mother would say: " 'There are no such things as true friends, your only friends are your husband and your children.' People have to be ultra, ultra perfect to be trusted" [Miss C.]. Another subject described the following:

> My mother always said, 'Don't tell that to your friends.' This fear of telling, you know, your secrets to other people, you know, just this sick, sick, sick idea that it was to be very controlled, just tell people certain things and not others [Miss D.].

Parents attempted to replace their children's sometimes more idealistic perspective with the idea that survival in the world requires extraordinary effort, strength, and self-reliance. For example, one subject described the following:

> My father tried to show me, how, I think, tough life is and how good I had it and to knock starry-eyed ideas out of my eyes. . . . I think what my parents always tried to do was to make me self-sufficient and to give me some sort of character, I think my parents view me as some sort of a lamb, that left to my own devices I would end up floundering around. . . . They were trying to build me up to the world in a nice way, you know. . . . If you want something in life, you have to work for it, no one's going to give you anything, you don't have to kill anybody for it, but rely on it. [Mr. G.]

Often the thrust of parents' communications about the world was to define an adversary relationship between their children and the outside world. The following statements reflect this position:

> That attitude of [long pause], you really have to, I don't know, it's mixed, you really have to, you deserve everything like making a lot of money, really striving and having lots of education and really putting yourself against the evil world. [Miss G.]

> Well, they really didn't tell me, but I see the only person you can trust is yourself, so you got to learn that yourself, it's something that people can't really teach you. . . . [Mr. A.]

> They've always tried to teach me to stand up for my own rights, my own interests, you know, not necessarily not to hurt other people, but not to be pushed around. [Mr. B.]

> You've got to get things by yourself, nobody's going to give you anything. [Mr. I.]

One component of parents' positions was that Jewishness was the focus of hostility and distrust in the world. For example, subjects described the following:

> My mother, I think, taught me, you can't trust people, especially who aren't Jewish. Yeah, I really sense and I've always sensed that my mother doesn't trust anyone, that you can't trust anyone, that you really have to, uh, like there's always this ulterior motive, you have to, uh, be careful. . . . [Miss G.]

> You can never really trust them [non-Jews] you can never really be sure. [Mr. I.]

> I've always heard comments like, it's always nice to have friends like that [non-Jews] but they'll be the first ones to turn on you. [Miss B.]

> Beware, you're a Jew and this [the Holocaust] could happen again. [Mr. C.]

Concomitant to their view of the world as actively malevolent, parents often expressed tremendous anxiety about the safety of their children. Parents were excessively preoccupied with all the dangers that might confront their children if they ventured out of the house, and therefore were overprotective throughout the child's life. This overprotectiveness was equally evident in parents who were otherwise inaccessible to their children. Many parents attempted to limit their children's freedom of movement. One subject described the following: "They [her mother and grandmother] think if you don't go somewhere, that's the best thing, just stay home because it's dangerous." [Miss J.] Other parents were extremely strict about setting limits on the extent of their children's commerce with the outside world. For example, they complained that they could not go to sleep at night unless their children were safely home and thus insisted that their children be home at an early hour.

The central demand made by survivor parents was that their children never leave them. Survivor parents, throughout the development of their children, potentiated whatever conflicts their children had about achieving separation and individuation. One subject described his mother's reactions to his attempts to become his own person as follows:

> She just took a much more active role in my life, just an incredibly much more active role, and in doing things that I thought jeopardized my self-assertion. I've had a feeling for a long time that she was intimidated by my sense of independence, you know.... [Mr. F.]

Another said:

> They're really over-anxious for me, and they can't let go. One thing that characterizes them is that they live and die for me, that's, that's their lives. [Miss D.]

Subjects remembered incidents from their childhood in which their parents greatly exacerbated their conflicts about entering the world. This was particularly true of the child's first experiences away from home. For example, one subject remembered that on her first day of school her mother had wheeled her to kindergarten in a stroller. At later ages, parents manifested the same difficulty in "letting go" of their children. For example, one subject remembered that in her early teen years, she had wanted to go to summer camp with her friends. Her parents, who otherwise indulged her in every way, reacted as follows:

> They would never hear of it because they could never stand the thought of my going away, they used to tell me that they didn't have the money, but I knew they did. [Miss E.]

While a number of the subjects could not directly comment on the pressures their parents put on them to inhibit their separation, the fact that they were still living at home and had never experienced a desire to live away or go away to college spoke for itself. Other subjects described the tremendous struggle they had had to engage in to leave home for college. After having left, they reported that they still had to contend with their parents' demands that they visit home often, and when they did, to stay for long periods. One subject reported that her decision to spend part of her vacation with friends resulted in a bitter argument with her parents. Another subject, whose parents live in the midwest, left her parents' home to go to graduate school. She reported that her parents continue to bombard her with their fantasy that she will marry and settle in their hometown. It is extremely important for her to please her parents. However, she has come to realize that:

> The major fact is, if I were this good girl, whatever this means, just dedicated to my parents, never opposing them or defying them or going against them in any way, then, maybe they'd be satisfied. [Miss G.]

Positive Elements

In contrast to some of the problematic and indeed pathogenic components of the survivor parent-child relationship, there also existed a profound reserve of emotional resources and positive relatedness. It is this capacity to manifest both extremes with devotion as the anchor at one end that is so striking. Even parents whose ability to relate to their children was grossly impaired were capable, if only briefly, to demonstrate genuine love and tenderness for their children. A few subjects, for example, described very moving episodes from their childhood in which their parents, not knowing any bedtime story to tell them, would make up one. In such stories, the child was a central figure who was loved and protected, if not by the parents themselves, then by some imaginary beings.

One central theme of many subjects' descriptions of their parents was that they had never doubted their parents' love for them. This theme emerged both when parents were described as emotionally distant and also when subjects described tension and angry feelings between themselves and their parents. For example, one subject described his father as quite brutal and himself as "hating the bastard." Nevertheless, he recalled many fond memories he had of his father throughout his life. Other descriptions of the child's faith in his parents were:

> I think that there's a lot of love between us but I don't think, it's very rarely expressed, you know, it's taken for granted. We know that it's there but we don't go around saying it. [Mr. J.]

> It's [her relationship with her parents] nice but it's very strained, too. It's like I can never really feel close to them, but you know, I appreciate like, they are very dedicated to me.... [Miss B.]

> They hold onto their feelings, don't show very much, but I really know that love is underneath. [Miss F.]

No matter how controlling and intrusive parents were, their children still felt that, at least consciously, their parents had had their best interests in mind. Some subjects had the understanding that their parents wanted very much to help them with their problems, even if they could not because they were too threatened or too unequipped to do so. Although the image of the parents' struggle to give their children what they themselves had been cheated of—even coupled with the constant reminder of the sacrifice—constituted a tremendous burden, it could also be taken as proof of the parents' love. Thus many children emerged from their relationships with their parents with a real sense of a stable and loving object. For example, one subject, who described himself as "missing" his father who had spent long hours working throughout his childhood, was able to say: "He was never much about but there was a real sense that, you know, you know, he was my father and he'd come through."

While many parents burdened their children with idealizations, some were also able to communicate a more genuine sense of valuing their children. Other parents, who were harshly critical, were also able to let the child know that, at least sometimes, they preferred him to any other imaginable child. Some were able to assure their children of their valuing them even as they were so critical. For example, one subject said, "They think that I'm lazy and I suppose they're right, but they have faith in me, you know, that I'll make something of myself, whatever that is" [Mr. E.].

5

The Influence of the Past on Identity

*The nature of the identity conflict often depends on
the latent panic pervading a historical period. Some
periods in history become identity vacua caused by
three basic forms of human apprehension: fears
aroused by new facts... which radically expand and
change the whole world image; anxieties aroused by
symbolic dangers vaguely perceived as a consequence
of the decay of existing ideologies; and the dread of an
existential abyss devoid of spiritual meaning.*

[E. Erikson, 1970, 1973]

This chapter will examine the imprint of the historical past, through the imagery of both the Holocaust and the European world that preceded it, on the identity of children of survivors. Identity is broadly defined as the person's basic organizing principles which determine his interactions with the world. Identity includes the beliefs, attitudes, and behaviors involved in the person's perception of himself, of others, and of the world.

Conscious Experience of the Influence of the Past on the Self

The extent to which subjects regarded issues of survivorhood and the historical past to have influenced their own identities ranged from those who consciously experienced such issues as central to their lives, to those who denied any impact at all of these issues on their identity.

Influence of the Holocaust

At one extreme, two subjects indicated a preoccupation with issues of the Holocaust to the extent that they regarded every personal action and commitment as if it were in context of the past. One of these subjects described herself as "haunted" by images of the Holocaust to the extent that she saw her right to exist challenged by the horrors of the past. She said:

> Sometimes you walk around and think you have no right to be alive and you have no right to have a coat because these people who were better than you, and in a sense, they didn't do a thing, they were all herded off, and you're left.... [Miss C.]

To a lesser extent, other subjects indicated that their political ideology and world view were influenced, to some degree, by their consciousness of the past. For example, one subject attributed a general pessimism about the world to the model of the Nazi domination of Europe.

Many subjects denied that the Holocaust *per se* had influenced their lives. Rather, they saw it as affecting their interactions with their parents, which in turn affected the development of their character. Some of these subjects felt that their extensive study of the Holocaust was in the service of understanding their parents rather than the historical events of the time.

Some subjects contradicted themselves when they reflected on the impact of their parents' survivorhood on their lives. For example, one subject, in answer to the question "Did your parents' having been survivors influence who you are, as a person?" said:

> I'd say again, I'm not sure if it's as much being a child of a survivor as much as the fact of being an immigrant. [Can you say something more?] I remember as a kid there was something glamorous about a real American family, they're different from how we are ... you know, I'd say maybe being an only child has affected me more than being *the survivor of a concentration camp* [emphasis added]. [Miss D.]

She did not appear to recognize her slip of the tongue. However, a bit later in the interview, contradicting what she had said earlier, she spontaneously said:

> It's what makes me tick, in part, the fact that my parents were in a concentration camp and were immigrants, and it had a lot of influence on how I look at things. [Miss D.]

At the other extreme, four subjects clearly stated that they felt that the Holocaust and their parents' experiences as victims had had no impact on them. One of these stated that it had "so little" impact on her that she made a point of avoiding anything which might recall the Holocaust to her. The second of these subjects described feeling "distant" from the whole area, while the third insisted that he avoided defining himself in terms of his parents' history so that he could define himself, above all, as a "human being." The fourth of these subjects, after denying any impact on himself, said, "Maybe I don't feel the depth of emotion [about the Holocaust] that I should."

Influence of the Past

For some subjects, images of the historical past retained a prominent position in their consciousness. For others, such imagery was blurred.

Subjects portrayed their involvement with the past in different ways. For a few, the vision of the European past was idealized. For example, one subject said, "Life there was just beautiful . . . it was very peaceful, like tranquil life." For some, early childhood memories were the vehicle through which they expressed their affiliation with the European past. For example, one subject who came to the United States from Poland in late childhood remembered the town synagogue with a continuing sense of awe. In particular, he remembered its beauty and size, and the fact that, though it had many rows of pews, only the front few were ever occupied. Another subject described the following early memory: "I remember going to my uncle's house and meeting the lady who my mother told me had saved her life, she died right after." In both these memories, one perceives the subject's feeling of an historical void, that becomes a personal loss. Another subject was more explicit. He described his continuing fascination with the world of the *shtetl*. His impression was of the richness of life and culture. At the same time, he feels that "It's dead and a lot of good things died with it." He feels his knowledge of the *shtetl* has contributed to his own life.

Other subjects described their affiliation with the past through a desire to visit their parents' native town or through the study of European history and Yiddish literature. One such subject said, "While I feel a warmth toward these things, I feel also a certain distance, trying to find my identity in this world." While concomitant involvement with the present characterized most subjects who portrayed an affiliation with the past, one subject, who had been born in the United States, described herself as having chosen to adhere to the values, standards, and ideas of the past. "I'm a typical European," she said.

Some of the subjects whose vision of the past was distant and negative had never made any attempt to study it. Some of them described having resented their parents' foreignness. Their general conception of Europe, if any, was one of a regimented, closed society in which a person's life revolved around nothing but his parents, his work, and his religion. Thus, for these subjects, affiliation with the past was repudiated as an aspect of identity.

The Importance of the Holocaust as Expressed through Thoughts and Behavior

In addition to the subjects' direct evaluation of the importance of the Holocaust to their lives, they also gave evidence of the importance of the Holocaust to them by describing thoughts and behaviors that were related to it. Subjects' reflections and attitudes about the Holocaust, their use of the Holocaust to provide the framework of a moral universe, their involvement in seeking more information about it, their interactions with others related to it, and their intent to tell their own children about their parents' experiences, constituted evidence in support of their statements concerning the importance of the Holocaust to their lives. Sometimes the quality and extent of these thoughts and behaviors were congruent with their self-report. At other times, their activities, for example, actually visiting the site of a concentration camp, betrayed their denial of their involvement in Holocaust concerns.

Reflections and Attitudes

The themes of subjects' reflections and attitudes about the Holocaust, from childhood to the present, will be described. Several themes can be identified as characteristic of different subjects during their childhood and adolescent years. The most prevalent of such themes involved wondering about relatives who had been killed. In particular, subjects wondered about and wished for grandparents.

Another prevalent theme of childhood thoughts involved conscious identification with the victims. For example, one subject said:

> I can remember seeing pictures, I remember a very famous picture of a little kid with his father's hat, short pants, torn coat around him, and he's very pathetic looking, and he's holding his father's hand, and they're going to go on a train and he doesn't know what's going to happen to him and I remember thinking, that could be me, I could be one of those kids. [Mr. I.]

Other themes were idiosyncratic to a few subjects. One subject recalled having thoughts about the tenuousness of his own life and its having been inextricably linked to his mother's survivorhood. He said, "I would think, gee, it's amazing that my mother is alive, and that maybe, in reference to me, if she had been killed, I wouldn't be here" [Mr. J.]. A few subjects articulated a theme that involved their own faith in the order and wisdom of the adult world being shaken. One subject said:

> How one man, Hitler, could kill six million, I wondered why six million didn't kill him.... I couldn't understand how it happened, my little head couldn't understand, it really couldn't. [Miss A.]

Another theme that ran through subjects' thoughts involved focusing hatred on Germans.

A final aspect of some subjects' thoughts during childhood and adolescence involved rejection of the idea that the Holocaust was a personally meaningful event. For example, one subject described his experience of having given a speech before a survivors' organization when he was 12 years old:

> It was all very bizarre because I had to give an impassioned speech, it was expected, and people were crying because of what I was saying, and I knew while I was up on stage, I was moving people to tears. It made an impression on me at the time because I was disinterested

by it. I didn't feel it was my experience, that I was justified in saying these things, I had gone through them or that I was as bitter or as moved as they were. I was really a prop to set these people off.... I had been more distant than the other people around me, other sons and daughters, I think. [Mr. F.]

The frequency of subjects' thinking about the Holocaust in the present was varied. Approximately one-third of the sample indicated that thoughts about the Holocaust were prominent in their consciousness. Other subjects reported that they did not think about the Holocaust spontaneously, but would be reminded of it. For example, several subjects reported that they often had associations to the Holocaust when they heard news reports that involved human suffering. Many subjects reported that they rarely thought about the Holocaust. One subject, as he denied thinking about it in everyday life, wondered why he didn't "hate more." Another such subject explained, "It's something that happened in the past."

Subjects' thinking about the Holocaust was accompanied by varying degrees of emotionality. Some subjects seemed to have isolated their feelings whenever confronted by Holocaust imagery, while other seemed to experience powerful and often conflictual feelings.

In the process of investigating subjects' present thoughts and attitudes, the interviewer focused questions on the subjects' location of the Holocaust within the general context of history, his identification of the most destructive elements of it, his understanding of how victims survived, and his perception of how survivors were affected.

Subjects were asked to compare the Holocaust to other historical events. It was the interviewer's impression that the attitudes maintained by the subjects were overdetermined by personal meaning. Twelve subjects believed that the Holocaust was a unique event in human history. Another two subjects believed that it could be compared to other events in Jewish history, but otherwise that it stood alone. Some of these subjects justified their positions intellectually. For example, they attributed the uniqueness of the Holocaust to the extent and methodical nature of the destruction. Other subjects made no such attempt and provided an essentially emotional response. For example, one subject said, "It was more horrible than anything else in the world put together. So much hate, so much hate...." Six subjects very strongly insisted that neither the Holocaust nor the concentration camps were unique. They compared both to other atrocities, past and present. It was the interviewer's impression that all but one of these subjects were struggling to repudiate the idea that they had been affected by their knowledge of their parents' survivorhood.

Subjects were asked their opinions about the nature of the destructiveness of concentration camps. Some had powerful reactions. For example, one subject said with a shrill voice that rose in pitch as she spoke, "The most destructive thing! I mean, well, if you kill six million Jews, isn't that enough!"

Most subjects, however, responded within an intellectual framework. Among the elements of the concentration camp experience that were considered most destructive were the harsh physical conditions. These included the deprivation of basic human needs, the wanton physical abuse of inmates, the constant fear of death, and the outright murders by gun, club, and gas chamber. One subject said, "The worst thing I could think of probably isn't half as bad as what they went through." At least one-third of the sample, while acknowledging the physical destructiveness of the concentration camps, felt that the most destructive aspect of them was the assault on human dignity. One subject said:

> It dehumanized them. It stripped them of values, of needs, of, it stripped them of what they were before they entered the camps. It turned them into animals just to survive. [Miss I.]

Another subject said, "Hope died, the faith in man died."

Different subjects had different understandings of how inmates managed to survive their experiences. A number of subjects seemed threatened by the issue and avoided it. Some subjects said that they could not imagine how anybody survived and were amazed that they had. Many subjects attributed survival to luck or prayer. One such subject said, "It was all in God's hands." Others attributed survival to "natural instinct" or "Jewish character." These referred to the idea that Jews had been trained to survive over centuries of persecution, and that it was a Jewish trait to act on the principle, "Where there's life there's hope." Another explanation of survivorhood was "the will to survive." Subjects said that people had to have "faith" to live and be willing to fight for life. One subject used the experience of his mother as an example of how people survived. He said: "She just stayed alive, she didn't even know what she was staying alive for, most of the time she just stayed alive." [Mr. J.] Some subjects said that the real test of strength was mental survival, not physical survival. Very few subjects mentioned the idea that some inmates exploited others in order to survive. One who did said:

> I'm not that certain that many people maintained a rigid self-protective dignified opposition to what was going on... people compromised and did what they could, there weren't that many heroes. [Mr. F.]

Subjects' images of the consequences of the trauma of the concentration camps were also varied. Some saw a wide range of possible effects that depended on the prior character of the survivor, while others saw specific effects that were true for all. Some used what they perceived in their parents as a general model, while others maintained that their parents were exceptions. Some subjects envisioned survivors as first having experienced a "jubilation that they were free," and then having been overcome by "sorrow, searching, and praying." Other subjects suggested that survivors' minds had been "killed."

A number of subjects felt that survivors would live with their memories of hell forever. Still others saw the consequences of survivorhood as ethnocentricity and racial prejudice, bitterness, distrust, and hate.

The Holocaust as a Framework for Understanding Morality

It was the interviewer's impression that, for many subjects, the Holocaust provided the framework for understanding moral responsibility and evil. What follows is a discussion of subjects' attitudes about the motivation of the crimes that were committed, the extent of culpability for those crimes, personal solutions to the moral dilemmas posed by the role of observing evil, and personal associations to Nazis as symbols of evil.

The motivation of the crimes. Subjects displayed a wide range of opinions about the motivation for the crimes of the Holocaust. Some of their opinions were characterized by exceptional perspicacity, which suggested that they were the product of more than casual thought. Others were characterized by a dullness which suggested unconscious avoidance of the issue.

A number of subjects seemed to have foreclosed consideration of the motivation of criminals. One said, "It's just a cruelty that's hard to understand." Another angrily denounced the Nazis and acted as if an attempt to understand them would be personally threatening. Other subjects, however, displayed a surprising tolerance, viewing the evil that had occurred as a very understandable human phenomenon. A number of subjects, for example, believed that the criminals of the Holocaust acted out of a desire to "do what was best for the good of Germany." Several subjects provided sophisticated sociological analyses of the conditions that had led to the persecution of the Jews. Other subjects affirmed a belief that those responsible for the crimes were normal individuals who had "adjusted" to the momentum of the times. One gave the following example, based on his medical studies:

> We were working with cadavers, o.k., and after we finished working we'd cut off the heads for a practical exam. They'll put metal tags with a number on different parts and ask you, What is this? . . . They put 'em in a sink and cut 'em in the middle and tag different things. Just before the exam, people were going over, sticking their hands in the sink and pulling up half a head . . . and the only thing people complained about was if there wasn't a tag on it. If six months before I'd walked into a room and there was a sinkful of half-heads underwater I would have gotten sick and run out and you know, now the only thing I can say is, 'Shit, I can't get close enough for the practical and there are tags missing.' You see the difference in just six months? [Mr. G.]

Other subjects approached the issue of criminality from the point of view of human psychopathology. Some of them used this approach to set off Nazis from the rest of humanity by labeling them "sick," "crazy," and "not very well-developed human beings." Others used their psychological approach to emphasize the universality of the dynamics that produced the Holocaust. Some of these subjects indicated that the crimes were motivated by a compensatory need for power on the parts of the people who felt inadequate. Others understood the crimes as having arisen out of basic human impulses which they, too, shared. One subject said:

> Ever been to an orgy? Ever feel orgiastic? Release all sorts of impulses? I think, in terms of violence, there was a certain orgiastic atmosphere in Germany that let those violent feelings and sadistic feelings take full-blown expression, really take over. Sexual feelings really overwhelm you, in that sense, violent feelings really took over. That's charitable, I'm trying to explain it. I really don't feel that charitable. [What do you feel?] I feel war criminals should be executed. [Mr. D.]

Another subject said:

> It's not only Germans who are like this, sometimes I think it's something wrong with us that permits those kinds of crimes. I think we can all be riled up and commit, something within man, I think, we can commit that because I see the African doing it, you know, and we, it was done in Vietnam.... So I would like to think of it as something unique about Germans, that they're really animals and it's only the Aryan race.... But it's me too, in that sort of situation I might be turning on, I don't know, terror, seeking to dominate and a teacher who, uh, had cats used to squeeze its throat to kill the fleas and imagined what it would be like if it's a man, not a lowly thing like a cat ... and you would dominate that and kill that and how would you feel? And I think of recently, that a girl was stabbed in New York, Uh, she came from Indiana, she was stabbed four times in the back, three times in the front, and I was thinking the way the guy must feel, he must have felt soooooo good.... He was really letting it out and feeling so superior to this person, really dominating, and I would take that and relate it on a mass scale to a whole nation, uh, they must have felt, doing to my parents, my nation, all Jews. You know, Jews have been the cats, you know, destroyed, to be killed like that, all people could do it. [Mr. I.]

The extent of culpability. Subjects were asked about both the Germans who claimed not to have been aware of the concentration camps and also groups outside of Germany who might have been in a position to aid the victims of the Holocaust. Very few subjects believed either the claims of Germans not to have known about the concentration camps or claims that the rest of the world had responded adequately to the plight of the victims. Many subjects empathized with the dilemma of German citizens, whom they saw as being essentially as helpless and as vulnerable as the actual victims of the concentration camps. Others condemned the German citizens for "letting it happen," and saw them to be as culpable as those who had actually perpetrated the crimes. Subjects, as a group, had harsher judgments about the rest of the world. Most expressed extreme bitterness about the failure of outside groups to intervene. Some subjects denounced American Jews in particular for having sacrificed so little for their European brethren. A few subjects, however, were more charitable. They compared the response of the world to the persecution of European Jewry to the present-day response of Americans to events all over the world. One subject who, interestingly, was a political activist, said he did not find the failure of the world to respond to the concentration camps "surprising" because:

> I think people are moved by what's closest to them.... It would be very difficult to live in New York if you were constantly in pain about other people's pain. It'd be impossible because there's so much pain in New York, uh. And I think people have to draw their own boundaries. [Mr. F.]

Personal solutions to the moral dilemmas of the Holocaust. Subjects were asked what they might have done had they been non-Jewish German citizens during the time of the Holocaust. Most of them felt that there was no easy solution to the problem of confronting evil at the risk of one's own life. Some of them said that they had often imagined themselves in a similar situation in contemporary America and honestly did not know what to do. Others indicated that they would have wanted to join an underground movement and actually fight the evil, but did not know if they would have had the courage.

Some subjects, however, felt they knew how they would react in similar circumstances. Many of these indicated that they would feel helpless and solve the problem by either pretending not to know about it or by fleeing. A few subjects indicated that under those circumstances, they too might have been swept away by Nazi rhetoric and have become Nazis themselves.

Personal associations to Nazism. Subjects were asked to say the first thing that came into their minds when they thought about Nazis. Many of them avoided the task by hesitating and then providing an intellectualized statement. The responses of subjects who complied with the task can be divided into three groups.

The first group consisted of subjects whose responses emphasized madness and hysteria. For example, one subject said, "Hitler on his tower talking to his people and the people going crazy." Another responded, "The crowds in the street screaming, *Heil Hitler*. [What feeling goes along with that?] Just the puppets running, and they thought he was like a god" [Miss F.].

The second group gave responses that involved brutality and sadism. For example, one subject said, "I don't know, I see somebody bending down and whipping him and whipping him until, and you know, and people pleading not to do it and they just mow 'em down" [Mr. A.].

The third group included subjects whose responses emphasized the appeal of Nazism. One subject said, "If you look at the pageantry and all these people marching along and the vitality, the animal strength that they had, yeah, it's interesting, even appealing" [Mr. G.].

Another subject said:

> The movie *Cabaret.* It's a blond, blue-eyed boy who gets up and he's beautiful to look at and singing an emotional song and you see everybody else in the place standing up and joining in and suddenly you see the boy's a Nazi. [Miss B.]

Involvement in Seeking More Information about the Holocaust

Most subjects had made some effort to learn more about the Holocaust era. The amount of effort ranged from undertaking massive studies to simply making a point of watching television documentaries. Many subjects, including those who had been referred from other sources, had formally studied the Holocaust in college. Others had chosen to write papers on it for general history courses or had done considerable independent reading. Several subjects had visited the sites of concentration camps which have been preserved as memorials. It became readily apparent that a number of subjects who had denied seeking information about the Holocaust had sought out information of events that reminded them of it. One subject who had read a number of books about Soviet prison camps said:

> Maybe I needed to read about dead bodies together because I can't imagine it, I can't see it. I don't know, I liked reading the books, I didn't get pleasure from it, I just got involved. [Miss I.]

Generally, subjects had difficulty explaining their interest and fascination. It was as if many subjects had consciously detached their studies from a personal referrent. For example, one subject, who had denied feeling that his being a child of survivors was part of his identity, described a visit to the site of Dachau as if it were accidental. He first portrayed himself as "happening" to be in Munich and "happening" to pay a visit to the nearby concentration camp. On further questioning, it appeared that he had, in fact, been having marginal thoughts about visiting the camp dating from the time, several months earlier, when he had decided to include Germany in the itinerary of his holiday. His feelings while there are worthy of noting:

> I felt threatened and attacked. These people were doing it to people just like me... really angry that human beings could deal with each other in that way, particularly deal with people I loved in this fashion and I wanted to cry and I wanted to scream out and run at the same time, tear the place down, just break out and I wanted to stop going through the same motions as you go through in a museum, just walking and looking, walking and looking, whether it's at great works of art or great monstrosities. I just didn't feel appropriate in that setting, behaving in a similar manner... wanting to assert some humanness and also rage, ambivalent feelings. [Mr. F.]

In contrast, a subject who had studied the Holocaust era rather extensively, and who had had fantasies of being in a concentration camp, described his visit to Dachau this way:

> I wanted to check it out... I wanted to see how the Germans as a people would leave the camps, how they would leave it for people to see, uh, I wanted to have some idea of what a big concentration camp was like. I wanted to see what a gas chamber was. I just, I just wondered about all of that. [How did you feel while you were there?] I was disgusted that the Germans made it look like a camp, like, uh, it was beautiful, I mean can you imagine anybody saying that? Dachau was beautiful? They, the houses were, well, I tell you, maybe I was expecting to go there and see lice crawling around and, and the place reeking from the odor of death, and you know, maybe, maybe, uh, that's what I wanted to see. And I went there and it was just like all the barracks were, concrete, whatever it is, barriers that high [gestures] around where all the barracks were, flowers, they had flowers planted. It was so nice, people were taking family pictures there which also disgusted me. There were crematoria, there were cham—, you know, gas chambers. They never used the gas chambers at Dachau, you know, they just made it look very nice, not at all bad.... [Mr. E.]

Interactions with Others about the Holocaust

The role of the Holocaust in subjects' lives was often portrayed as they described their interaction with others about it. All but three subjects reported having had some communication about the Holocaust with other people. Some subjects described having such interactions with people in general, while others reported having such interactions only with people they considered close friends, while still others reported having such interactions with only other children of survivors.

For many subjects, one important function of their interactions with others seemed to involve public identification of themselves as related to the Holocaust. The interviewer's impression was that such identification was covert. That is, subjects attempted to let others know about their history without appearing to have, or indeed being conscious of having, any investment in so doing. For example, a number of subjects indicated that they had told others, during first meetings, that their parents had been in concentration camps during the course of exchanging details about their own lives. One subject, after denying that she ever discussed her parents' survivorhood with others, added, "But most of my friends are aware of what my parents went through." Other subjects described discussions with others during which they had "educated" others to the history of the Holocaust. One such subject said:

> I think I could almost imagine how it was to be in a concentration camp. When people ask me, I think I can almost tell them what it was like as if I were in one. [Mr. D.]

The interviewer's sense was that such interactions were also a vehicle of identification of self as a child of a survivor.

This seeming need to identify oneself publicly in these terms is open to many possible interpretations. One subject described a typical interaction he has had with others since the fifth grade, which suggests that ego-aggrandizement somehow resulted from such identifications with overwhelming suffering. He said:

> Most of my friends wanted to talk about it and it even got down to the point that we were vying for 'my parents went through more than your parents' and what not. [Mr. C.]

He went on to describe interactions with black people, the theme of which was competition for the status of having suffered more.

Another prominent theme that emerged was the use of the response of others to issues related to the Holocaust as a vehicle for becoming isolated from, or developing negative feelings about, others. In some cases, the subjects' responses to others were thinly veiled. For example, one subject described the response of others to his revelations about the Holocaust as follows:

> People are interested, I think. I think they sort of tell you, 'That's too bad,' very emotionless, which you know, I tend to do also most times, uh, they might ask me a few more details. [Mr. J.]

In his statement, there seemed to be a rationalization of his feelings of disappointment and anger in the response of others to him. Another subject, speaking in a tone of voice that can best be described as indignant, said:

> When I'm with my friends and they say, 'Look how terrible this is,' I'll tell them what my mother went through and how they killed her little brother in front of her. [How do they respond?] Well, they listen, pretty, you know, 'I can't believe your parents went through that.' [Miss B.]

Another subject described his friends as having difficulty understanding his consideration for his parents. He went on to describe an incident during which a girl, one of a group of friends visiting him in his parents' home, asked for something to eat:

> I said 'the dairy dishes are here,' and she said, 'What are you giving me this shit for,' and I said, 'Listen!' And I gave 'em the whole rap my parents had been through, this, and they said, 'Wow!' She's a 19-, 20-year-old girl and she doesn't understand this. She goes, 'That's stupid, you know.' And you might not believe this but I got to the point where I went and I had to get some pictures of a concentration camp and show 'em to this girl and say, 'Look, what do you mean it's stupid, look at what my parents went through so they could stay kosher.' That's one of the reasons, a small reason, they want a kosher house and I had to show this picture and it

totally amazed her, she was just so sheltered. It really just flipped me out. [How were you feeling toward her?] I hated her, I wanted to kill her. I couldn't believe I had to go to this extreme to make her understand, you know. I thought it was thoroughly disgraceful that a person of that age couldn't understand. [Mr. E.]

With different emphasis, another subject described going to a documentary movie about the Holocaust with a group of non-Jewish friends. Her response to the movie was:

I was very ripped apart inside.... They've got one scene that's phenomenal, it's bodies upon bodies upon bodies being bulldozed into a big open pit. When you see it, it seems so incredible that you can't, you know, it just sort of seems that out of all these mounds of arms and legs, it just hit me, you know, 'That could be your grandmother.' It made me feel very sick and I had to run out. So along with that was the question, If you can't sit through that, how do you expect other people to sit through it? You've got to sit through it just to understand your parents.

At the same time, she described her reaction to her friends' reaction:

My friends weren't moved at all, which kind of upset me because, not that I expected them to cry or anything, but they would cry for a stupid movie like *Love Story,* and here they were watching the story of 10,000 Jews in the Warsaw ghetto being killed, and they weren't moved at all and, I just asked one of them, you know, 'Like why?' and uh, she said that when she saw it, she, it seemed so incredible that she couldn't believe it. [Miss B.]

A final function of subjects' interactions with others seemed to be reparative in nature. That is, some subjects used interactions with others to help them gain an understanding or express their feelings of the impact of the Holocaust on their lives. Subjects described having made efforts with intimate friends and other children of survivors to analyze the role of the Holocaust on their characters and personalities. One subject described discussing "how crazy we are because of it." Another subject described the following all-night conversation she had had with three friends:

The theme of the conversation was, 'Why I never got to go to camp,' only it was concentration camp.... It was death upon death, maiming, killed, died, blood. Just so awful that we were hysterically laughing because there was no other way to incorporate it. [Miss A.]

The feelings described suggest an attempt to deal with the trauma of the horrors that had occurred in their own families and to overcome the psychic numbing that had frozen those feelings.

Telling the Next Generation

The role of survivorhood in the lives of the subjects was also revealed by their responses to the question "Do you intend to tell your own children about your parents' experiences?" Of the eighteen subjects who were asked this question, all answered in the affirmative. Three main themes of their responses may be identified.

The first theme involved a desire to preserve the past in some way. Some subjects, for example, said that, by telling their own children about it, they would insure that the Holocaust was never forgotten. Other subjects emphasized that they wanted their children to have a sense of Jewish identity, and that they regarded the Holocaust as part of the history of the Jewish people.

The second theme involved subjects' desires to use the example of the Holocaust to educate their children about the nature of the world. They emphasized the desire to alert their children to the dangers in the world and to the consequences of succumbing to a false sense of security.

The third theme involved subjects' desires that their children know and understand them. These subjects emphasized the impact of the Holocaust, directly or mediated through their parents, on their outlook and personality, and their desire that their children understand their background.

The Holocaust as a Source of Unconscious Symbolism

Holocaust imagery clearly appeared in the manifest content of the dreams, daydreams, and marginal thoughts of 15 of the 20 subjects. Included among these were three of the four subjects who denied that the Holocaust had affected them.

In some cases, subjects were quite defended against experiencing the personal importance of Holocaust imagery in their lives. For example, one subject, who had denied that his parents' experiences had had an effect on him, also denied that he had ever had dreams related to the Holocaust. He then remembered that a roommate had once overheard him say "Hitler" in his sleep. Another subject recalled having had "thoughts" precipitated by discovering photographs of concentration camp inmates in the middle of an album of baby pictures of herself. She could not, however, remember what these "thoughts" were. Other subjects recalled having had dreams and daydreams, the themes of which directly involved the Holocaust, but could not or would not recall the specific content.

The Holocaust imagery of subjects' dreams, daydreams, and marginal thoughts revealed symbolic themes regarding identification with the victim, the experience of loss, and the exertion of mastery.

Identification with the Victim

By far the clearest referent in subjects' dreams and daydreams about the Holocaust was identification with the victim. For example, although one subject could not recall details, he said that he had "fantasized the horror occurring to me." Another subject described having had, during early adolescence, fantasies of being "a young kid in concentration camp" and of imagining "how I'd have to smuggle food in." He described the following as characteristic of him from the age of 15 and continuing through the present:

> You know, you always see these pictures of these little kids. They're just typical Nazi concentration camp pictures, little kids with frightened looks on their faces, their hands up. I had these horrible images of sewers and getting trapped in sewers and having rats. I used to daydream like that. [Mr. E.]

In addition he said that, while he was taking a course on the Holocaust, he would imagine himself in the situations described by the lecturer. He summarized his description of his daydreams by saying, "I guess in a very mild way, I feel some of the things my parents feel."

Another subject described having had dreams from childhood to the present, of "a big, strong guy coming to drag me away." The only specific relevant dream he could recall was the following:

> They were, uh, I just remember being lined up and being marched along, you know . . . essentially what I remember was this utter feeling of helplessness and nothing that you could do, being packed on a train, being marched in camp, being told to do whatever they want, not knowing all the faces around me. I never got killed in any of these dreams because you never die in your dreams, but I just remember utter feelings of helplessness and terror. People pounding on the door and stuff like that. [Mr. G.]

He understood these dreams as a derivative of his interest in the Holocaust era and all the reading he had done about it. He had also had daydreams which involved Holocaust imagery. The following is one:

> I remember I went to an exhibit at the Jewish museum and I walked up and they had a uniform, like they have pictures and photostats but they're not really real, you know. They had a uniform on a board and I went up and I was afraid to even go near it. Finally I got up enough guts to touch it. [What was it?] A blue-striped cotton uniform and then I would have daydreams about it, I wondered what it would be like to stand in a long line of people wearing one of these things. I'd wonder what would have happened if I had lost my glasses, I have really bad eyes, in concentration camps would they take my glasses away, I'd be a dead man, I'd be a helpless sort of thing . . . and I had daydreams about these big, tall, strong guys because if you're not all that strong, I'm not weak, but I know that if a 200-pound guy came along and tried to drag me away, he'd have no trouble. . . . [Mr. G.]

A number of subjects, when asked to describe "phobias" they had, described special fears which were clearly related to Holocaust imagery. For example, one subject reported that he had a fear of "rabid dogs" which recalled to the interviewer an incident this subject described earlier in the interview, in which his father had been bitten in the neck while hiding, by a man who went "mad."

Another subject, who had reported no dreams or daydreams related to the Holocaust, described himself as "maybe claustrophobic." However, he had no fear of closed places. The only object he could relate his fear to was what appeared to be a fantasy. He described the fear-producing stimulus as "the thought about being in a tunnel that's barely bigger than I am." He has, to his memory, never been in such a place, though he thinks "possibly it might happen." His association to this image is "the kind of tunnel dug to escape." Concomitant with the image is a fear of its "caving in." One may speculate that this tunnel represented a joining of the imagery of the past and present through the vehicle of the tunnel which might have been used to escape from the imprisoning forces of Nazis in a concentration camp in the past. This fear was experienced in the present as a vivid emotion of constriction and imprisonment, but the image was drawn from the past and the concentration camp experience. Given that this image belongs to a subject who was particularly constricted in his feelings and thoughts, one may well understand his fear of the tunnel caving in.

Subjects also described "worst fantasies" which re-evoked Holocaust imagery. Some of these worst fantasies involved direct threats expressed by the subject making an explicit connection between the fear and the crimes committed by the Nazis. For example, two subjects described the worst thing that could happen as being or having been the victim of the Nazi experiment. Other subjects described fears of dying violent, unexpected deaths. One subject elaborated such a fear with the fantasy of "some crazy guy coming into my home and scaring me first for a couple of hours, and then shooting me in the spine." One may speculate that the "crazy guy" is a translation of Nazi criminals into a contemporary representation. Other subjects' descriptions of their "worst fantasy" re-evoked dilemmas which, in reality, were experienced by concentration camp inmates. For example, one subject's worst fantasy was being in the situation of "my life depending on either 'he lives or I live.'" Another subject's worst fantasy was "probably being in a position where I'd hate myself."

The Experience of Loss

Some subjects expressed acute anxiety about loss, particularly in childhood and early adolescence, through the vehicle of Holocaust imagery. For example, one subject reported having had the following dream at approximately the age of fourteen: "We were in World War II, and we were all taken away . . . we were all separated and there was a big red smokestack belching out smoke." [Miss C.] Her association to the dream was of having gone through a period around the age of eight to nine during which she was "afraid to go to sleep because I was afraid of losing everybody I loved." She said that she would go to her mother during this period and cry, "Mommy, we're never going to die."

Another subject described having had the following dream:

> I remember one dream in which we escaped about, we left my sister behind and I went back to get her, uh I realized I was a little kid at the time and I realized I was neglecting her, Oh I lost my sister, how much I really love my sister, and I was good to her for a day after that. . . . [Mr. G.]

An important element in this dream, revealed by the subject's guilt and atonement for it ("I was good to her for a day after that") is that, coexisting with the anxiety, there is a wish to lose the sister to the Nazis.

The Exertion of Mastery

Some subjects' dreams and daydreams reflected their attempts to exert mastery over Holocaust symbols. For example, a number of subjects described having daydreams about finding Nazis who had escaped punishment and then killing them. One man, an atheist, recalled his childhood belief in God, heaven, and hell as having been based on his incredulity at the idea that Nazis would escape eternal punishment and victims would not be compensated for their suffering. Others had daydreams about finding relatives who were thought to have been killed in the concentration camps.

One dream which involved the theme of mastery was described as follows:

> A dream I had a very long time ago, I've always remembered it, of, um, walking down the street. There's a parade, there was like a big tall building and on top of it was a Nazi flag. I remember going up, trying to get the Nazi flag down. [Miss G.]

The subject reported having had this dream at about the age of 17 or 18. Her association to the dream was "strength, overcoming some tremendous fear to be able to do that."

Other subjects described having fantasies of going back in time and saving people from the Nazis. For example, one subject, while in the fifth grade, read about a woman paratrooper who had parachuted into Nazi-occupied territory as a saboteur. Ever since, this subject has been having fantasies and dreams about being a "super-secret agent through espionage, destroying the Nazi war machine." She described a recurring dream that involved different episodes:

"One night we'd bomb Nazi headquarters, ski away, another night throwing bombs from bicycles, be dressed in black, blowing up gas chambers . . . " [Miss B.]

Political and Social Attitudes

Some subjects' world views, that is, the general ideas and images of the nature of the world they lived in, were vague and undifferentiated. Many other subjects had a clearly articulated set of beliefs about the world in which they lived. In both cases, the investigator often sensed that subjects' approaches to the world could be traced back to the influence of the Holocaust.

In general, subjects tended to be cynical about institutions. In the extreme, they portrayed rage at a world they perceived not only as unjust but also as actively malevolent. A number of subjects seemed to equate ignorance with wickedness, and characterized people in general as either ignorant or wicked. One subject described having gone through a period of what he called "political realism." He said of it, "I hated everybody around me because they were happy and people were starving."

Several subjects articulated a sense of the world as being overwhelmingly unstable. They seemed to be living under the constant threat of imminent doom. One subject, describing a "cataclysmic and depressed view of the world," attributed it directly to the influence of the Holocaust. He paid vigilant attention to the "political wind" and said he was ready to "get out" at any moment. Another subject said, "I live from day to day, If the bombs were to fall tomorrow I'd say, 'Yep, I knew it,' If they didn't fall, I'd say, 'Yep, I knew it.'" The interviewer's feeling was that the same theme was being portrayed as other subjects expressed their sense of vulnerability to immediate influences in their lives. Such influences could be a mugging, the loss of job, or even receiving poor grades. A number of subjects expressed a need to design their own lives in a manner that would be secure from outside threat. For example, one subject said of her college education, "That's something they can't take away from you."

It must be noted that at least three subjects were more optimistic about the world. They expressed a fundamental trust in the idea of the good will of others and a belief that change was possible in institutions.

The sample represented a wide political spectrum both in terms of active political involvement and political belief. At one extreme, subjects described themselves as uninterested in politics to the degree of never reading the newspaper or watching news reports on television. One such subject, when asked to pick some issue in American life that was important to her, said:

To tell you the truth, I really don't care. I live off the fat of this land. It's not correct to say that I guess, all right, inflation. That bugs me, who wants to pay 35 cents [for bus fare] four times a day? [Miss H.] [Author: at the time of the interviews, the bus fare was indeed 35 cents.]

Other subjects described a general interest in politics but could not imagine themselves taking political action of any kind. For example, one subject said about politics, "I keep up with it, but I keep out of it." Other subjects reported a profound interest in politics, but only from the point of view of intellectual exercises with no personal commitment.

At the other extreme, a few subjects described or portrayed intensive involvement in political activities. Each of these had been active in causes associated with the political left. These subjects had participated in, among other things, demonstrations against the war in Vietnam, against racism, and against Soviet policies on the emigration of Jews. Some had leadership roles in campus organizations which organized such demonstrations. However, even most of these subjects felt fundamentally impotent to effect change. They often explained that their political activity was a means of making a personal moral statement.

While the statements of some subjects broadly identified them as either radicals or conservatives, the interviewer could not categorize any subject in terms of a commitment to any established, organized political ideology. They all tended to share cynicism about the motives of politicians. In spite of the radicalism of some subjects, commitment to alternate political systems was not attractive. For example, one subject, who had held a leadership position in a campus political organization, said, "I see little difference in being kicked by the boot from the right as the boot from the left."

Subjects were asked to describe their attitudes about "things that go on in the world that might be called atrocities." If subjects did not spontaneously describe such an event, the interviewer asked about their thoughts about then-current events such as happenings in Biafra, Bangladesh, and Vietnam. A wide range of responses was elicited.

Some subjects indicated a feeling of distance from other atrocities. For example, one said, "I don't want to think about them, I got my own problems, nobody is going to help me out." Another said:

I don't care about it. I mean, I feel bad that people are being killed but they're not my people. That's not really right to say. I read of 60 people killed today, but if I hear one guy in Israel was hurt badly, that would affect me. [Miss H.]

Other subjects responded, whether or not they were directly sympathetic to the victims of "atrocities" by identifying with them. For example, one subject said, "It makes me think I'm not so bad off." Another said, "If you suffer, you have to sympathize with other people's suffering." Still another subject said that she felt "compelled" to respond emotionally to the suffering of other people because of her own involvement with the Holocaust. She said that if she did not, she would be "the biggest hypocrite in the world."

Subjects were asked about their attitudes toward minority groups, in order to explore the relationship between their own identification with being a member of a persecuted minority group and its effect on feelings about other such groups.

It was difficult to place subjects' attitudes into clear categories. Most subjects acknowledged that certain groups in the United States were "oppressed," but had varying degrees of sympathy for such groups. Some subjects were content with the position that people had to be judged on the basis of their individual traits and not on the basis of race or religion. Others were very aware of racial prejudice, but regarded racial conflicts as "unfortunate and inevitable" with "no solution to the problem in sight." The full range of attitudes went from hostility to, for example, black people, to support for the most radical spokesman of minority groups.

At least seven subjects drew some parallel between Jews and other minorities. One subject said that he sometimes wondered if blacks were "dumber." He then added that similar things had been written about Jews at the beginning of the century. Another subject said,

> Any type of prejudice is a curse. Sometimes I feel badly when I speak an off-color word about any group of people because I feel guilty about doing the same kind of thing that other people did to Jewish people. [Mr. J.]

Another subject said: "People have to be judged on the basis of who they are, not color. You can't stereotype them. That's what being Jewish taught me more than anything else" [Miss B.]. However, a few subjects, as they identified themselves as minority group members, used this fact to rationalize disregard for other minorities. One of these said, "I don't sympathize with them, we're a minority group also. First feel sorry for myself."

Jewish Identity

With only two exceptions, all subjects included the dimension of Jewishness in their definition of themselves. The two subjects who did not, explicitly rejected the idea that Jewishness was a relevant category of their identity. For only four subjects did Jewish identity include an orthodox religious dimension. For the rest, it involved cultural, nationalistic, and racial aspects. One subject described his sense of being Jewish as:

> Inwardly I know I'm Jewish. It's more a tradition and racial sort of feeling than actually going through the tenets of Judaism and deciding this is what I believe. [Mr. G.]

Another subject said, "I'm very Jewish but in nationalistic terms. I feel chauvinistic about Jewish history. I'm a violent supporter of Israel but I don't believe in God" [Mr. D.].

The Jewish identity espoused by subjects did not emerge without evidence of accompanying conflict. For example, many subjects reported that, while they had done very well in school as children, they had done quite poorly in Hebrew school. Several subjects who had been sent to Yeshivas described struggling with their parents to be allowed to go to public school. For some subjects, the attenuation of Jewish identification was concomitant to separation from their parents. For example, one subject reported discovering that he no longer believed in God as he moved out of his parents' house. Another subject reported that, because of his extensive religious education, he was invited to sit on a panel, the purpose of which was to discuss religion publicly. He described the following: "I had an interview with someone, and it really came out. I had a violent opposition to this Jewish thing. It was a part of me that I had to purge myself of" [Mr. I.].

Although no subject had renounced a belief in God because of it, the Holocaust clearly affected the conception of God maintained by several subjects. For example, one subject described her belief in God as follows:

> A supreme being who has the world at his fingertips. A spiritual thing that can do whatever He wants at any time. Man doesn't have to question, I mean I have to question in regard to the deeds that I do. But when someone is killed, like a nine-year-old child is taken away, there must be some reason for it and man can't question that reason. [Miss H.]

The reference in the above statement to a "nine-year-old child" is to her mother's brother who was killed by the Nazis. Another subject said that she had once challenged her mother's belief in God on the basis of what her mother had suffered. Her mother had responded, and the subject was satisfied by it, that proof of God's benevolence was her survival. Another subject said, "I can understand people who love God and who hate Him for what they went through, I can't understand people in the middle."

The experience of persecution was an integral component of most subjects' Jewish identification. They tended to regard Jewish history as the history of one pogrom after another. They saw the historical role of the Jew as being the scapegoat. One subject said, "Jews have always been different ... there isn't as much hate for any other group." For this reason, many subjects saw Jews as especially vulnerable to continued persecution. However, an equal number of subjects felt it unlikely that Jews would ever again allow themselves to be vulnerable, because they "have history to look back on."

One of the few characteristics shared by all subjects was a pro-Israeli political stance. Some subjects had visited Israel, and others were definitely planning to go, or fantasizing about emigrating. The interviewer's sense was that even those subjects who did not verbalize intense feelings about Israel indicated such feelings in some way. The interviewer sensed that a few subjects were committed to Israel in some organic way, almost against their conscious will. It seemed to him that, for many, Israel had become a symbol for either themselves or their families. As such, Israel could be seen to represent both a survivor and a child of the Holocaust. Like their parents, subjects saw Israel as struggling to establish a life for itself in a difficult world. Like themselves, they saw Israel as asserting itself in a world fundamentally different from the past. Many subjects displayed what might best be described as pride in the existence and achievements of the State of Israel. In spite of any sympathy for Palestinian refugees, subjects felt Israel's existence to be justified—if by nothing else, by the Holocaust. A few subjects went on to say that they felt personally safer because of Israel's existence. That is, the existence of a Jewish nation decreased, in their minds, the possibility of another Holocaust.

The verbal distance of some subjects from acknowledging a feeling of personal affiliation with Israel was belied by a number of other factors. For example, a number of such subjects reported having become frightened for Israel during the Six-Day War. A number of subjects who denied intense feelings about Israel spontaneously mentioned that they could become citizens of Israel by virtue of being Jewish. One subject, who seemed to be a hesitant Zionist, was asked if he felt that his pro-Israeli position in any way contradicted his leftist positions on other issues. He responded by making a number of nervous political jokes about Israel. The interviewer's sense was that he might have preferred to, but could not bring himself to, espouse a pro-Arab position. Another subject, also among the more lukewarm in his support for Israel, explained his idiosyncratic nickname to the interviewer in the following way:

> I tell my friends I was born in an airplane over Israel. My father went and told the pilot and said———. [A Hebrew word, phonetically similar to the subject's nickname.] [Mr. E.]

Needless to say, the subject was born in the United States.

That subjects were committed to the existence of Israel did not mean that their attitudes were entirely positive. While some subjects felt that Israel "has done a miracle," and was "a noble social experiment," they were also quick to point out social inequalities in Israeli life. Some subjects had difficulty accepting what they defined as the arrogance of the Israeli character. For example, one subject, although struggling with it, was more comfortable with the image of the Jew as victim. She said of her discomfort with the image of the Jew as aggressive, "I always thought this too. You should be humble, meek, you should suffer, and if you don't, if you fight for what you want, you're doing something wrong" [Miss A.].

Subjects' attitudes about the Arab-Israeli conflicts included varying degrees of sympathy for Arabs. At one extreme, a subject said quite simply of the Arabs, "I hate them." At the other extreme, another subject, referring to Israeli raids on Arab territories, said:

> Killing people, Arabs are people. It's disgusting. I don't feel, maybe it's they're going to get things done. It's wrong. I can't stand it. It doesn't make me pro-Arab in any way, it just makes me against them. [Miss I.]

For some subjects, the Arab-Israeli conflicts re-evoked images of the Holocaust. For example, one subject identified the position of modern Israelis with the "position of Jews going to the gas chambers." He saw the Arabs as anti-Semitic rather than anti-Zionist and said, "My response to anti-Semitism is not to turn the other cheek, it's to kick back." He felt that Israel had the atom bomb and "If it goes, it should take half the Arab world with it." Another subject described his feeling that Israel's retaliatory raids on Arab lands was "very good." He explained, "It shows the other countries that Israel will not just stand back and let the other countries do what they want." It was clear that underlying his position was an image of unchallenged Nazis "doing whatever they want" to the Jews.

Some subjects experienced the Arab-Israeli conflicts as involving them, not because of their commitment to Israel, but because of Arab hostility to them for being Jewish. They explained that they could easily see themselves the victims of terrorist attacks. Some said that when they read about such attacks, they experienced the attacks as directed against themselves.

While subjects felt personally threatened by assaults on Israel, not one subject felt that Israel would not survive as a nation. On the contrary, the sentiments of many subjects were summarized in the proud comment of one who simply said, "We'll make it." Other subjects went further and envisioned the Israel of the future as a powerful, prosperous nation. One of these said that she thought Israel would one day become a great world power.

At the same time, many other subjects felt that Israel was in danger of losing its unique identity. Some of these described their fear of Israel becoming "like any other country." Variants of this belief included the idea that Israel would continue to "swallow up" more Arab territory until it was no longer a Jewish state. Another was that Israel would become "torn apart" by internal strife, particularly among the many different Jewish subgroups.

One may speculate that at least some subjects' views about the future of Israel had highly personal meanings and may be interpreted as fantasies. For example, the view that Israel would become a great world power represented not only a chauvinistic stance, but also an expression of the person's own grandiosity and unfulfilled expectations of self. The view that Israel was threatened by internal strife represents not only evaluation of Israel's problems, but also an expression of the person's own conflicts about maintaining a Jewish identity at the expense of other possible identities.

The Imagery of the Past as an Organizing Principle of the Present

Even though they were not aware of it, the imagery of the past provided children of survivors with a central organizing principle for their present interaction with the world. The specific imagery they so integrated involved those images that had been transmitted to them both by their parents and also by their culture in general. This imagery was used by subjects in various ways, according to the particular dynamics of their evolving characters. The focus of such imagery was that it became the implicit basis of what may be called a survival strategy in the present world.

While describing his parents, one subject noted that they rarely voted for Jews who ran for political office. They believed that the visibility of Jews in Europe had resulted in the exterminiation of European Jewry. The subject himself was typically shy with other people. He felt extremely intimidated by authorities and felt especially uncomfortable when singled out for praise by them. Although he had a superb academic record, he had been satisfied to take a rather mediocre job within his profession. Though unhappy with it, he was not contemplating any plans for advancement.

In attempting to understand his feelings and behaviors, a number of psychodynamic interpretations come immediately to mind. However, the relationship between his sensitivity to persecution and his behaviors was not immediately apparent. Then, at one point in the later part of the interview, the subject was asked if he thought that he might one day become the victim of another Holocaust. His answer was "No." He then added he sometimes felt a need to be outspoken but suppressed it, so that, if society again needed scapegoats, he would not be among those chosen. He had not connected his shyness, his intimidation by authorities, and his failure to seek professional advancement to this belief. However, each of these behaviors, whatever else their dynamics, is organized around the issue of maintaining anonymity. Thus each betrays his strategy for living in a world that has had a Holocaust.

Another man described his mother as having survived the concentration camps because she had managed to convince the Nazis that she was a Christian. His father had survived because he had managed to smuggle money into the concentration camp and used it to bribe guards. He prided himself on his capacity to manipulate his environment; and he boasted of a number of incidents in which he had outwitted competitors or authorities in order to achieve success for himself. He seemed to have no awareness that his own considerable intellectual talents were as valuable as his guile. Again, the imagery of the past provided the basis for a stategy for living in the present.

A third subject's mother had come from a rich, progressive family. She was delighted by a story her mother told about a rabbi who had criticized her grandmother for providing her mother with dancing lessons in the Christian community. The grandmother agreed to interrupt the lessons, but only if the rabbi would agree to provide them himself. The mother had gone on to a medical career which was ended by her incarceration in a concentration camp. She herself was a premedical student in a prestigious university and supported her ambition to become a physician with an A-average. She spontaneously denied that her career choice was related to her mother's aborted medical career. She, however, described a second life goal. If she could not become a doctor, she wanted to become a "bohemian." She had a fantasy of "wasting my life away" with hedonistic excesses. Her fantasy included having an old English sheep dog. She experienced it as a startling coincidence when her mother told her the poignant story of returning to her farm after her liberation:

> The first thing she saw running to her was the dog [specifically, an old English sheep dog]. And that kind of made her feel at home, but when she walked into the house, it wasn't her home anymore. Things change. [Miss B.]

Implicit in the above account is the subject's unconscious identification with her mother. The subtlety of the identification was suggested by the fact that she must somehow have learned (and then forgotten) that her mother had had a sheep dog years before she fantasized having one herself. The identification provided her with a strategy for warding off her fears of not attaining her ambition and with a fantasy which provided an alternative. This alternative also took her back to the past, since her bohemian objective can be seen as an elaboration of her mother's dancing lessons. For her, the medical profession was a choice that led to an uncertain future. Paradoxically, the bohemian life she envisioned, symbolized by the dog, represented stability.

Another man described being proud of his father's heroic behavior while a prisoner. He believed that his father's scrupulous integrity had resulted in his defeat of the Nazis' attempts to murder him. At the same time, he was disturbed by literature he had read which described the childlike regression and identification with the aggressor of some inmates. A third image that was prominent in his consciousness involved his father's having organized a theater group in a displaced person's camp immediately after his liberation. At that time, his father was reunited with a nephew, his sole surviving relative, who was terminally ill. The night of a performance, it was not clear if it was the first performance, it was apparent that the child was on his deathbed. Nevertheless, the father went on stage, and the child died while he was acting. This man described his fathers' behavior with the words, "It was a choice."

The subject's own life has been characterized by a deep commitment to social justice. Throughout the interview he gave evidence of his dedicated, active pursuit of social values. At the same time, his worst fear was of:

> Probably being in a position where I'd hate myself, I don't know who'd put me in that position or how I'd come to hate myself, uh, going insane or compromising to such an extent that I'd think I'm disgusting. I don't think that physical damage would bring that about in terms of self-hate. [Mr. F.]

Another important characteristic of his was that he had been able to achieve an extraordinarily painful and difficult separation from his family.

One sees the thread of the past woven throughout these three elements of his life. His own political activities can be seen as related to images of his father's integrity and heroism. His own worst fear can be seen as related to his image of concentration camp inmates who compromised themselves. His own separation from his family can be seen as related to the image of his father insisting that life must go on, as he performed while his only link to the past died.

In each of the above examples, an image from the past was an underlying organizing theme of present behavior. In each example, past and present were integrated idiosyncratically, according to each subject's particular personality structure. Finally, in each example, the subject was unaware of the relationship of past and present.

6

Psychodynamic Themes and Characterological Issues in the Lives of Children of Survivors

About the children they can feel no certainty whatever.

[O. Handlin, 1951, p. 240]

This chapter will describe the themes and dynamics of character and development which emerged during the course of interviews with subjects. The aim of this chapter is to present psychological issues which, while universal, may have been exacerbated by the particular histories of the subjects interviewed.

The evidence supporting each of the intrapsychic themes to be discussed, particularly dream fragments and screen memories, resembles evidence which might emerge during psychoanalysis and would be used to generate hypotheses about the character organization of patients. However, the limitations of circumstances prevented the investigator from confirming his interpretations in the same way as might have been done during the course of treatment, that is, by repeated observation of the person's own associations. Consequently, the interpretations made are at a higher order of inference than might otherwise be desirable. In many cases, alternate interpretations may strike the reader as being as likely as those offered.

The Process and Vicissitudes of Separation and Individuation

Difficulties Achieving Separation

Subjects' difficulties in achieving, maintaining, and, in some cases, tolerating separation from their parents were portrayed at every level of development. For example, one subject's earliest memory involved her profound vulnerability to loss. She described the following:

I remember my father leaving, I guess I don't know how old I was, I must have been like a year old, um. I remember my father leaving, something about a train to leave me, anyway, and I was taken to my real mother's brother's house, and I remember like crying hysterically the entire time and wanting my father to come back, and the whole time, and like being very happy when he came back. [Miss G.]

Another subject, when asked to describe her first day of nursery school, remembered her "horror at being left and being miserable and having no one to comfort you." She described herself as "just so distraught about it...I was hysterical, I was a maniac, I was crying my head off." Another subject could not recall how she had felt when she went to kindergarten for the first time. However, she represented the psychic upheaval caused by this separation by remembering, "There was a hurricane, I just remember it was really bad weather."

During childhood and early adolescence, a number of subjects were sent by their parents to summer camp. Their experiences were uniformly negative. In some cases the experience was accompanied by the "terror" of being confronted with the hostile forces of the outside world. For example, one subject who was sent to camp twice, between the ages of four and eight, while he still lived in Europe, remembered that, during his first experience, he was convinced that a group of nuns was trying to convert him to Catholicism. He recalled being forced to go to Mass. He described how he responded to this assault as he said, "I threw up all over the place." His only memory of the second experience was:

The house across the hill burnt down and I was terrified and couldn't wait to leave, I was terrified and couldn't wait to leave, I was afraid the building would burn down, I couldn't wait to get to my parents. [Mr. D.]

At somewhat later ages, subjects described experiences which suggested that they had girded themselves to face the world. For example, the subject quoted above described a third experience in summer camp during his early adolescence: "It was O.K., but I couldn't socially hold my own, I was not isolated but retired, I would rather read than go with people." Another subject described going to summer camp at the age of 12, his first experience away from home, as follows:

I didn't miss my parents that much, believe me, like it was a different atmosphere 'cause you slept with other boys. It was like being home, you had people watching over you. You were out in the country but I really didn't like it that much. [Mr. A.]

In both the above examples of separation during early adolescence, the subjects engaged in denial of their feelings. One said spontaneously, "I didn't miss my parents," while the other said, "I wasn't isolated." Denial served to protect both from the onslaught of feelings connected not only with separation from parents but also with facing the world alone. This is not to say that subjects were unambivalent about achieving separation. For example, another subject described himself as constantly pestering his parents to send him to a summer camp. However, when they finally did, he described himself as immediately wanting to return home. Another subject who went on a tour at the age of 17, clearly as an attempt to achieve her first physical separation from her family, recalled the following:

> It was lonely. . . . I also got to appreciating my family, I didn't appreciate them before, and you realize that you're not, you know, going to live forever and that really, your family is really all that you've got, 'cause I went out there and you realize that you're not related to anybody and nobody out there is going to do anything for you because they like you much, and everthing that was done was done through great effort. And you realize, I got those letters [from her parents] with all the spelling errors, and those are the letters that make you feel like you want to be home, back where you can sleep comfortably. [Miss C.]

Similarly, another subject, at approximately the same age and in similar circumstances, described her experiences by saying, "It was O.K., but there were times I needed my mommy and daddy."

Subjects were most directly confronted with the difficulties of separation when they reached the age of having to choose a college. With only four exceptions, they chose schools which they could attend while continuing to live in their parents' homes. Often subjects insisted that their parents could not financially afford to send them to residential colleges. At the same time, they did not investigate the possibilities of earning a scholarship. One subject, who at first claimed that money was the factor determining his choice of a local university, later admitted that he had been offered a full scholarship to an out-of-state university. On reflection, he said, "I think I wasn't ready to leave home." Other subjects blamed their parents' hesitations for their own choices. One of these, who, after graduation from college, enrolled in a professional school in a different city, said that she had never considered applying to the Ivy League college that she wanted to attend, because of what she assumed would be her parents' position. Now she wonders if perhaps her attitude was a defense against her own difficulty with separation. She said:

> I knew I never could go to ———. I took it for granted that I'd have to live in ———. I would have never thought that at the time but I had such a hard time leaving when I did that, maybe, I don't know. [Miss G.]

Some indication of subjects' difficulties in achieving and maintaining separation from their families was manifested by the fact that, at the time of the interview, eight subjects were living with their parents. Of the 12 subjects who lived apart from their parents, two had left their homes to be married and lived in the same neighborhood as their parents. Most of them visited their parents at least once a week. All of those who lived in cities different from their parents were in school. All but one of these visited their parents on every school holiday. Some of these subjects described a "seesaw" or "approach-avoidance" between their desires to visit their parents and their desires to stay away from them. Similarly, all but one subject telephoned their parents at least once a week. Some described calls which lasted for long periods of time, while others described brief, unpleasant, and highly ritualized interactions. One subject described her reaction to her phone conversations with her parents as follows:

> My friends could always tell when I finished calling. I'd walk into the room, throw everything in sight at various people and doors and windows and scream for a couple of minutes and then be very calm. [Miss B.]

Although she overtly depicted acute distress as characteristic of her response to these contacts with her parents, she has made no attempt to change the nature of these interactions. Although the self-representation of a passive victim of her parents' aggression was implicit in her description, it is clear that she maintained her half of the interactions with them. Clinically, one may assume that, for her, these conversations represented her own efforts, in collusion with her parents, to continue her childhood relationship with them.

The Struggle for Separation and Individuation

While some subjects seemed to have physically matured within the context of a symbiotic relationship with their parents, and seemed to have made minimal efforts to establish independent identities, others seemed to have mobilized extraordinary resources in order to achieve some degree of individuation. The picture that emerged from these latter subjects' life histories was of a constant struggle, not only with their parents, but also with themselves.

While they described many of the same behaviors that characterize normal struggles for individuation—acting out through defiant behavior in school, plans and fantasies for travel and adventure, rejection of parental values, experimentation with a counter-culture—each of these behaviors seemed to have been imbued with an intensity and dedication that was extreme. For example, one 22-year-old subject insisted on smoking marijuana in his parents' home to "force them to accept who I am." Another subject planned his first trip away from home for a full year. He was 15 at the time, and he saved all the money he had earned from a part-time job he had taken in order to make the trip. He said that he had originally secured his parents' permission because "they never thought I'd do it." To the same end, another subject described her continuing attempt to shift her understanding of her parents, which at one time had been based solely on their past sufferings. Concomitant to her coming to experience herself as more separate from parents, she was able to say about them, "I guess I've attributed a lot of things to it [their past suffering] that's just them."

Some subjects gave the impression of having thrown off parental restraint relatively early. For example, one subject said, "I developed really independently, they [her parents] couldn't help it." She described that, as she grew up in a homogenous community, she had always made a point of "not conforming," and of choosing friends who "would not be accepted" by either her parents or the general community. In the process, she described having had "tremendous rows" with her parents which continue through the present.

Often, similarities between the subjects' struggles and compromises could be identified at different levels of development. For example, one subject described his first day of kindergarten as follows:

> I remember being frightened but I think that passed. I think I had a great desire to go and, uh, I basically sent my mother away. I think I said, O.K., that's cool. Leave. [Mr. J.]

Implicit in his memory was his having to master not only his own fears of being away from home but also his mother's interference with this task. As he prepared to make another step toward separation, by choosing a college, he decided that for his "development" he needed to go to a residential college. He explained:

> I didn't want to go to ——— [a local college] because that would be too much like high school, I wanted to meet different people and manage my own business. That's basically why I wanted to get away. [Mr. J.]

In explaining his final choice of a college, he mentioned that he had taken into account the financial burden he feared he would impose on his parents. In saying this, it was the interviewer's sense that he was saying that what he had taken into account was his parents' hesitation to allow him to leave. He went on to say that he chose a university that was "close enough to home so it wouldn't be a hassle getting back and forth."

Another example of the struggles involved in separation was provided by a subject who had been offered an extremely prestigious opportunity to advance himself professionally which involved his having to move to a different area of the country. The decision to accept the offer and leave his family was made all the more difficult by the fact that his father had just died. His mother's reaction to the idea of his leaving was described as:

> She was very against my going away, she tried to pressure me by repeating her feeling that it wasn't a good idea and suggesting that wasn't it time I had a family and settled down. I think she wants something stable in my life so she can have something to lean on. [Mr. F.]

He described his response to her pressure as follows:

> I told her I thought about her reasons. She was most bitter about the fact that in recent years, like last summer, I sublet an apartment in ——— and I didn't live with her.... And I tried to tell her why it was important for me and probably good for her that I don't [that is, continue to live with her]. [What did you tell her?] Well, in terms of her, that her husband's death is something she's going to have to come to terms with . . . and my living with her would only make it more difficult for her to realize that she's going to be alone, and, uh, to come to terms with this and, uh, that she knew she could reach me at any time, that is, if anything important, that I'd be available . . . that I had the opportunity to be away from the pressures that were around me, and it was just so important so I could develop the way I wanted to develop. That it was very important to me, and, uh, I asked her to accept this. [Mr. F.]

Implicit in his account of his decision to accept the offer were clues that he himself was ambivalent about it. This is suggested by the isolation of affect that characterized his description. In addition, his statement to his mother that "she's going to be alone" represented a neurotic distortion based on his own continuing attachment to her. Nevertheless, he clearly mobilized the resources to master the pressure put on him by his mother and to separate himself from her. The success of this effort became all the more impressive when he described his history, which included, among other things, the fact that his mother had fed him until his baby brother was born when he was six years old. And his success was adumbrated by the fact that then he struggled with his mother by "holding a piece of food in my mouth . . . for two hours just so they couldn't put another piece in it."

The added difficulties of survivors' children in achieving separation from their families, and the fact that their struggles for it did not always succeed, was dramatically portrayed by one subject. Around the age of 16, she began to change from a child who was passive and compliant in her attitude toward her parents to one who felt "everything they said was wrong." She began to have heated arguments with them, usually about the strict restrictions they imposed on her. Concomitantly, she began spending more time with school friends and also discovered that she was interested in boys. By the time she was 17, she began to challenge her parents' expectation that she would continue her education in a Yeshiva and demanded to go to a public rather than a parochial college. Although she continued to live in her parents' home, she won a major victory as she entered the college of her choice. During her first year of college, she formed her first serious attachment with a male, and carefully hid this fact from her parents. As she spent more time away from home, though she never spent an entire evening out, her parents began to call her friends and check the excuses that she had given them. They also hired a private investigator to follow her. Not only did they eventually discover the relationship, they also forced her to break it off. Her reaction to this episode was a feeling of extreme guilt at "having lost my parents' trust." She contemplated suicide, had an unsatisfactory consultation with a psychotherapist, and finally decided to "turn over a new leaf." She experienced this decision as a "rebirth." She said that her relationship with her parents was restored because, "They see I've come to my senses." By this she meant that she abandoned her attempts to live her life in any other than the manner prescribed for her by her parents.

Subjects' Symbiotic Attachments to Their Parents

A number of subjects described personal histories in which the investigator observed minimal efforts to achieve separation. These subjects may be described as living in symbiotic relationships with their families. While certain features overlapped, three patterns of such relationships emerged.

The first pattern involved the subjects' conscious representations of the relationships between themselves and their parents as distant. Subjects had tremendous difficulty describing either themselves or their parents. That is, their capacity to represent self and object was extremely limited. Therefore, on the basis of verbal information, consciously provided, the nature of their relationship with their parents was elusive. However, on the basis of certain other information, it was possible to ascertain hostility and profound dependency as characteristic of their relationships with their parents. For example, verbal battles, unacknowledged or denied by the subjects, were detected by either the interviewer or the referral source. In addition, the themes of dependency and frustration at unsatisfied dependency emerged, usually out of the subjects' awareness, as they described their lives. For example, one subject revealed that it was his habit to leave notes for his father, asking him to wake him up in the morning. His father would frequently forget to do so, provoking one of the few contexts for the subject's overt expressions of anger. The subject never considered the possibility of his setting his own alarm clock. Another subject revealed a similar situation as he described his expectation that his mother would have his meals prepared when he was hungry. These subjects also spent a great deal of time in their homes, usually in their own rooms. Their contact with the outside world was limited to going to school. The thought of moving out of their parents' homes was foreign to them. The distinguishing characteristic of this pattern was the failure of the subject to experience himself as existing apart from his hostile, dependent relationship with his parents.

A second type of symbiotic relationship involved the subject's presentation of himself as undifferentiated from his parents. Such subjects incorporated their parents' views, attitudes, and even moods, making them their own. One such subject described herself, *vis-á-vis* her mother, as follows:

> My mother and I are exactly alike. [How so?] Every respect, we think alike, we're very much alike, I mean I can picture my mother at my age, we were one person in every respect. [Miss H.]

The third pattern of symbiotic relationship involved the subjects' appearing on the surface to have achieved some degree of physical separation from their parents and some involvement in the outside world. On closer examination, they continued to be compliant to parental demands, perhaps at the very same time as they gave the impression of having struck out on their own. Many of these were following the careers and life styles that their parents had wanted for themselves. One such subject said, "Essentially, quite by accident, I turned into exactly what they wanted." His comment reflected his incorporation of his parents' wishes for him and his treating these as if they were his own.

Characteristics of More Successful Resolutions

In spite of the serious difficulties in the process of separation-individuation experienced by all subjects, some nevertheless appeared to have achieved an identity of their own which was distinct from that of their parents. A characteristic of these subjects was that, while they sometimes seemed more mature than their peers when younger, they tended to be still engaged in the interpersonal behaviors associated with separation and identity formation at ages older than their peers. For example, many of these subjects first started dating and joining groups, both formal and informal, during their first years of college.

The major theme throughout these subjects' lives was a willingness to be influenced by the world outside their families. That is, some of them, on their own initiative, may not have been willing to turn from their families to the world, but, once forced to, they were willing to have commerce with it rather than continue to guard themselves from it. For example, a number of subjects, after the trauma of separation, were able to relish their experiences in school. Others continued to seal themselves off. At older ages, other subjects portrayed dramatic growth upon leaving the physical presence of their parents. One subject, for example, who lived in his parents' home, said that he "needed" to sleep between 10 and 12 hours each night. He said that his father criticized him for "being like my mother" and for being "lazy." However, for a period of time every summer he worked as a busboy in a hotel near his parents' vacation home. In passing, he mentioned that he thought his parents would be "amazed" if they saw how "hard" he worked, and if they knew that, during this period, he felt refreshed after only five hours of sleep. Another subject described himself as changing from someone who was "closed" to someone who was "open" when he entered college. He said of his first year of college, the first time in his life that he had experienced himself as away from the influence of his parents, "Freshman year was a momentous year. I became aware I was a person."

Some subjects provided evidence that, as a step toward individuation, they had turned to real or imagined others in an attempt to fill the void created by their disappointment with their parents' inadequacies. For example, several subjects reported having fantasized that other people were their parents. For example, one subject said:

> When I was really younger, I would have fantasies on people's homes kind of things, like I'd really want a home with a lot of people coming in and out and, uh, understanding parents and a more relaxed environment. [Miss G.]

Another subject located fantasies that other people were her parents as occurring as early as seven years of age. Other subjects reported actually seeking out adults who parented them in a more satisfying and nurturant manner than their real parents. One of these described a couple whom she called "grandparents" who "fulfilled needs for me that my real parents didn't." She hid this relationship from her parents. Parental surrogates, whether real or imagined, may be considered to have represented transitional objects who prepared and enabled the child to turn from his family to the world.

For some subjects, it seemed that precisely those parental attitudes and behaviors that had inhibited other subjects' individuation had motivated their own. For example, one subject said:

> When I was growing up, they were really hung up about a lot of things, like I say, they were really paranoid about it. I mean they would never let me out of their sight for five or ten minutes. Their upbringing was so different that, um, I suppose I resented a great bit and my parents and I would argue about a lot of things and I feel bad because I know that I'm hurting them when I do what I think is right and how that I'm old enough to know what, to have opinions of my own. I don't want to succumb to others. I had to get away to school in order to develop on my own. [Miss B.]

She seemed to be saying that she experienced her parents as so suffocating that, in spite of other feelings she also had (about hurting them), she felt that, in order to survive, she had to achieve distance from them.

Often subjects had to pay a price for having achieved the separation that they did from their parents. It seemed that some subjects, to be allowed to maintain distance between themselves and their families, could not also enjoy themselves in the process. For example, one subject reported that her parents would complain to her that she did not write letters to them often enough. She went on to say, "But they would always add, 'If you're studying instead, don't worry, we understand.'" As a consequence, she adopted the strategy of complaining to them about the amount of work she had. Similarly, another subject, who was contemplating going to a professional school in a distant city, seemed to be able to anticipate only the work that would be expected of him, and could not experience any pleasure in looking forward to his move. However, the price most often paid for separation was guilt. Many subjects described feeling guilt as a consequence not only of moving out of their parents' homes, but also of engaging in any behavior that they maintained in the service of their own individuation and at the expense of their parents' symbiotic demands on them.

Interpersonal Relationships

Many subjects described or portrayed difficulties in their relationships with other people. As a rough indication of the extent of such difficulties, 12 of the 20 subjects may be described as having severely limited social interactions. Each of these had no more than one person, if any, of the same sex whom they would call a close friend. Five of these found their lack of relationships with others to be ego-syntonic. Seven subjects had never had a relationship with someone of the opposite sex that had lasted more than eight months. Six subjects had had at least one such relationship at some time. The other seven subjects, including two who were married, were in such a relationship at the time of the interview. Subjects' difficulties in their interpersonal relationships were characterized by isolation from others, mistrust of others, and fears of and desires for merging with others.

Isolation

Many subjects described themselves as having been isolated from others throughout the course of their development. Several subjects reported that they had spent their childhood in virtual seclusion, playing by themselves in their homes. The theme of isolation was reflected in a number of their earliest memories. For example, one subject's earliest memory was of sitting on the darkened steps to the cellar of his house, banging on pots and pans. Another subject described the following memory, which he located in his third year:

> I remember being in a bungalow colony one summer. I just remember being engulfed in tall grass, like weeds. [What mood do you associate with it?] It's just like an image more than a memory. [Mr. J.]

A number of subjects related their isolation in childhood to their perception that they did not "fit in." Many of these subjects described themselves as having felt that they were "different" from their peers. These included both subjects who were born in the United States and those born in Europe. At some point during their lives a number of subjects recalled having gone through periods of resenting their parents for being foreign.

Another aspect of subjects' isolation from others was revealed by some subjects' use of the word "miserable" to characterize their adolescence. These subjects described themselves as either having had no friends during their adolescence or as having had acquaintances whom they did not like. Other subjects described themselves as having been extremely shy and therefore having had trouble making friends. One subject who described himself as "retired, tired, and shy" throughout his adolescence reported that he did have friends but that "they were all like me."

A number of subjects' descriptions of their interpersonal isolation was characterized not by loneliness, but by a feeling that can best be described as existential aloneness. For example, one subject said that she understood that the only people in the world who would care about her were her husband and her parents. Another described herself as having acquaintances but no friends. She insisted that this did not trouble her because she knew that "you're always alone." Other subjects portrayed their feelings of aloneness in the difficulty they had responding to the interviewer's request that they describe someone they considered important to them. For example, one otherwise cooperative and open subject said that not only did he not want to think about who he considered important to him, but that he also experienced anger when the interviewer asked him to do so.

Mistrust

Basic mistrust was a dimension of many subjects' interpersonal lives. It emerged implicitly or explicitly as they described their relationships with others. For example, one subject explained her isolation from others in terms of others' being unwilling to accept her because "I was too honest and wouldn't say things to make friends. I wasn't like them, and they hated me for it." When asked to say more about her being different from others, she responded by telling many spiteful stories about the failings of other people. Implicit in her portrayal was the image of others as dishonest and unreliable. Other subjects described people they knew as "back-stabbers," "untrustworthy," "mean," and "envious." One subject, for example, said he would neither ask for nor do favors for others because in both cases, he said, "They'll hold it as a grudge."

In a number of cases the interviewer had the impression that the subject typically portrayed himself as the victim of other people's aggression or deceit. For example, one subject who had been engaged three times experienced bewilderment at the termination of two of these engagements. She said that she had concluded that she was "gullible" and "too trusting," and that thus people took advantage of her. Another subject, a male, described women as "untrustworthy," and as typically taking advantage of him. Still another explained that she did not become close to people because she anticipated that they would "hurt" her in some way. A number of subjects, when asked to describe interactions that were characteristic of these relationships with other people, described incidents during which they felt they had been abused or during which they became deeply mistrustful of the motives of others.

Conflicts over Mergence

A number of subjects' descriptions of their relationships with others, especially their difficulties becoming close to others, suggested that their basic difficulties on the one hand involved a desire for a symbiotic relationship with others and, on the other hand, a fear of being engulfed by the other. For example, one subject said that she understood her difficulties in becoming close to others as a consequence of her desire to "cling to" and be dependent on people. Another subject described herself as most comfortable in casual relationships with people and becoming "anxious and withdrawing" when others passed a certain "boundary" of intimacy. Other subjects, who in fact had few close friends, described their basic expectations of a friend as someone who would be willing to "die" for them or "come in the middle of the night" if they were in need. One such subject also described his fantasy of a possible love object as someone who would know what he was thinking without his having to say.

Similarly, a number of subjects described their friends as remarkably similar to themselves. One subject, for example, described her only friendships as those she had had during college. The only activities she and her friends had engaged in were frantic and unsuccessful attempts to plan opportunities to meet males. After college, none of these relationships endured. Another subject described her best and, besides her boyfriend, only friend as having interests and attitudes identical to her own. One such attitude was, "We decided that most people use each other, and we really don't." The two of them have not only decided to travel together at the first opportunity they have, but also to go into business together at some point in the future. In addition, the subject reported that, when asked out on a date, she often insisted that her date agree to take her friend as well.

At the other extreme, some subjects chose to pursue love objects completely different from themselves. For example, a striking theme in one subject's life was his having, from childhood to the present, chosen only those female playmates, and later, girl friends, who were Christian. At the same time, he explained that he would never marry a non-Jewish woman because of his parents' objections. While interesting at many levels of analysis, his history suggested that he chose only love objects whom he could not have. Still another subject described his only sexual relationships as being with women whom he met casually, while traveling. He was quite perplexed, because none of the relationships he had had with women who were available to him in his home town, in spite of his conscious desires, had never led to anything more than a "friendship."

Dynamic Themes

A number of dynamic issues emerged as especially prominent in the lives of these subjects. These were conflicts related to the expression of anger, the need to control, the experience of shame, the inhibition of the gratification of impulses, grandiosity, sibling rivalry, the experience of fearfulness, and the representation of the self as a victim in dreams.

Conflicts Related to the Expression of Anger

Anger emerged as a particularly conflictual area for many subjects. On one hand, subjects produced evidence that suggested they experienced massive rage. On the other hand, they produced evidence which suggested they were quite as massively defended against such feelings. Subjects' conflicts will be described in the context of, first, anger at parents, and second, anger at peers.

Anger at parents. Some subjects denied having had angry or aggressive feelings toward their parents, while other subjects not only owned up to such feelings but also seemed immersed in them. It seemed to the interviewer that many of the former subjects, even as they were affirming their compliant attitudes, gave evidence of their passively aggressive behavior toward their parents. For example, one such subject described the only area in which he ever resisted his parents as involving food. Since he so adamantly refused to eat her food, his mother would become desperate to provide whatever food he was willing to eat. Thus he would often demand dishes which she had never even heard of. He described, with great humor in his voice, her searching the streets, "in the middle of the night," for lasagne. Other subjects reported that the only exception to their uniformly good conduct during childhood had been misbehavior in Hebrew school. The choice of this locale for the expression of aggressive impulses suggests that it was the most immediately accessible symbol of their parents. A number of subjects, already described, were observed to express anger at their parents by the interviewer or the referral source. Each of these denied having had or having expressed any such feelings toward their parents. The interviewer did not feel that these subjects were consciously distorting their responses but, rather, were involved in repressing their angry feelings through isolation and denial.

Subjects' conflicts and defenses about the expression of anger became more manifest as subjects described their management of such feelings. For example, one subject reported that he did not get angry at his parents because

"I can just as easily say, 'Leave me alone,' and walk out." Other subjects described efforts to be "more tolerant" of their parents. One of these described herself as often shouting at them, and as trying as hard as she could to "control" these outbursts. Another reported having periods during which she would say things like "I wish you never had me," and then regretting "the stupid things I said." Still another subject made the following contradictory statement:

> I don't think I've been angry for a long time. I've felt bad, like, you know, I've never felt like killing anybody if that's what you're asking about. . . . I holler at my mother. [What kinds of things do you holler?] 'You ignorant bitch or refugee'. . . . [Mr. C.]

When subjects described expressing angry feelings to their parents, their portrayals were often dramatic. For example, one subject repeatedly used the word "violent" to describe his arguments with his father. Another subject described often having wished for his father to die, and on one occasion having hit him hard enough to knock him down. Still another subject insisted, in an exceedingly bitter tone of voice, that the only reason she could "forgive" her parents was that they were survivors. In some cases the subjects' dream life belied their denial of angry feelings. For example, one subject described having repetitive dreams of an atomic explosion in which "she's [her mother] the first to go."

Anger at peers. Many subjects portrayed themselves as having had minimal angry or aggressive outbursts at peers during childhood. For example, a number of subjects (both male and female) described their "first fight" as having been challenged or attacked by another child and being unable to show angry feelings in return. Several of these subjects reported having been struck, kicked, or scratched by another child, and having been unable to respond in any way other than fleeing or crying. In these incidents, subjects clearly portrayed themselves as having been the victims of the aggression of others and as having had no aggressive feelings themselves. A number of subjects, all males, described themselves as "cowards" who would frequently be beaten up by other children. Subjects also reported difficulties tolerating their aggressive feelings when these did emerge. For example, one subject recalled having been goaded into a fight by another boy, and finding himself sitting on top of the boy "begging" passersby to help him get off.

Subjects' anger and aggression was also inhibited during adolescence and adulthood. For example, when asked to describe what made them angry, a number of subjects described conditions under which they had become angry at themselves. Several subjects described as having been depressed and, because they were in therapy, later recognizing that they were really angry. Other subjects described being "frustrated" and "disappointed" rather than angry.

One described herself as "an easy-going person. It takes an awful lot to make me angry but I get upset inside."

Some subjects described having adopted strategies for dealing with their angry feelings without having to express them directly. For example, one subject said:

> Most people don't know it when I'm angry, see, I'm very lucky in that I found out … if you smile and look like you're joking around, you can say awful things about someone and you can get away with it. [Mr. G.]

A number of subjects described becoming "arrogant" or "sarcastic" or "biting" as a way of letting others know they were angry. Others described becoming "quiet" or "holding in" their feelings or going to a person different from the one they were angry at to whom to express their feelings. The inhibition of angry feelings did not mean that such feelings were not intensely present. For example, one subject indicated that he often experienced "a rage" at other people, and also often felt very vindictive, but had tremendous difficulty communicating these feelings. Another subject recalled having repetitive daydreams about "devastating" other people by using the powers of his mind. Other subjects, while denying having angry feelings toward other people, portrayed a profound contempt for and rejection of other people.

A number of subjects expressed a desire to be able to vent their angry feelings. In one case, this desire was expressed symbolically as the subject described his desire (which he has never acted upon) to learn karate. Another subject described the following feelings about an incident:

> We were playing basketball and some guy thought I was playing it rough and he and his friend got together and one guy kneeled down and, uh, pushed me over [the other's back], tried to, you know, hurt me. I fell over. I was a little hurt and I could see myself, if I were a different kind of guy, I couldn't come up swinging and I didn't, I didn't fight. That bothers me somehow. [Mr. H.]

The Need to Control

The need to control the self and the need to control the environment, based on fears of losing control, were prominent themes in the lives of the subjects. For example, the interviewer's impression was that control was an important characteristic of many subjects' relationship with him throughout the interview. He often noted that subjects would interrupt both his questions and his answers to their questions. In addition, a number of subjects seemed highly invested in presenting a particular image of themselves and their relationships with their parents rather than allowing a more mutual process of exploration to occur. It was also the interviewer's impression that a number of subjects maintained a need to control their feelings tightly throughout the interview. A few subjects were able, themselves, to comment on their need to maintain such control over their feelings. For example, one subject described herself as being very anxious before meeting with the interviewer for the first time, because she was not sure that she would be able to keep from crying. Other subjects portrayed their need to maintain control of their feelings by denying feelings about events in their own and their parents' lives. These same events provoked intense emotions in the interviewer. For example, one subject described a suicide attempt made by his father and described his reaction to it as "I didn't want to be bothered with it." Another subject described the blasé reaction of "I knew it all the time" to his accidental discovery, during adolescence, that his father had had a previous family that had been killed by the Nazis.

Other evidence of subjects' need to control came from reports of fantasies, dreams, fears, and incidents. For example, one subject described his worst fantasy as "going crazy, I'd get scared that I'd totally lose control of myself." He described the worst thing that had ever happened to him as waking up from a nightmare and thinking that he was "going to go crazy." He said of it, "I feel like I can't get into this, I feel like I must be defending, I thought I was going to lose control." Another subject, although he was hesitant to describe his dreams and fantasies, described the following about his adolescence: "I guess I fantasized a little bit about being terribly strong and in control of whatever might come up." [Mr. J.]

Other subjects described specific fears that may be understood in terms of conflicts over maintaining and giving up control. For example, one subject described a fear of "deep water." She said that she enjoyed swimming and diving as long as she could "touch ground." The moment she cannot, she said, "I'll panic." Another subject described a fear of "walking down dark stairs." When asked to associate to "dark stairs" she said, "I get scared, I can't see in the dark." Both the above subjects struck the interviewer as being constricted during the interview. Two other subjects, who seemed less constrained in their behavior during the interview, had experimented with a wide range of behaviors and life styles. One of them described a fear of heights. At the same time, he had made plans for the future to go sky-diving. The other described an intense fear of snakes that sometimes transformed itself into a "fascination" with snakes. Both subjects can be understood as manifesting behaviors underlying which was a conflict over issues of control which was resolved by a counterphobic adaptation.

One focus of subjects' need to control was the feeling of vulnerability to a capricious outside world. Many subjects described feeling helpless in the face of threats posed in the form of receiving bad grades or losing a job. One such subject described a "terror" of receiving bad grades because she felt such grades would jeopardize her future. Other subjects described feelings of vulnerability to inflation and increasing prices. One such subject described the following dream:

> I had this dream I went to the gas station and gas was 60 cents a gallon and I was really upset and really worried because I have to commute next year and won't be able to afford it. [Miss G.]

The dream occurred in June 1973 before the "energy crisis."

Another focus of the need to control involved the control of ego-alien wishes. For example, one subject described what seems to have been an intense struggle to interrupt compulsive, grandiose daydreams. After describing such daydreams, the themes of which were his superhuman powers and achievements, he said of his having given them up, "I have this gyroscope that forces me to be realistic because otherwise you can just lose control." Another subject reported the following dream:

> I just had a dream that there was a submarine and I had to stop it or I was in it. I just had to stop something and I woke up yelling, 'stop it, stop it.' [Mr. E.]

Implicit in the dream is the subject's attempt to control impulses, most probably aggressive impulses, represented by the submarine. Another subject reported a dream which she has had recurrently since the age of eight: "I always dream of being killed in a car crash, I wouldn't be sure who was driving and it goes out of control and hits trees." [Miss B.] In her association to the dream, the subject reported that she has often thought it quite likely that she would be killed in an automobile accident. She has also thought that such an accident would occur while someone else was driving. Implicit in the dream, and the lack of affect with which it was told, was a wish to give up control. Concomitant to that wish is the representation of its consequences.

Shame

Feelings of inferiority and vulnerability to humiliation emerged as a theme in many, but not all, interviews. Such feelings suggested that shame was a personality characteristic of many subjects.

Several subjects had memories of events in their lives which represented the prominence of shame as a central theme in their lives. For example, one subject's earliest memory was of "taking off my tights and they got stuck in my shoes." Although she could not remember any feelings associated with the memory, it may be inferred that the memory represented a central theme in her unconscious experience of herself. Another subject remembered that, when he was six years old, he was seen urinating in his back yard by a little girl. He described being "so embarrassed I ran away for a whole day." Another subject reported that he was quite threatened by the question "What was the worst thing that ever happened to you?" He finally described having made an error, which he would not specify, during the course of a ball game, while in the eighth grade, which produced in him a profound feeling of humiliation.

Other subjects described or portrayed intense feelings of inferiority to others. For example, one subject portrayed this feeling as he described his parents as having done "a good job" with him, "considering what they had to work with." Another subject described feeling extremely "timid" with people in authority and always "amazed" when "important people" were "nice" to him. Still another subject described that, throughout his adolescence, he was ashamed of being older than most of his classmates. He described the following about his four years of high school:

> I was extremely alienated . . . and I never told anybody my age . . . I was so glad to get out of high school, I just didn't feel a part of anything. It was always as if I had something to hide. [Mr. I.]

Grandiosity

As had been described, subjects, in their childhood, were often the center of their parents' lives. This role fed their grandiosity and infantile omnipotence. Thus, the earliest memories of some subjects emphasized this aspect of their unconscious lives. The following are two such memories, both located in the subjects' second year:

> I think I remember it because it's been described . . . a little baby in our apartment. I'm sure it's because my mother told me about it, and having toys around me and the center of attention. My aunts and uncles, my mother and father, standing around me. [Miss I.]

> I guess I remember being in Poland, like a lot of people around, like the nun who took care of me, sort of like hovering over me and attending to me and stuff like that. [Miss G.]

Other subjects described the importance of feeling special at different times in their lives. For example, one subject said of her kindergarten year, "It was great." She explained, "I was the smartest kid in the class." Another subject, who also described her high school years as characterized by "having no other interests in my whole life except getting good grades," said:

> It [high school] was very good. I liked it. [What did you like about it?] I was number one. [What do you mean?] I was valedictorian. I always did very well. I was very good. I had a good time. [Miss D.]

Other subjects expressed the theme of grandiosity through their daydreams. Although most could not or would not share the specific content, they described these as "power-oriented daydreams," "success grandiose daydreams," and "fantasies of success."

Sibling Rivalry

A number of subjects described relationships with their siblings which suggested the possibility of intensified sibling rivalry in their families.

For oldest children, the arrival of a sibling was most often an unexpected event for which they were not prepared. For example, one subject remembered herself, at the age of four, sitting on a fire hydrant in front of her house, waiting for her mother to return from the hospital. Although probably involving considerable distortion, the memory reflected her feelings of abandonment in favor of the new arrival. Another subject said that when her baby sister was born her father was unable to care for her. She continued to say:

> And they took me to a place, I always thought it was an orphanage, and I was two and a half. They put me in diapers and I didn't like it too much and I started pulling them off. [Miss F.]

Several subjects remembered greeting their new siblings with contempt and anger. One subject remembered thinking that her new brother was "the stupidest thing that I ever saw." Other subjects remember physically attacking their infant siblings with bites and punches. One subject remembered that she threw her baby sister out of her crib.

Conflicts about Achieving Gratification

One theme that was absent from many subjects' descriptions of themselves involved the portrayal of a capacity to enjoy life and gratify desires without shame or guilt. For example, few subjects described themselves as gaining pleasure in the pursuit of their own interests and careers. A number of subjects who had defined pastimes that they found pleasurable had foreclosed the possibility of pursuing these as careers.

Some subjects, in their memories of childhood, represented their renunciation of wishes of their fear of gratifying their wishes. For example, one subject remembered the following event from his childhood:

> I was hit by a motocycle when I was three years old. A girl who lived in our courtyard noticed a man mending pots and pans in the street. It was very exciting to watch because he would grind metal, making noise and throwing sparks. She ran across the street, I chased her and got hit. [Mr. H.]

Interpreted symbolically, the memory portrays the juxtaposition of impulse gratification with the idea of severe punishment. Another subject was asked to remember her first fight. She responded that she never fought, but that she could remember her "first sin." She came from a religious family that observed strict dietary laws. She described the following:

> I ate meat, I wanted a candy bar, I don't eat meat and milk together and I had eaten a drumstick, and two minutes later I had eaten a Hershey's chocolate bar, and I felt bad. [What do you mean?] I thought I was going to die. [Miss H.]

The process of the subject's response to the original question has two interesting features. First, it suggests the confusion of aggressive impulses with oral gratification. Second, her thought of dying after having gratified her impulse suggests an excessively harsh and punitive superego. The same subject recalled dreams which she located in her fourth and fifth years:

> They were dreams that I was in Candyland, fun dreams. Candyland was colors and lollipops and sugar canes and that bunny rabbit, What was his name? He always used to come around. We used to eat candy together. [Miss H.]

Her present response to these dreams was indicated as she continued, "It was a sick dream. [Why?] Because it was nuts. [Why was it nuts?] Who dreams of Candyland with colored lollipops?" [Miss H.] Her comments clearly indicated a repudiation of pleasurable wishes as "sick," that is, unacceptable.

The theme described above was also reflected in the prevalence of depression among subjects. Although few subjects were able to observe their own suffocation of their pleasurable desires, one subject was conscious of experiencing pleasure as "getting away with something." She went on to say, "It's like I got a ledger in my head and I can't get away with anything, if I do something, there should be pain in it." A final manifestation of the inhibition of gratification was that, although many subjects were quite successful either professionally or academically, few showed any enjoyment or pride in their successes.

Fearfulness

Implicit in many subjects' life histories was the portrayal of a profound fearfulness of the outside world. Many of their earliest memories, for example, involved the portrayal of danger. The person's role in such memories involved either vulnerability to and helplessness in the face of direct threat or passive observation of the omnipotent, impersonal force of the outside world. One may assume that the latter role involved a translation of terror into detachment. For example, one subject's earliest memory, located at the age of two, was "being on a table ready for an operation." His memory of the feelings he had was "I was probably sitting there waiting, wondering what was going to happen to me." Another subject's earliest memory was of his village in Poland. He remembered hogs being slaughtered. He described:

> Whenever they would slaughter the hogs, the people [*sic*] would put up an awful squeal, would make an awful sound. I never really saw a skinning. I recall one night, I was listening to it, a terrible sound outside in the courtyard. [How did you feel?] I don't remember, only the awful screeching sound. [Mr. H.]

Another subject's first memory, which she located in her second year, involved the idea of invasion by hostile forces. She remembered being "in a swimming pool and a dog jumped in... I was scared, scared of the dog." Still another subject's first memory, located in his sixth year, involved passively watching a scene of destruction. It was of walking down a broad avenue, seeing a large truck hit a concrete pole and "things slowly falling off."

As subjects described their later childhood and early adolescent years, the objects of their fears became more associated with people. For example, several subjects described themselves as being afraid to go out of their homes because they were afraid of being beaten up by other children. One subject described taking off his yarmulka as soon as he got outside of Hebrew school because he was afraid it might provoke other children to attack him. These and other subjects described themselves as "cowards." Another subject remembered that when he was 11 years old he saw a fire alarm and pulled it. He said of the incident, "I ran so fast and I didn't come out for two days... I was wondering if they would take the fingerprints off it." He still has a vivid memory of the incident and described his fear of imprisonment and a thousand-dollar fine as if it were a realistic punishment for his crime.

Fearfulness, as a dominant affective theme of childhood, was also portrayed by a number of subjects who described themselves as exceptionally well-behaved. While many of these subjects presented this description of themselves in the context of having lived a bland and emotionally uneventful life, one subject indicated that he understood the dynamics of his behavior as he said:

> I was a very good child. I did anything anybody told me to and I was completely nonrebellious but very introverted and frightened of what people would do to me. [Mr. F.]

Representations of Self as Victim

Many of the subjects who reported dreams revealed through the manifest content of the dreams a preoccupation with the ideas of invasion, of threat to, and violence against the self. In their dreams, they portrayed themselves as the victims of the aggression of others who were specifically defined or only vaguely outlined.

An early example of such content was reported by a subject who described recurrent nightmares, some of which possibly were hallucinations, around the age of six years. He described them as follows:

> I always used to remember seeing things that weren't there. I remember I saw this man, he was coming, I heard noises in the hall. Then I heard the door open. I heard a man coming toward me. I yelled for my father and he came and then he opened the light and I saw nothing was there. [Mr. A.]

The importance of these dreams in the subject's life was indicated by the fact that the above was the only dream he could recall ever having. Given his constriction in other areas (for example, the inaccessibility of his feelings, his denial of having a fantasy life, and his self-imposed isolation manifested by his never venturing from his home except when absolutely necessary) his memory of this particular dream was remarkable. The outstanding characteristic of the dream involved his terror of being attacked by "things that weren't there." One must immediately raise the question, What was the dreaming child unable to see? The answer to this question was suggested by the subject's identification of a male figure whom he then denied seeing. The memory of his father rescuing him supplies the answer. Implicit in it was the conscious representation of the father as savior. Behind this was the unconscious representation of the father as the threatening aggressor.

While the feeling of terror often accompanied their dreams, in their reports subjects tended to intellectualize, deny, evade, and detach both the terror and other feelings implicit in their dream imagery. In other words, the feelings in their dreams were unintegrated, ego-alien, and defended-against. For example, one subject reported having the following dreams throughout her adolescence and in the present:

> A lot of dreams of escaping or running away from people, it wasn't that anyone was chasing me in the dream but I do remember these running sequences and really being afraid that I wasn't going to make it or that I was going to exhaust myself. [Miss G.]

In the description of the dream was an explicit denial of it, "It wasn't that anyone was chasing me." Another subject, after describing recurrent nightmares she had between the age of five and seven, said of them, "I can't imagine why I had these dreams." She described them as follows:

> I had a very old uncle, a grand-uncle or something. He was a very scary looking old man with a hunchback and I had these dreams of him running, chasing me up the stairs and through a very long tunnel. [Miss B.]

The source of threat in her dream was a "very old uncle." At one level of interpretation, he represented the threat of her sexualized attraction to her father whom she saw as crippled. At another level of interpretation, he, as an old man, represented the historical past reaching into her life.

Imagery related to the Holocaust was sometimes translated into more modern terms. For example, in the following dream, the Nazi threat to Jews was re-evoked in imagery of the Arab-Israeli wars:

> The night after the Fourth of July, I imagined I was in a war. I was behind a fence and people around me, and bombs going off all around me. For some reason I thought it was the Arab-Israeli war. [Mr. E.]

The exploding bombs can be understood as the subject's experience of the undifferentiated malevolence of the environment around him as well as his own diffuse, internal anxiety. The following is a more complex dream also involving the translation of persecutory symbols of the past into a more modern context:

> I went to, in a brand-new car that belongs to my parents, to some vacation resort, kind of beach, race track, resort with somebody, can't remember who, got stopped by the police who said that I couldn't drive a Connecticut car with a Connecticut license and all of a sudden, they took out a rifle from the back seat of my car and they took my car away, and all of a sudden, there was this routine with pullovers and jerseys and trucks and someone was going to teach me to ride a truck. Then in some disconnected way, I don't know how, there was a group of Russians in Connecticut who were holding me prisoner, and I had to prove that I could read Hebrew to prove that I was American. They were holding our passports and I couldn't make sense of it because I knew I was in Connecticut. I woke up having difficulty reading Hebrew. [Mr. G.]

In the above dream, Russians were substituted for Germans and the dreamer's release was dependent on his Jewishness. Other important elements of the dream are threat as a consequence of the use of parents' possessions (the car) and an accusation that is irrational (the crime of driving a Connecticut car with a Connecticut license). Identity confusion was evident in the dual representations of aggressor (police and Russians) and of the victim (American and Hebrew). In addition, the "routine with pullovers" may have been an association to the subject's mother's survival of the Holocaust by passing for a Christian (that is, changing her identity, represented in the dream by changing clothes). However, the key to the dream was the rifle found in the back of the car. It symbolized the dreamer's own aggression that was denied throughout the dream as he maintained that he was a victim.

The aspect of projection of the subject's own aggression onto others was evident in other dreams. For example, one subject reported the following dream: "I can remember a dream about burglars coming into the house and I got knifed in the throat. I remember seeing the blood coming out."[Mr. C.] The dream may be translated into the statement: "I cannot be a criminal who wants to murder others because it is I who am attacked." Another subject reported frequent dreams of running away from something or somebody whom he cannot identify. Such dreams usually ended with his being shot. In addition to the projection of his own aggressive impulses, the dream also involved the externalization of the subject's own internal conflicts. The statement implicit in the dream is: I am not running away from my feelings which are inside me; I am running away from somebody outside me.

Several other attributes of the dreams reported above deserve mention. Typically, no explanation was given in the dream for the dreamer's being attacked. The aggressor was typically male, probably an older person and, if identified, a criminal or military figure. The dreamer was most often alone and portrayed as having varying but limited capacity to deal with the threat to himself.

Evaluation of Psychopathology and Assessment of Character

Evaluation of pathology was based on subjects reports and portrayals of specific symptomatology. Assessment of character was based on the quality of subjects' object relations, rigidity of character, and degree of parataxic distortion of present reality based on their relationships with their parents.

In evaluating pathology and assessing character, the investigator was often faced with the problem of making distinctions between those subjects who were open and in touch with their unconscious lives, and subjects who— through being guarded—revealed very little about themselves. While some of the symptomatology reported by the former suggested deeply rooted difficulties, the investigator's final assessment was often that they were dealing with the world in an effective way, and that they were sufficiently well integrated to portray a capacity for growth. In contrast, the latter subjects were often evaluated as having difficulties which impaired their capacity to function as well as they might otherwise.

Specific Symptomatology

Subjects described or portrayed a wide range of symptomatology that included depression, somatic complaints, and anxiety.

Depression. The most prevalent symptom reported was depression. Eleven subjects reported periods which they described as having been characterized by "extreme depression," "moping around," "I know I was in a rut," "A black vacuum," "I was dead." At least four of these subjects have had various suicidal wishes. These periods of depression were often accompanied by difficulty in sleeping, difficulty in awaking in the morning, poor appetite, and withdrawal from others. In addition, four other subjects reported episodic depression. However, the interviewer was not able to ascertain whether the severity or the frequency of this depression would justify deeming it a symptom.

Somatic complaints. Frequent headaches were reported by three subjects. These occurred at least once a week with no apparent precipitating event, and were of suffcent intensity to incapacitate the subject. Two other subjects described less frequent but equally severe headaches. In both of these cases the symptom was precipitated by some interaction with parents.

Anxiety. Eight subjects described difficulties which suggested extreme anxiety. Two additional subjects described tossing and turning for several hours before they finally fell asleep. Two others described difficulties concentrating. Another subject complained that he sometimes began to "tremble" for no apparent reason. Three other subjects stated that they often felt extremely tense.

Character Assessment

Although no one specific character type emerged as representative of the sample, some broad descriptive summaries may be used to define groups within the sample. The boundaries of such groups are vague.

A proportion of the sample may be described as rigid characters with well-established ego-syntonic modes of relating to the world. They tended to be alienated from others as well as harsh in their judgments of the world around them. They had rigid defenses and manifested a brittleness when they were asked to describe themselves. Their affect was constricted.

Another group of subjects can be described as typically guarded and mistrustful of the motives of others. They tended to be extremely sensitive to hostility and exploitation by others and often experienced themselves as "victims" in their encounters with other people.

A third group of subjects can be described, in spite of clear evidence of neurotic conflicts, as highly integrated individuals. Their view of the world was characterized by flexibility rather than rigidity or diffusion. They had a stable sense of who they were, which included the idea of personal growth as an important dimension. They were insightful and capable of responding empathically to others.

All subjects, even those who seemed impaired by severe psychopathology, were able to meet professional and academic requirements. The group, as a whole, must be characterized as exceptionally successful and intellectually outstanding.

Attitudes toward Psychotherapy

Eight subjects had consulted a psychotherapist at some time. Five of them were in treatment at the time of the interview. Of these five subjects, four reported that they had become deeply attached to their therapists and conveyed the sense of valuing the exploration of themselves in treatment. A fifth subject, who had been in treatment for two years, continued to resent the fact that she was charged a fee. She was ambivalent about continuing treatment in spite of chronic difficulties.

The other three subjects had dropped out of treatment after no more than two sessions. They shared a resentment that their respective therapists had had expectations that they would spend much of the hour talking. Each expressed a variant of the sentiment that the therapist's silence meant he had nothing to offer. They may have fled treatment either out of fear of becoming dependent on another person or out of frustration of their need for a more nurturant therapeutic approach.

Six subjects were at least cordial to the idea of possibly entering treatment, while the remaining six had foreclosed the idea. In the former group, one subject indicated that he would consider psychotherapy if "anything came up." The others expressed an interest in psychotherapy as an opportunity to know themselves better. The remaining five subjects were antagonistic to the idea of psychotherapy. They insisted that they either had no problems or that they could cope with whatever problems they had.

7

Case Study 1: A Powerful Sufferer

Gone, gone. The earth ate them.
Why, why? I don't want people to die.
My uncle shrugged his shoulders. "When you grow up,
you'll find out why."
I never did find out. I grew up, became old
*   and never did find out.*

[N. Kazantzakis, 1966, p. 46.]

Each of the following three chapters will describe the life history of a child of a survivor of the Holocaust. The three subjects were selected for in-depth presentation on the basis of the clarity they provided about the organization of the themes of survivorhood into the total context of their lives. Each of them highlights particular themes of second-generation survivorhood.

The first subject, Miss A., was a remarkably open and introspective young woman who, through her capacity for insight, provided a detailed picture of the interaction of normal themes of development with the special context of survivorhood. Her life also illustrates a masochistic adaptation, prior to the intervention of psychoanalytic therapy, to the problem posed by her parents' history. Her life also provides a picture of successful integration of images and themes of the past into identity.

The second subject, Mr. B., was also extremely open about himself. His identity revolves around an obsession with the images of the Holocaust. His history illustrates an adaptation based on projection and an attempt to master inner conflicts on the field of the external world. That is, for him, absorption in the images of the past provided a solution to intrapsychic conflicts. Examination of his life provided an insight into the symbolic significance of historical images. Finally, both he and Miss A. illustrated the formulation of prosocial commitments based on the experiences of the past.

The third subject, Miss E., was representative of those subjects who had great difficulty talking about themselves. In contrast to Miss A. and Mr. B., she had rejected the idea that having been the child of a survivor influenced her in any way or was a relevant dimension of her identity. Nevertheless, it became clear that her heritage had had a major impact on the development of her character. She illustrates an adaptation to the second-generation effects of the Holocaust which is based on denial. In addition, she was distant from the social concerns which characterized both Miss A. and Mr. B. It was as if the very knowledge of the past which motivated them left her without the resources to empathize with others.

It must be noted that these three subjects who shared the heritage of the Holocaust also had important differences in their backgrounds. Among these differences were the degree of psychological impairment of parents, the degree of explicit communication about the past by parents, the socioeconomic status of the family, and the degree of homogeneity of the community in which they were socialized. At the same time, these three subjects (who appear to live their lives in such different ways) share many of the same basic conflicts, particularly in regard to separation, trust, aggression, and identity.

Description of Miss A.

Miss A. is an attractive 25-year-old woman who has been living on her own since she was 18 years old. She is a college graduate and holds an administrative position in a social service agency. She has decided to switch careers and become a clinical psychologist. Miss A. has been in psychoanalytic psychotherapy since the age of 17.

Miss A. was interviewed over the course of three meetings, each of which lasted approximately one and a half hours. She was eager to participate in the study, of which she had learned from another subject, because she anticipated that it might be helpful to her. She seemed to use the opportunity provided by the interview to think about herself.

Miss A. manifested an ability and willingness to move back and forth between primary process ideation and evaluative ego functions. She also displayed a lively sense of humor, an acute sense of irony, and an engaging manner. During the interview, she talked of many things that were painful to her, and at times came close to tears.

The interview was conducted in the context of a warm, mutually respecting relationship. The interviewer experienced his meetings with Miss A. as very moving.

Family Background

Miss A. considered her family to include her father, 73 years old; her mother, who had died when Miss A. was 15 and who was between five and ten years younger than her father, and a half-brother (on her father's side) who died in a concentration camp.

Miss A.'s parents were distantly related and knew each other before the war. She described their relationship in the following terms:

> i can't figure it out, what can I think of, I never ever got the feeling there was love. It was more like helping each other through life. I remember, as a matter of fact, as a little kid asking, I remember her saying, 'Of course I love him, my husband,' you know, never any display of emotion or affection for each other. I can't figure it out. She was the supporter and he did a lot of leaning on her, but he also scapegoated her a lot. Everything that went wrong was her fault, and she put up with it, so I don't know.

At the time of her birth, Miss A.'s parents were living with her mother's sister. Miss A. reported that her birth was a hardship on her mother and that her aunt told her that her mother had spoken of suicide when she learned she was pregnant.

Miss A. described her closest family relationship at present as being with an aunt, her father's sister: "She's a sweet old lady, she's a nice old lady, the closest thing I ever had to a grandma; she was very positive about everything, the way grandmas are." Though this aunt did not parent her as a child, another aunt—her mother's sister—took care of her on weekdays throughout her childhood. Miss A. described this aunt as "very fucked-up."

Miss A, grew up in a predominantly but not exclusively Jewish neighborhood. Although neither of her parents observed Jewish traditions, they did send her to Hebrew school for over five years. The family was poor. Her father was an unskilled laborer who had difficulties maintaining a job for a long period of time; her mother worked full-time as a seamstress.

Miss A.'s parents were both survivors, and they met and were married in Europe immediately after they were liberated. They came from Poland and spoke Polish in their home. Miss A. is fully fluent in Polish.

Relationship with Parents

Miss A. described her father as follows:

> The first things that come to mind are bitter, crazy, a broken man, never rebuilt his life after the war ... paranoid, paranoid delusions; for example, he goes shopping, 'they cheated him'; there's intent behind everything; he couldn't hold a job, 'they didn't want me to work,' been like this ever since I can remember.

Miss A. went on to say that her father has no friends and no interests. She characterizes his life as "Work when he has it, and to survive, like get by ... he doesn't do anything, won't give himself any pleasure and he takes pride in that." Miss A. reported, poignantly, that when she was younger she remembered that her father seemed to have one pleasure: watching wrestling matches on TV. He is no longer interested in that. He now spends his time watching give-away shows on TV.

This vision of a "broken man" involved Miss A.'s awareness of the quality of her father's life before the Holocaust. He had come from a poor family, moved out of the Jewish community to become an overseer on a large farm. Miss A. was continually surprised whenever she thought of prewar pictures of her father that she had seen. These portrayed him as a handsome man.

Miss A. has difficulty remembering her mother. "I don't [remember her] and I should because I was old enough [when she died]. She liked to play cards, she had lots of things, she was really different than he was, she was basically the supporter of the family, she had lots of friends."

Although she spoke of her mother with great affection and communicated a sense of her mother as the more nurturing, caring parent, this affective tone was contradicted by specific memories of her mother's beliefs about child rearing. For example, Miss A.'s mother told her that when Miss A. was an infant and cried for a bottle, she would let her cry because she believed that, if she indulged her, Miss A. would become spoiled. Miss A. also remembers the attitude both parents had about children, "They want to carry on, let them carry on . . . they'll get tired and they'll stop."

Miss A. described her relationship with her father at present as:

> I kind of take care of him, take care of, you know, his physical needs, apartment I got for him, signed him and moved him. His demands on me are very clear-cut, any time something bad happens, take care of it, there's no closeness in a way I think of a father and daughter and I, at this point, don't even try to show myself to him.

When the interviewer asked if her relationship with her father had been different in the past, she asked, "When he was younger?" There was mutual laughter when the interviewer replied, "No, when you were younger." She went on to say: "I guess it's always been that I thought he was younger. Even when I was little because he couldn't speak English when I was little. I knew very definitely that I was looked to as the authority."

Miss A. gave the impression that she shared the caretaking responsibilities with her mother: "When my mother died it was very different because she took care of many things but my father never. As soon as she died, things fell on me." Her mother's obligation to her father left little room for nurturing Miss A. as a child:

> I think it was like me always trying to reach her. I didn't feel like I was trying to take care of her, there was none of that. I felt very clearly that she was the mommy and I was the baby, and all you needed from her, but there didn't ever seem to be enough for me. She had to take care of Daddy, she had to and it was always me 10 paces behind, running, and there was a lot of resentment for that and a lot of hate and a lot of longing. . . .

The feeling she described was compounded by the accusation of ingratitude: " ... and a lot of guilt for wanting so much when she had to, 'cause it was like I shouldn't expect so much she had to do so much anyway."

The idea that Miss A. didn't deserve more from her parents was reinforced by the idea that because she was born in the United States, she was different. Also, although she was a child, she had the responsibility of explaining the new world to them: "I have a special connotation in the family. [They talk] ... about me being American and therefore different. It was always like if they didn't understand something, I should explain it to them." She was further mystified when her parents said things like:

'We're not important anymore, my life is finished, everything is for you now, I don't need nothing, my whole life is you ... ' and they very much tied it in with being in a concentration camp, that they died there and that the only thing good about their life now was that they had me. ...

This mystification was compounded by her neighbors who said things such as: " 'look how they struggle, look how they sacrifice, look how grateful you should be'. ... " She described her reaction: "and there I was thinking I had nothing to be grateful for, where the fuck were they anytime I needed them. ... "

Miss A. was asked how she understood the contradiction between the idea that her parents gave so much to her and her profound feeling of being deprived. She responded:

What I did with it then was I felt guilty. What I'm coming to believe now is that the message that I was getting and the realities weren't the same at all ... I'm not sure, there's something I can't quite put my finger on, everything was for me, but there wasn't enough because they had very little to give, they weren't the kind of people who took pleasure in having a child or who knew how to relate to a child and so the things that I needed and the things they were giving were like this [indicates her meaning with a gesture]. They were giving me clothes, they were giving me food, these were the things they were so into giving and these were the things I was not craving or needing or appreciating, really, and the way I dealt with it all was guilt. What do I want, listen to this, you're everything and it's not enough, you see, greedy little kid. It was also, this is something I'm just coming to in my therapy, very strong demands they needed from me. That there was never, you know, it was like the rule had been established of sacrifice. Everything they sacrificed for me and I sacrificed for them. I mean there was this tremendous responsibility of, if I'm their whole life, I have to do certain things because they have expectations that have got to get met because it's their whole life. They keep telling me that.

Miss A.'s parents' expectation of her, as she was growing up, centered on her being "a mature little lady, very grown-up and proper." She remembered an incident that occurred when she was five years old. A children's TV show producer had come to her nursery school to select a child to appear on the show. After his visit, her parents were asked to bring her to the studio. She described what happened:

> All the way down they told me, 'I want you to be serious, I don't want you to fool around, be a good girl, do the right thing,' and I got there and I was a little Miss Proper, a little Miss Muffett, as good as gold, so grown-up, I was like a little old lady, and that's what they told my parents, 'I'm sorry, we can't use her, she's too grown-up, she's not a little girl.'

The above incident, besides portraying the strictures her parents put on her behavior, also portrays the confrontation between her parents' values and those of the world outside the family. In these terms, it is related to an incident that occurred later on when she was 15 and experienced her first "crush." The first boyfriend was "goodlooking and smart, he was perfect," and he came from a "rich, American family, he was very poised and polished, he was everything I wanted." Their relationship lasted three or four months, and it broke up because she wouldn't sleep with him. She explained that she had learned from her parents, "This whole moral type thing and the firm belief that if I slept with him, I'd lose him." A year later this boy started dating one of her friends who did sleep with him. She described her feelings:

> He married her, after that, man, my parents, I didn't respect a word they said, they were wrong on everything, it didn't matter, you know, shit, nothing, didn't trust them anymore, the foundation of society, you should be a virgin, they were wrong, that's how much they knew about the world they were living in. . . .

Miss A. summarized her relationship with her parents as she grew up by saying that they gave her the feeling that:

> Being a parent wasn't a joyful, loving thing, but a duty, an obligation . . . there were injunctions, a parent does, a parent doesn't. And a child does such and such for her parents, not because she wants to, not because she loves them, but because she should and she must and therefore she will. . . . A child does not lie to a parent, a child has respect for a parent regardless of how fucked-up a parent is, you know there were all sorts of injunctions about how I was supposed to behave to them and one of them curiously enough was a child is to help the parent, almost the kind of European expectation, the more children you have, the more comfortable your old age will be. . . .

Developmental History

As a young child, Miss A., for the most part, satisfied her parents' expectations of what a child should be. "I was a little goodie-goodie," she said of herself. Concomitantly, she had a sense of never having had a childhood or even childhood friends. On this score, she described how, throughout her life, her friends have always been older and how, even now, she includes among them her parents' friends. When she was younger, she was bored by people her own age and considered the things her peers paid attention to trivial:

> I had real concerns as a child, I was burdened by many problems.... My parents would talk about money with me, with the result being that I thought about them, I was concerned about things like life and death and these kids never were...I could never get into frolicking....

She always felt confused about how old she was because nobody treated her like a child or talked to her like a child.

Until her mother died, Miss A. was always a religious child, not so much in terms of religious observance as in these terms:

> I felt that God was up there counting what I did and didn't do, if I did something wrong, I was going to get it, I mean I believed and I was afraid and that's what I mean by religious. They had instilled in me the wrath of God, they instilled in me that there is a right way and a wrong way and your feelings don't count. There's a right way and a wrong way and you'd better do it the right way.

An interesting contradiction to the above emerged, however. In spite of being a "goodie-goodie," Miss A. was not allowed to re-enroll in a Hebrew school during her first grade because she was a behavior problem. She got A's in all her subjects except conduct: "I remember I hated my teacher, she was a bastard, she was a tyrant, she was a mean lady and I probably screamed and yelled and ran and wouldn't do what she told me."

It is not clear if she had tantrums in a way that could directly be perceived by her parents. It is clear that she experienced tantrums in relationship to them:

> Whenever I had a tantrum, in my head was, 'I'll fix her [my mother], I'll punch myself in the belly and make myself sick'.... Whenever I wanted to get even with them, the thought was, 'What can I do to myself to get even with them? I would self-inflict something; I'll make her sorry, I'll die, I'll make her so sorry.'

Another preoccupation Miss A. had as a child was death:

> I thought about death...I used to lie in bed at night and think and try to imagine being dead. I was six years old at the time, and I used to imagine being dead, and what I used to do was close my eyes and squeeze, and you know when you close your eyes, it's black and with little, like after your eyes look, there's a flash, you look at a light bulb like, close my eyes and squeeze and try to imagine nothingness and no matter what happened there was always something, like even the consciousness of me imagining nothingness but after doing it for a while I would get very scared, like trembly scared....

Later in the interview, the interviewer asked Miss A. how she understood her childhood concerns about death. She answered, "There hasn't been anything in my life to warrant an obsession with death." Immediately after having said this, her eyes lit up, and she said, "I never made that connection before." What she was referring to, of course, was her parents' history of survivorhood and its impact on her.

One image of Miss A.'s childhood that continued to stand out was of "little Donna housewife." She was a woman on television who was very blonde and did an advertisement for a soap company. Miss A. saw her as representing the essence of the American woman in the American family. All through childhood she yearned to be like her. In Miss A.'s fantasies she was "little Donna housewife" rather than the dark-skinned daughter of immigrant parents. Miss A. also said that she resented very much being foreign, and, as will be seen, this antithesis of "little Miss Donna housewife," the American, and the less desirable Donna, child of immigrant parents occurred throughout Miss A.'s life. She sees, at present, a major developmental milestone insofar as she has ceased to yearn to be "little Donna housewife," or even to find the image attractive. In any event, she described the early resentment:

> I always blamed my parents for being foreign, the implication was I wasn't like that [here she is referring to a childhood friend, Janet, who in the third grade was "perfect"; for example, "on a rainy day, Janet never looked wet, she came in her little rainsuit never mussed, and me, no matter how many raincoats and boots and umbrellas I came in, you knew it was raining out, I don't know, I was just bedraggled and she seemed like wrapped in cellophane"] for being foreign, they didn't speak the language, they didn't know how to dress me, I blame them for the most absurd things, although a lot of them were true.... I also wore hand-me-downs, I wouldn't take a hand-me-down after that, it could have been a used ring, forget it.

The interviewer, struck by the idea that Miss A. would not consider a "used ring" as a gift, asked her what her associations to this were. She remembered that when her mother died, she left her a wedding ring, and Miss A. had planned to get married with it until it was stolen in a burglary.

Another thread of Miss A.'s childhood that bore a close affective resemblance to her resentment about being foreign involved her always having been in the position of waiting for her parents. She remembers, for example, she was always the last child to be picked up after nursery school. By the age of six years, when she was old enough to come home alone, she remembered having to wait on the doorstoop for an hour and a half until her mother got home. Once there was a hurricane and, as other parents came to pick up their children, Miss A. waited and waited and was afraid that no one was going to come for her.

Miss A.'s first friend was Nancy, whom she met when she was three years old. She most remembered Nancy's father who was "good looking" and "nice." Nancy's mother was "not a very good looking woman, a good woman, but somehow they seemed a very unlikely couple." She later heard stories that

Nancy's father had married because of the mother's money, which to her seemed: "... although it was not fine, to me it was very American [and] seemed a better reason to get married than my parents which didn't seem any reason at all."

Miss A. remembered spending a great deal of time at Nancy's house. In early adolescence, Nancy's father died. Miss A.'s reaction was to be very "wiped out." She remembered looking at his body at the funeral and having been puzzled by what death was. Her feelings about Nancy, whom she had always considered to be "very American," changed with her father's death: "I remember feeling Nancy was more like me after that, incomplete, no longer eligible for the Donna housewife role. There was a taint in her history and her life, she wasn't normal any more...."

For the most part, Miss A. remembered being quite isolated in school. Most of her friends were two to three years older and also children of refugees who lived in her apartment building. She said of her early schoolmates: "Yeah, it was a very traumatic thing for me to make friends with those little white things in school, they were somehow pristine and pure, and I felt much older than they." In contrast, she experienced herself as "black somehow, tarnished, dirty, impure, somehow sullied."

Miss A. went to nursery school for three years before starting kindergarten. She was also sent to camp at four years of age. This confirmed her sense of being "thrown away, abandoned." It also confirmed her sense that, as a child, she had "had to fend for myself." Her memories of being at camp recapitulate some of the themes that run through her develoment:

> It was the worst time in my whole life, early memories from then include eating dirt, they made me drink milk although I was allergic, I was the youngest kid in camp, tagged along with the counselors because I had no friends. I remember a woman who I thought was a witch, I was afraid of my counselor, finally the camp called my parents to get me.

Miss A. was a precocious adolescent. She entered college when she was 16. In high school she was in the honor class and experienced that time as "an up." She says, "I think it bolstered my fantasies of being special." Perhaps more importantly, although the school was predominantly Black and Puerto Rican, she was well liked and ran for president of her senior class. She even went to parties. At the beginning of her senior year, her family moved to a new neighborhood, and she felt that she was living a "normal teen-age life." However, soon after, her mother fell ill, and Miss A. retreated into her home and spent her time worrying about her mother.

The summer before she entered college, her mother died. No report exists *vis-à-vis* her immediate reaction; however, she had a "fabulous time" throughout her four years of college. She did "an incredible amount" of socializing, had friends and boyfriends, and maintained ties with her high school friends.

At 17 she entered psychotherapy on her own initiative at a community mental health service because of problems she was having with her father. She felt that she used her treatment primarily to gain enough support to move out of her father's house into an apartment of her own. She did this during her second year of college.

The longest relationship Miss A. has had with a man was for two years between the ages of 20 and 22. It included living with him for six months. She characterized this relationship as tempestuous. The attraction it held for her was that she felt that he understood her completely. The major conflict of their relationship, as she described it, revolved around dependency. For much of the time, she felt a continuous need to assert her own independence, and in different ways would act out the theme, "You don't own me." After a brief period of separation, she decided to move in with him and give in to his demands to be allowed to take care of her. As she saw it, he became threatened by this shift. The relationship broke up, leaving Miss A. feeling angry and bitter. Her subsequent relationships have been with men she either hasn't been particularly attracted to or who weren't "eligible" for any number of reasons.

The Concentration Camp as a Theme in Miss A.'s Life

Information Exchange in Miss A.'s Family

Miss A. felt that her knowledge of her parents' having been in concentration camps "has always been there, like the numbers on my father's hands just seem to have always been there." Though she remembered the fact, she cannot remember the details of "horror stories" told to her in childhood. She also had a vague memory of learning that she had had a brother: "I remember being seven when I found out I had a brother or I once maybe had a brother; there was some talk then of some guy who was my father's son; I'd say it was before then, I'd say it was very early."

Miss A. reported that her mother never brought the issue of concentration camps up spontaneously with her, but that she overheard conversations her mother had with other people. On the other hand, her father, at least now, brings the issue up very often. The quality of her father's communication was described as follows: "He often gets into the lousy deal he got from life and when it starts, it starts from way back when he was a kid...he harps, that's what he does, he doesn't bring it up in conversations to talk about it." She also perceived guilt in her father's telling of anecdotes about the camps on the basis of what she describes as a "belligerently defensive attitude." "Every time he tells me something, it's 'I did this but it's all right, you understand, it was all right.'" Another feature of her perception of her father's talking about the camps was his "talking about it as though there was nobody in that concentration camp but him."

Other sources of imagery about the concentration camps were relatives, who would bring up the issue in the context of all the hardships they had endured. A cousin would bring up the issue in the following context:

> in terms of whenever she has any problems, 'this is nothing after what I have lived through, this is nothing. I'll get through this too with no hassle,' you know, if she's talking about anything that bothers her, anything that's bad, she raises that, 'All's well, I'm thankful, I can live with this, I've lived with worse.'

That Miss A.'s parents used the concentration camp experience as a major organizing principle in their lives was suggested from the fact that they, as Miss A. described it, "use it as a time marker, before Hitler, after we were liberated, like B.C. and A.D." Nevertheless, Miss A. said that she has only a fragmentary notion of her parents' experiences and that she very much wanted to know more. She remembered having asked her parents questions but "they didn't like to talk about it, they didn't like to tell me." A recurring incident occurred when the concentration camp would "invade" their home via television. Miss A. described the following:

> All these creepy shows with skinny people and bald heads and dead bodies coming out of an oven, and I used to be fascinated by it and wanted to watch them, and they would get very nervous and wouldn't want to watch or, if I insisted, they wouldn't watch, and they would tell me I was crazy to look at that, what do I want to look at that for, what do I need that for.

These interactions produced in Miss A. the feeling that "They could neither one of them want to be reminded of it, they could neither one of them forget it, but they didn't want to be reminded of it." She describes how she grew to feel about her own curiosity concerning her parents' experience:

> Like I'm touching something I shouldn't touch. There was also something, not just about the camp but also the whole life back there. That it was something special and sacred that I very much wanted to see but that I couldn't. You very much had to belong to a special club of people who were born on the other side and there was an envy about that.

Although she could satisfy little of her curiosity through her parents, Miss A. would ask questions about their experiences from friends of the family. One friend in particular, a woman who had gone through Auschwitz with her mother, would tell Miss A. how some people had stolen food in order to stay alive, but how she and Miss A.'s mother had "maintained their dignity." This report was very important to Miss A. She said that it made her feel like crying, and, while describing it to the interviewer, she indeed seemed close to tears. She also reported that she had been asking other people more about her parents' experiences since her mother's death.

Effect of Knowledge of the Camps on Perception of Parents

Miss A. felt that she understood the impact of the Holocaust on her father more than she understood its impact on her mother. Her fantasy of what her father would have been like if it had not been for the Nazis was:

> My father would have been a petty bourgeois, landed Jew; he had property, he owned a vineyard; he would have been, by his standards and those around him, prosperous; he would have been an authority...he would have been happy, he would have been proud of his possessions, he would have been very proud and he would have been, temperamentally, I think, the same, very stubborn; he knows what's right, very moralistic.

She went on to wonder if, in fact, he would have lived "happily ever after," or whether perhaps "there was something in him before that made him turn out the way he did." On the other hand, she said of his manifest paranoia:

> After the war, he had nothing, not his looks nor his strength, nor his skills, nor his money, nothing. And he never reconciled himself, I think there's his paranoia, how could this have happened to me? There must have been something tying it together; he couldn't accept that it just happened, he had to attribute it to something.

She also understood that her father's reminiscences, in which he continually emphasized how much authority he had, and how many people he had supervised, was his way of making up for the "powerlessness" he now feels.

Although it was very difficult for Miss A. to recall what her mother was like, Miss A. has the sense that she withstood the impact of the camps better than her father had. There are two stories that have a major emotional impact on her sense of her mother. The first is the story that she could have escaped the Nazis but chose to remain behind to care for her own ailing mother. The second was told to her by her mother's niece, Miss A.'s cousin:

> They managed to hold on to their dignity...they never fought over food like others, they were always kind of saying, you eat it, no you eat it, no you eat it and those are the kinds of things that really make me want to cry when I hear them, I don't know why.

Feelings and Thoughts Generated by Knowledge of Parents' Experiences

During the interview, Miss A. stopped to reflect about how she was feeling as she talked about her parents:

> I feel sad when I think about their past, I feel sad for them [sniffing, near tears] and I think I feel somehow responsible, like I owe them something, like I have to make something up to them because they had nothing else, they had to get from me, and I feel like it was my responsibility toward them. I hate to keep coming back to the same old word but it's there and it's very strong—it's guilt.

Prodded by the interviewer's questions, she elaborated:

> There was a certain amount of guilt for not having been through it like they were; things were often thrown at me like, you never went through what I went through, you don't know what it means to be hungry, you don't know what it means to be cold, you never had an ache in your belly for days on end that didn't go away; and it was, you know, what I said before, about hate and a lot of resentment, that was when I felt it, it was almost like I should have known, I should have been there, I should have suffered like my parents suffered, then I could have been part of that special club, but I didn't so I couldn't understand anything. There was a special little private club and the dues you had to pay were very high.

She remembers that when she was preparing to move out of her father's house, she experienced "incredibly intense feelings of guilt over abandoning" her father and "leaving him to die." As she sought support from friends, she talked about his incarceration in a concentration camp "as a background to what I was feeling."

Miss A. reported that she rarely talks with friends about "the concentration camps *per se*" but does talk to friends about how her parents' incarceration affected her as a person. She recalled one all-night conversation she had had with friends, in which surprising feelings emerged along with ones with which she was more familiar:

> [We] were laughing hysterically about it, talking about horrors in general and also in each of our own families. The theme of the conversation was 'Why I never got to go to camp'.... It was death upon death, maiming, killed, died, blood, just so awful that we were hysterically laughing because there was no other way to incorporate it.

Miss A. said that she would not like to be like her father in any way and that she was like her mother to the extent that she has "a lot of friends thinking highly of me, a kind of gregarious, active, bubbly person and competent, strong and competent, that's like her." She often thought about the question, would she have survived concentration camp? She felt, "If I had survived, I'd be pretty rotten, and I like to think I'd be dead." She also recalls her parents having said, in Hebrew: "It was the good ones who died."

Another aspect of her reaction to her parents' incarceration had to do with her father's seeing the world as "Very hostile, with powers lying in wait, you know, like trying to trick him up . . . and an incredible distrust of people, my father always tried to make me mistrust my friends." She remembered that, when she first entered psychotherapy, she was "terrified of falling into" the way her father saw the world. She described the experience: "I was able to think like him, to turn it on and to turn it off, and the fact that I could scared the hell out of me." Sometimes something would happen, and she would react by saying to herself, "My father would react da da da." By this she meant that she would react by imagining what her father's reaction would have been had the same thing happened to him. It is important to note that she remembered her mother as not having been at all like her father in this respect.

Another aspect of her reaction to her parents' experiences was her thinking about relatives who were killed during the Holocaust. She says that she always "resented terribly not having grandparents because grandparents were the ones who gave you the goodies and just loved you a lot." Miss A. was named after her mother's mother. She did not know why, but she took great pleasure in this. Her grandmother was supposed to have been "a real nice lady, not nice, good, a good lady." Miss A. has photographs of her dead relatives and to her, "They all seem so saintly." In the same way, she thinks about her brother and imagines that he would be "tall, dark, and handsome," and that he would be a professional if he were alive today.

It is evident from the above that several different and conflicting attitudes are a consequence of Miss A.'s knowledge of her parents' experiences. Some synthesis of these was expressed in her desire to tell her own children, when she has them, about what her parents went through:

> I have very fucked-up feelings about what I am and where I came from and I want my kids to have a very good sense of who they are and to feel good about it and you can't have a good feeling about it if you're not sure, I mean, it's not like I'm going to tell them, you see, you see, you see. I just want them to know because it's part of them . . . it's certainly part of what makes me, me and if they're going to know me, they're going to have to know me, they're going to have to know that. . . .

Another reason she wants her children to know about her parents' background is that she wants to give them something from the past, from another culture. She related this to her own early desire to not be different from those around her:

> Something that I'm realizing about myself, which I always thought was a bad thing, now strikes me as not a bad thing. I have a yearning to know differences, differences of people who aren't like me, people who aren't me. I don't like, I guess I'm through wishing I was little Donna housewife. It finally happened.

Conscious Reflections on the Meaning of the Concentration Camps

Miss A. remembered that, as a child, she was bewildered by the Holocaust. She recalled: "I had a lot of trouble understanding how one man, Hitler, could kill six million. I wondered why six million didn't kill him. I couldn't understand how it happened; my little head couldn't understand, it really couldn't." She also remembered: "I couldn't understand how God let it happen; I think that was one of the reasons I was so afraid of Him. He couldn't have been a nice God. I mean all those people dying and He didn't do anything."

Although she says that she has a "morbid fascination" with the Holocaust, she has never gone out of her way to learn more about it. What she knows is what she has gleaned from what she described as "passive" activities, like watching movies and documentaries. She said: "I think there was an ambivalence, I wanted to, but not enough to do it. . . . I was comfortable with wanting it and not doing it."

Miss A. did not think too much about the Holocaust *per se*:

> I mean I rarely think about it in its entirety. I mean my father lost a wife and a son, about four brothers and sisters, and a mother and a father and what, there's nobody left in the family except a few people who came out before the war, everybody else died, and the horror, it doesn't sound like anything now because I've said it so many times before, but the horror of that, that's a lot of people.

Miss A. was very clear about the fact that her conscious intellectual thoughts about the concentration camps and the Holocaust were inextricably linked to her identity as a child of a survivor. These thoughts have changed over time, and she discussed them in this context. One major feeling she has now was that the crimes committed by the Nazis were not unique in human history. However, she had not always believed this:

> Until now I always used to think of it as something special . . . the older I get, I'm inclined to think about it as not any more horrifying than a lot of other things that happen in this world. I think I used to, I tend to wear it like a badge. [What do you mean?] Like, you know, my parents went through this, and it made them special, it somehow makes me special and almost righteous, like the righteous victim, and I don't feel it as strong anymore, I feel it leaving, like there's nothing righteous about being stupid like that, and sometimes I try to get back to that feeling because it's warm and comfortable and I like it. . . . I mean I'm not saying it wasn't horrible and horrifying and destroying and all that but it wasn't the only time it had ever happened, and Jews aren't the only ones it ever happened to and there's nothing so righteous about being a victim, like I expected people, I expected a hush to come over the room if I said, 'My parents were in concentration camp,' and that I should suddenly be touched very gently.

At the same time, it is extremely difficult for Miss A. to envision the Jews as innocent victims. She also believes that Jews could again be persecuted in the same way, and that it would be unlikely that other groups would be persecuted. She explained her thoughts:

> Sometimes I think the Jews asked for it with this holier-than-thou, I am a victim, I mean if you go around telling everybody you're a victim, when there's a slaughter coming, they're going to know where to find you. I think the Indians aren't eligible for a full-fledged slaughter any more, it wouldn't be worth the effort. I think the Blacks'd fight back faster and if they needed somebody to put in an oven, I think they'd find us again. I think we're a conspicuous minority just because of talking about it. You know what I'm getting out of [saying] this, a lot

of self-hate. I'm sitting here listening to myself talking about this and I sound incredible, like I've really got a lot of anger at them, me, us....

I guess maybe I'm angry at them because I blame a lot of my personal hang-ups and fuck-ups on what I got from my parents, because they went through this and they went through this because the Jews were so stupid, therefore fuck the Jews, it's their fault. What I still don't understand about the whole thing is that they were so powerful, to lose so much power so quickly, I don't know, I guess a lot of the rich ones and the ones with power and money just left, they didn't bother to stay and fight it, they just checked out.

Much of her childhood bewilderment about the Holocaust, and also about her relationship to her parents persists today:

Not enough is known about it [World War II], you know. I have the same sense about it, the war and the concentration camps that I have about my childhood...the difference between what everybody said, and what was really true, like when I was a kid and everybody said, see how much they're sacrificing, see how much they're suffering, see how much you're getting, I kept thinking, what am I getting, what are they sacrificing, they're doing what, I don't understand and I get the same feeling now about the war and the stories that I heard, the way I heard World War II retold wasn't the way it really was, it couldn't have been so simple. It wasn't like the Jews were the angels and the simple little folks, and this bad guy came along and suddenly slaughtered them all. I mean, it doesn't make sense, one man does not a Holocaust make, and to have murder, you have to have a victim and a murderer and they both have to be willing participants.

Miss A. felt that the most destructive aspect of the Holocaust was the "uprooting in time and space...the no reason, the not understanding." She saw the horror as being so severe that she said, "I think the ones who died were the fortunate ones." She explained:

I don't know how anyone lived after that. I don't know how anybody lives with the sight of dead bodies, I don't know how anybody lives with the thought, if I held on to my mother's hand, I'd be dead today, that it was only because I looked older than I am that I'm still alive today, or because that day, this woman had her period so she was weak that day so she's dead, and this woman was my mother, again, nowhere a reason, no way to understand it, and just, just to look back at the life you had and the life you had now.

Miss A. feels overwhelmed by the imagery of being helpless to save the lives of loved ones. She said:

I don't know how every one of them doesn't have nightmares every night that someone's going to kill them. There was no reason to expect it then and there's no reason to expect it now. I would wake up in a cold sweat every night.

Miss A. felt that a reasonable way to deal with survivorhood was by "going crazy."

Miss A.'s attitudes toward the Nazis was, on the one hand, understanding, and on the other hand, pure rage:

I think people are capable of incredible cruelty if it's accepted. I don't imagine that anybody took pleasure in killing, but I don't think they lost any sleep over it. When I was younger, I used to think this had to be a country full of crazy people, Germany, I mean, they all had to be crazy to do it, I don't think it's craziness now, but a craze, like a fixation. Yeah, I don't know, I guess maybe even death becomes unreal when it's on that large a scale that you don't even have a sense that you're really killing people, even if you're the person pulling the switch in the gas chamber; there are just too many of them, the whole thing becomes like surrealistic, it can't really be happening, so it's not happening, so I have no reason to feel guilty. I often feel bad, I feel bad, ugh, I'm such a schmuck, for old Eichmanns and people like that, because I think, What terrible consciences they must have today. I don't know whether that's true for him, but I feel bad for him and I wonder, should they kill him, and I think about things like that and recently, who was it that they found in Argentina but they didn't find, Bormann, Bormann, right. I think maybe he's a different man today, maybe he's a nice man, why should they want to kill him for something 30 years ago, and I think, why, why, because it would make me feel good, it, I would feel good to see, to see him die, I would feel maybe a little bit of hate leave me and be satisfied and it would be worth it, I'd like to see him die with his tongue hanging out of his mouth, hanging down to here, his eyes bulging, I wouldn't really because I could never escape that vision. I mean I would and I wouldn't.

Miss A. does not believe Germans who say that they were not aware of the atrocities being committed. However, she tends to exonerate them from culpability on the grounds that they, too, were helpless. She could understand this because of her own feelings of helplessness. On the other hand, she said: "Sure, they're all to blame and so are a lot of other people in lots of other countries and everybody knew everything and if they didn't know it was because they wouldn't look." When asked to put herself in the place of the Germans during the war, she said:

I might have killed people or I might have been one of the guards. I have a tremendous abhorrence of any physical violence, either doing it to somebody or having it done to me, I mean real, I can't stand the thought of it and I'm a coward, I don't think it would have been something I would have looked for to do but I think that scared enough I might have done anything, I don't know, and maybe scared enough I'd probably shiver and shake so long there's be no decision to make.

Aims, Interests, and Beliefs

During college, Miss A. majored in sociology with a minor in Balkan and Eastern European affairs. She reports having had a fascination with political systems and Eastern European literature. She saw her interests in this area at least partially an "attempt to recapture the past." After graduating from college, she almost decided to pursue these interests for a Ph.D. but she was deterred in part by not knowing the required languages, but also by a curious lethargy in regard to taking steps toward obtaining an advanced degree. She was also disenchanted with political science because she saw it primarily as an "academic exercise" that could not result in effecting change in the world.

At present, she is pursuing her education in psychology because of a fascination with the workings of the human mind. She compares her interests in psychoanalysis to her enjoyment of reading detective and mystery novels. Both, for her, involve putting together the pieces of a puzzle.

Miss A. continues to be very much interested in politics, but feels she is not as politically active as she was in college because of a growing disillusionment and cynicism. One consequence of her earlier political involvements was to come face to face with a feeling of impotence. She became convinced that peaceful protest could not lead to change; and that the only means of effecting change was through violence, something she did not feel prepared either to engage in or to condone. Intellectually, she continues to be fascinated by issues of power and its application in political systems.

Miss A. feels very strongly about issues related to oppression of minority groups. She described a feeling of "incredible guilt when it comes to blacks or Indians . . . guilt about what was done to them as if it were my fault and guilt about not doing anything to correct it, being passive."

Miss A. also believes very strongly in the need for the state of Israel to exist. This belief is related to her fear that Jews might be persecuted again. Knowing that Israel exists makes her "feel safer." At the same time, she was disturbed by the displacement of Palestinians, saying that she felt "it isn't right, but it's necessary." Miss A. is pessimistic about the fate of Israel. Her thoughts are not that it would succumb to the Arab nations. Rather, she feels that it would expand and "swallow up" more Arabs and thus lose its identity as a Jewish state.

Another significant difficulty she experiences in relationship to thinking about Israel stems from her awareness of "a whole new Jewish culture growing up there." She is "ambivalent" about it: "I thought . . . you should be humble, you should suffer, and if you don't, if you fight for what you want, you're doing something wrong."

Miss A. has a wide range of interests and often spends her spare time reading the classics, doing pottery, painting, and sculpture. She is not religious, nevertheless feels cordial to Jewish tradition and feels robbed of it by her parents. She is not sure if God exists, although He played a prominent role in her childhood and adolescence: "I talk to God, all those nights my father was going around the house, ranting and raving, and I was in bed crying, I was crying to someone."

Miss A. sees herself as about to make some important life decisions. It is important to her to maintain her identity as a person, "not easily defined." She feels unwilling to fit herself into an "established life style." At the same time, she does not feel identified with what has been called the counterculture; she also does not feel identified with the culture at large. However, she does feel that she has an identity as an American, insofar as, for all her cynicism, she still has not "given up" on the American political system.

Fantasies and Dreams

Miss A. reported two dream specimens, one from childhood and the other one from about a month before the interview.

As a child, she used to have nightmares of "this giant bug standing in the foyer coming to get me." She described her associations and behavior related to the dream:

> In my own little head I thought he was death, and I would wake up screaming, no no, I would wake up feeling like screaming, for the longest time I had to have a light on...in that foyer...so he wouldn't come.

She described a more recent dream, also a nightmare, as follows:

> ...lying in bed, felt the room move and imagined that the building collapsed on top of me, and I was buried in the rubble, and the problem in the dream was whether I should struggle out from under it or just give up and die, and knowing that if I did struggle out from under the rocks, I'd be bleeding and torn and deformed for the rest of my life....

Miss A.'s childhood fantasy of being the lady in the soap commercial has been presented. Two other childhood fantasies that she remembered are that she would find her lost relatives and that "a charming prince masquerading as a peasant" would fall in love with her, and she would go off with him, "leaving behind everything."

A recurring fantasy that Miss A. has had more recently is as follows:

> If somebody came in at night, would I allow myself to be raped, would I put up a struggle... and assuming that he left, who I would call, who I would tell, you know, I had a fantasy of running out into the halls and just bowling, these little old ladies [who live in her building] over.... I think I pretty much decided on my girl friend Anne's parents.... I trust them to take care of me in a situation where I am at a loss, where I'm helpless, they're parents, they are to me what my parents should have been and never were.

When Miss A. was asked to generate a fantasy of the worst thing that could happen to her, she produced the following:

> Pain inflicted from the outside, I can handle pain pretty well, cramps, toothache when I have it, I can go for a week with a toothache that would drive somebody else up a wall.... I'm afraid of being hurt by somebody else...a cut like when my face was scratched [during a childhood fight with a friend] it was like a cold feeling of raw skin, like my insides coming out, of horror, of gore....

Her associations to the above involve remembering stories her father told her about German atrocities and her vague memory of accompanying her father, when she was eight or nine, when he filed a deposition for compensation from the German government.

Miss A. cannot remember any fantasies, the manifest content of which involve Holocaust imagery. However, associations in the present world often take her back in time. For example, referring to street violence in her city, she said:

> To me, they all fall into the same category, Hitler, Nazis, the big black guy on the subways who says "Hey, don't push me, man,' and the thing they all have in common is strength and violence and cruelty. They'd rip your arm off as soon as look at it, and they all kind of come together and I have a tremendous fear of all of them, a very vulnerable feeling.

Another related set of images is her fantasy about helping people who are attacked. She felt that she was "a physical coward, afraid of being beaten or hurt," and that this is wrong. Related was a fantasy she had when driving in a car with her niece. She wondered if she would save her father or her niece in case of an accident. She remembered deciding on the niece because she was younger.

Another association to the past that stems from events in the present occurred after she saw the movie, "State of Siege." She remembered being very nervous and restless afterward, so much so that she did something unprecedented for her: she drank herself to sleep. Her reaction, she felt, had to do with an association of the torture portrayed in the movie to the tortures of the Nazis. She felt ineffectual and dismayed by the thought that if she were in Chile, she probably "wouldn't have done anything."

Though Miss A. has participated in a number of political demonstrations, she has always been afraid of being "confronted by having to say this is how much I believe." To her, this confrontation involved having to decide to put herself into physical danger. In large measure, she has become "apolitical" because of the knowledge that "if push came to shove, I wouldn't fight, I'd run."

Other Manifestations of Unconscious Process

Miss A. reported, as a major psychological symptom, that she was often depressed. Sometimes she became so after something positive happened to her. One difficulty she has always had is sharing her good fortunes with her family. She felt that they much preferred to hear complaints, and that in general, "They don't like to talk happy."

She sees some of her unhappiness as a way of not leaving her family behind: "I have to suffer, I have to somehow martyr myself to stay with them, to be part of their world."

She has had at least one major episode of self-destructive behavior. This involved becoming pregnant and having an abortion. She reported that, afterwards, she was overcome with a feeling of well-being which she interpreted as having to do with punishing herself successfully.

Miss A. was also aware of guilt in connection with her mother's death. She said that, even though she knew it was irrational, she felt that somehow her bad feelings had killed her mother. She also says, "It's a guilt trip for me to be alive if she's [her mother] dead."

Miss A. did not want to be married or to have children until she felt more sure of who she was. She particularly felt that she could not have children while she still felt "needy." This feeling, she said, "drives me up a wall." She also connected it to her feelings of helplessness and being unable to take care of herself.

Discussion

The central themes of Miss A.'s development were deprivation of self and obligation to others. Her parents clearly failed to deliver essential emotional supplies. As an infant, she was allowed to cry without succor. When she was a child, her parents were often physically absent or unable to meet her emotional needs when they were present.

At the same time, the idea was communicated to her that they were continually sacrificing for her, and that, rather than experience deprivation, she should experience profound gratitude. One consequence of this communication has been her experience that her needs were somehow not legitimate. The idea that she should feel grateful also represented her parents' demand that, rather than expect to be fed by them, she should feed them with her gratitude. The message that her parents' lives were over and that everything that they did was motivated for her (while overtly a statement of self-sacrifice) in reality constituted a tremendous burden. It required that she give up all claim to the parental nurturance that seemed to be so freely offered. Moreover, the central, most devastating requirement was that she offer her life so that her parents could live through her. Thus, her parents' overt demand that she be a more mature and bright little girl was not a manifestation of concern for her development. It was a requirement that she give up her self to become their fantasy of their little girl; that is, their fantasy of the possibility of redeeming their own ruined expectations and self-esteem.

The demands made by Miss A.'s parents defined the fostering of a symbiotic relationship. While these demands constituted an almost overwhelming burden, the potential destructiveness of them most has to do with the fact that they interfered with the already arduous developmental task of achieving separation from parents. As critical as this task is in the process of normal development, it is performed only with ambivalence. In Miss A.'s case, the difficulties inherent in fulfilling this task, already inhibited by her parents' demands, was even further inhibited by the fact that those demands were reinforced by guilt. Specifically, the portrait of her parents as already having been so deprived and abused itself constituted—even without further elaboration—an obligation that the child should somehow "make up" for it. Although an impossible task to fulfill, its failure represented a serious crime of omission, insofar as the parents experienced its failure as yet another persecutory deprivation and communicated this feeling to the child. For the child, this crime of omission then led to (in the unconscious) the recognition of a more serious crime, one of commission: the crime of having angry and destructive wishes toward the parents. As such, the child took the responsibility for the crimes the Nazis committed as if she had committed them, and felt that she must punish herself for them. Evidence for this in Miss A.'s life was her feeling of being responsible for her mother's death and her feeling, upon having made the decision to leave her father, that she was abandoning him to die. Thus, the guilt demanded that Miss A. remain tied to her parents in order, first, to undo her failure to make up for their shattered lives (thus mirroring the deprivation they had suffered at the hands of the Nazis); and, second, to undo the deeds done by the Nazis which stood for the deeds she herself might have done because she had thought of doing them.

The pathogenic potential of the developmental dynamics described above is far-reaching. Miss A. was scarred by psychological symptomatology that suggests powerful, unresolved, pre-Oedipal conflicts. However, the lack of chronicity of impairment in everyday life and her ability to experience insights with appropriate affect, suggest a strong and resilient ego. In addition, though she has difficulties with men, her interpersonal relationships suggest a capacity to form enduring attachments to others, that is, a capacity for genuine object relations.

One is indeed struck by the strength that Miss A. portrays despite the serious strains she endured. These must be accounted for.

In the sense that Miss A. emerged from her family psychologically intact, she, like her parents, was a survivor. In an attempt to understand her survivorhood, one is struck by a critically redeeming aspect of her parenting. While other survivor parents communicated and enforced the view that the only haven of safety and caring that existed was the home, hers did not. That is to say, although her parents starved her, abandoned her, and mystified her, they did not prevent her from turning elsewhere for supplies. Her history is one of turning to surrogates: parents of her friends, older camp counselors, and ultimately a psychotherapist. Moreover, she responded to her felt neediness not by spitting out what was offered but with the capacity of being able to swallow and be nurtured by whatever was available—the ability, like a concentration camp inmate, of surviving on a crust of bread.

In addition, while other children of survivors lived in homogeneous cultural systems, predominantly Jewish neighborhoods served by parochial schools, the culture she grew up in was sufficiently heterogeneous and she was not faced with images of her parents everywhere she turned. To some extent, she was able to yearn to be like someone different from her parents.

Facilitating this alternate model of identification was the fact that her parents failed her when they did attempt to provide proper parenting. The two major examples she gave—in childhood being rejected by the TV producer for following her parents' instructions, and in adolescence, being rejected by her boyfriend because (as she saw it) she followed her mother's moral code—must have represented many more portrayals of their inadequacy to care for her. Because these inadequacies were highlighted in the arena of the external world, they were accessible to the ego as perceptions. Thus the stranglehold of her parents, and their representations as introjects, was loosened and she was allowed and impelled to search for objects that would not fail her.

At the same time, one may speculate that the balance between Miss A.'s striving for individuation and her having been undermined in this effort by her parents, was affected positively by her parents' demands that she take care of them. First this overt element in their relationship reversed the roles between parent and child and decreased the latter's dependency on the former. Second, it forced the premature development of her ego functions as she was called upon to make judgments and decisions that reinforced her reality testing. Although she had to pay considerable psychic costs, perhaps even give up her childhood, this ego that was prematurely forced into being by her parents could, in turn, help her deal with them. Third, another function of her parents' demands on her was to feed her own grandiosity and infantile omnipotence. And, while not a substitute for other supplies (and though it generated problems of its own), it did provide an important source of self-esteem.

Another major factor determining the positive outcome of Miss A.'s character had to do with the introjection of the parent. On the one hand, the fact that as Miss A. developed out of infancy, her parents' inadequacy must have become more and more evident, she must have experienced this inadequacy as a profound narcissistic blow. That is, their inadequacy, because it was inside her, was experienced as her own. On the other hand, Miss A.'s parents provided another introject. That is, as survivors, they represented images not only of survivorhood, but also of the triumph of humanity over what in reality was the ultimately conceivable devastating experience. This parental image became an introject and represented a pool of strength from which she could draw sustenance.

Finally, in considering those aspects of Miss A.'s character which provided her with strength, one must remember that her two parents were, in fact, very different. Although she was not as clear about her mother as she was about her father, the interviewer had the distinct impression that the mother provided a much more stable and constant figure than did the father. From one perspective, it seems as if the mother parented both the father and daughter, or perhaps mother and daughter, together, parented the father. In either case, the message to the child provided by the contrast between the two parents was that life can be utterly devastating (as it devastated the father), or life can be confronted with dignity (as it was confronted by the mother).

The clearest element of Miss A.'s character was her wish to suffer, which was manifested by her depressive symptomatology and the masochistic themes in her primary process ideation. In the unique elegance and economy of the unconscious mind, this wish was overdetermined by a number of other wishes, defenses, and conflicts.

At the layer closest to consciousness, Miss A.'s wish to suffer represented an identification with her parents. If she suffered as they had, then she could be like them and thus acceptable to them, a full-fledged member of the family. She could join what she called "the special club."

In this respect, one notes that the themes of her fantasies, dreams, and marginal thoughts recapitulated themes of the Holocaust. These included the obligation to save others, the brutal choice of whom to save when one can live only if the other dies, the dilemma of opting to survive when one knows that one will be scarred for life, the problem of resisting or not resisting, and "the immersion in death." In the episodes in which these themes were portrayed, Miss A. relived the experiences that she imagined her parents must have experienced. In doing so, she expressed her attitudes to themes in her own life through the symbolism of themes of the Holocaust. In each of the fragments she reported, she suffered. In each fragment she was confronted by her own helplessness as she faced the overwhelming power of the outside world. The only difference between her own unconscious experience and her parents' real experience was that she translated the instruments and symbols of malevolence of their historical era into those of her own. As such, Nazis became muggers and rapists, and the concentration camp a building that fell on her. Rather than choose whom to save with a piece of bread, she chose whom to pull from a car wreck. These fragments illustrate Lifton's (1971) construction of the "psychohistorical dream" [p. 25], insofar as they portray both the dynamic issues of the unconscious and the sociohistoric context in which these take place.

The same wish to suffer served not only Miss A.'s wish to be identified with her parents, as discussed above, but also the wish to separate from them. As such, it was an attempt to deny the role they imposed on her of being so strong that she had to stay with them to care for them. As long as she maintained her own vulnerability and cathected her own helplessness, she could justify a position of not fulfilling her parents' symbiotic demands. That is, the strength of these demands was based on the power held by one who has suffered over one who has not. As long as Miss A. herself suffered, she was no longer obliged to honor the rights and privileges that might have accrued to her parents because of their suffering. In fact, she had earned some of her own.

At the level least accessible to consciousness, Miss A.'s suffering represents the mechanism by which she returned to her own childhood in three different ways. First, suffering allowed her to recreate her childhood experiences of deprivation which were cathected because they represented one of the defining characteristics of her relationship with her parents. Second, it disguised her response to that deprivation, which, to her, was ego-alien. Specifically, it evoked aggressive, destructive, and sadistic impulses toward her parents which she redirected inward toward herself and toward the parental introjects within her. The childhood memory which best illustrates this was of hitting herself in the stomach with the idea that, by doing so, she would "fix" her mother. Third, the above incident reveals a failure of self-object differentiation. This failure emerged out of a symbiotic relationship which was gratifying to the parents and, at some level, to the child. Thus, by discharging aggression against herself, that is, by suffering, Miss A. not only discharged aggression against her parents, but also recreated the confusion of self and object.

Miss A.'s identity emerged from the interaction of the influence of three different cultures: that of Europe of the past, the America of the present, and the culture that formed the bridge between them, namely the concentration camp. Miss A. may be seen as struggling to resolve her identity confusion as she struggled with the contrasting themes, images, and models provided by each of these cultures. Her confusion may be expressed as being caught between the extreme poles of two different but overlapping dimensions.

The first involves establishing her identity along the dimension American-European. Identifying herself as the child of immigrants, she saw herself as a European and as having an identity basically different from the majority of those around her. This experience of difference fed her grandiosity, as it represented a sense of herself as more worldly and having more serious concerns than those around her. It also involved her having been possessed of a rich, full heritage that others did not share. However, being European also fed her negative self-image. It meant that she was an outsider, unable to participate in the images of perfection, for example, a classmate "wrapped in cellophane" and a woman on a TV commercial that her adopted culture afforded.

Miss A.'s parents identified her as an American. This signified that she was special and privileged. She was better than her parents and they looked up to her. However, this also meant that she was alienated from her family, unable to share their experiences and also burdened with obligations to be the interpreter of her culture to them.

The second involved establishing her identity along the dimension Nazi-Jew. Insofar as she identified herself as a Jew, she identified herself as a martyr. This identification gave her "power" over others insofar as it meant that they had to treat her "gently." She also took pleasure in her affiliation with Jewish rite, ritual, and intellectual tradition. Being a Jew, like being a European and like being a child of her parents, made her special. On the other hand, being a Jew also meant that she saw herself as the Nazis saw her. It meant that she saw herself as "dirty" and "worthless." Because she was a Jew, she was "tainted"and contaminated by death. She could not believe that the Holocaust could have happened if the Jews were entirely innocent; that thought was too hideous. Thus she condemned Jews for the presumed crimes that brought the Holocaust upon them, and in doing so, expressed her own feeling of being condemned. Finally she felt that "it could happen again" and felt vulnerable as a Jew. Though not a Zionist, she fervently believed that Israel must continue to exist because it made her feel safe.

Along this dimension was the identity of non-Jew. Non-Jews represented those who failed to save Jews during the Holocaust as she failed to save her parents after it. She put herself in the same position in relationship to Jews before and during the Holocaust. She experienced what she imagined was their helplessness to help the Jews at the same time that she experienced an obligation to help these groups, with whom she also identified as she displaced her sense of vulnerability to them. At the extreme, she identified herself as a Nazi. In her thoughts, she treats Nazis as she treats herself, first with understanding and then with sadism. Her unrealistic expectation that she "ought" to be able to stand up for others against an overwhelming enemy, and her guilt for not doing so when it might well be at the cost of her own life, betrayed not her helplessness but her grandiosity. As such, her fantasy of her own powerfulness is at issue, a fantasy that must be denied because it involves her identification with being a Nazi.

To understand the confusion that has attended the emergence of Miss A.'s identity, one must appreciate it not as a static entity but an evolving structure. At present, she has made great strides toward resolving the question, "Who am I?" with a creative synthesis of the elements involved in that question. In the service of this task, Miss A. set out to overcome the lamentation that she is different in order to be able to enjoy her uniqueness. Her fantasies of raising her children by giving them the gift of their past as she helps them in their present, emphasized her own growing integration of the American-European dichotomy. Accompanying this was her ego-ideal of "not being easily definable" which recalls Lifton's (1971) description of "Protean man." Miss A. resolved the Nazi-Jew dichotomy by the act of mobilizing her psychological sensitivity and understanding the Nazi and the Jew that is alive in all of us. Thus, as she examined the issues of criminality and victimization from a humanistic perspective, she testifies not to an ideology but a genuine commitment to justice.

8

Case Study 2: A Nazi Fighter

... They then poured kerosene over him and set him on fire. And because my father was so weak and thin, he burned only a moment; almost as soon as he was lit, he was burned out. And I, who saw him, who saw it all, swore that if ever I was put to the same test, I would not let them get away so easily. I would show them that a Jew does not go out like a miserable skinny candle. No. When I burn, I shall burn so long that they will burst with anger. That is why I eat so much; all my energy, all my passion is devoted to eating. Not that I am hungry, you understand....

[from a dialogue between Baal Shem Tov and his future neighbor in paradise, cited by Wiesel, 1973, p. 28.]

Mr. B. is a 20-year-old college student. His father had escaped from a Nazi slave labor battalion and spent the later part of the war in hiding. Mr. B.'s mother escaped from Europe to come to the United States in 1938.

Mr. B. is moderately tall and quite thin. He spoke articulately and eloquently about those things which occupied his thoughts. At times, however, his speech had a pressured, breathless quality. He was sloppy in his dress and wore a yarmulka. He had drawn Jewish stars on his pants legs and on one of his boots.

Mr. B. was referred to the interviewer by the teacher of his class on the Holocaust. He was eager to participate in the study, and during the first phone contact he said, "This should have been done a long time ago." However, during the first interview, he announced that he did not meet the criteria of the study because his father had only been in a labor camp. After the interview ended, Mr. B said that he felt very warmly toward the interviewer, but was somewhat surprised about how revealing he had been about himself. The interviewer felt a great deal of affection for Mr. B. but found himself nevertheless feeling quite uncomfortable at various points during the interview. Some of this had to do with Mr. B.'s passion as he described his beliefs. This discomfort may also have been a consequence of Mr. B.'s expressing in an ego-syntonic manner themes that existed in the interviewer's own primary process or themes which he could not admit.

Developmental History and Family Relationships

Mr. B. lived with his parents in an exclusively Jewish neighborhood. His parents both came from Rumania. His mother was 46 years old, his father was 53, and he had a sister 17 years old and a brother 13 years old. The family was supported by a jewelry store owned by Mr. B.'s father and uncle which produced a modest income. All of the family's friends and acquaintances were Orthodox Jews, and most were also refugees from Europe.

In the abstract, Mr. B. spoke of his family in glowing terms. He described "closeness" and "openness" as the characteristics of the relationship between himself and his parents. The family always spent Friday night together and went to synagogue on Saturday. However, Mr. B. also said that he had never been able to discuss his feelings with his parents, a fact which he attributed to his own "make-up" and which he regarded as "sad" and "strange." For example, although he "knew" his parents would approve, he never told them that he was in psychotherapy.

Mr. B.'s descriptions of his father were far more clear than his descriptions of his mother. He said that he "respected" his father more than he did his mother. He was quick to add that this did not mean that he loved his father more. Mr. B. could not see himself as being at all like his mother, but felt that he took after his father in many ways. He said that both he and his father had volatile tempers and were capable of going into "violent" rages, were both quite cynical, and both were interested in politics.

In his youth, Mr. B.'s father had been both a Zionist and a Socialist. His views were particularly radical for his place and time, since the Jewish community in his town was Hasidic. (Hasidic Jews were antagonistic to Zionism for religious reasons.) However, he had become rabidly anticommunist and uninterested in going to Israel. Mr. B. was puzzled by this change. He said:

> I've asked my father if he was this crazy militant Zionist in his childhood, how come he chose to come here instead of go to Israel? I really still don't understand, but what he told me was he was really so tired of ideology, he became like a nonpracticing Jew after the war, this lasted for a couple of years. He really wasn't interested. I guess he was just shattered by the whole thing. . . .

When Mr. B.'s father first came to the United States, he had not wanted to have children. However, his wife, whom he met in the United States, threatened to adopt, so he gave in.

Another consequence Mr. B. attributed to his father's wartime experiences was a weakened heart. His mother continued to tell him not to aggravate his father for fear that he might cause a heart attack. Nevertheless, his father often lost his temper and frightened Mr. B. with his outbursts.

Mr. B. was thankful that his mother's disposition was calm. He felt that her role as the family mediator prevented fights between his father and himself. They often argued about politics. Even though the father has supported his son's activism, he also has gone into rages when he has learned of Mr. B.'s plans to be arrested during demonstrations.

Mr. B. wanted to be more like his father. He admired him for having "experienced a great deal" and for his "understanding" of politics. In contrast, Mr. B. perceived his mother as naive. For example, he sided with his father about an argument his parents typically had concerning their friends. His father, described as being likable, often insisted that he didn't care to have friends. His mother was described as follows: "She's very, very naive and very innocent . . . she'll believe anybody, and, uh, she thinks she has a lot of friends. My father's always saying she doesn't have any friends and, "You should realize that.'"

One quality that both parents did have, though the mother perhaps more than the father, was that they were "sensitive." Mr. B. said that both his parents cried easily and that neither of them was afraid of showing emotions. Though he could not be specific about what his parents cried over, he said, "Family things, Jewish things, and certainly Holocaust things." Mr. B. said that his parents' only expectation of him was that he be a "good Jew." He added they were quite liberal in their interpretation of what being a "good Jew" meant.

He was emphatic that his parents had always been very involved with him in spite of the fact that his father, who always came home late, was often tired or busy in the evenings and his days off. Comparing himself to his sister, to whom he felt "close," Mr. B. said, "They've had more problems and also more involvement, and I guess, more reason to be proud [of me]."

Mr. B. saw his sister as very different from himself and as being like his mother. Two of his early memories revolved around her. The first was of having thrown her out of her crib when he was in his second year. The second was of having been bought a costume which included a whip when he was four years old. He hit his sister with the whip, and his parents threw the costume out of the window.

Another of Mr. B.'s earliest memories was of hearing choir music as he lay in bed. He used to wonder if he was hearing angels sing. Anxiety was associated with the memory. For years Mr. B. wondered if the music he heard was real or if it was mystical or supernatural.

Around the age of three and four years, Mr. B. asked his father to tell him stories before he went to sleep. The stories his father told were about the Holocaust. Mr. B. said:

> He would tell me stories about what happened 30 years ago, and you know, I really grew up with this whole thing, you know he would tell me these stories, and he told me later that all

the members of the family used to tell him, let's say my uncles, they would tell him, 'What do you want, you're just going to give him nightmares, forget it,' you know, and my father says, he feels I could never really be happy unless I knew what happened, and he feels that he would not be doing what he felt would be a proper way for a Jewish parent to raise his child, would be to tell him what happened.

There was some confusion with respect to the actual events which defined his father's experiences. Mr. B. insisted that his father had been in a "labor battalion" as opposed to a slave labor camp. Some of the words Mr. B. used indicated that he regarded it as part of the army. For example, Mr. B. said that his father "deserted" rather than "escaped."

Mr. B. said that he was always "tremendously interested" in his father's stories. He added: "I guess the clue to the way I felt was that I became active in Soviet Jewry demonstrations ... as soon as I heard about it. ... " Mr. B. remembered three incidents related to him by his father. The first concerned his father's return to his native town, which had not yet been ravaged by the Nazis, after his escape. He related the story and its implications as follows:

When he did return home in 1944, a trainload of Polish Jews passed through the town. It was the first day of Passover; it stopped for a few hours and they made an announcement in the synagogue, 'Everybody go home and bring food and blankets for the Jews,' you know, so they all, my father, went to the train and saw the Jews, and he knew where they were going, and everybody gave them food, and that was it, you know, they absolved themselves, they didn't care and they didn't think twice about it. They went back to the business and they went back to the prayers and that was it, they, and it was if the train was never there ... and it was things like that that must of really made an impression on me from way back.

The second story told to Mr. B. by his father concerned the father's attempts to warn his parents: "He told his parents to run away but they called him irresponsible. They told him, 'Don't worry, this'll pass,' so my father went into hiding, and this was like a week before the ghetto in the town was liquidated."

The third major story related to Mr. B. concerned his father's hiding in an underground bunker with two friends. They dared not stir for fear of discovery and were brought food by a friendly peasant. Mr. B. described his understanding of the experience:

I can see it as a tremendously maddening experience, knowing that your whole family is being wiped out, and you're sitting in this bunker. You can't move, you know, and you don't know when you're going to be caught, and once in a while German patrols go by.

Mr. B.'s father had a scar on his neck which resulted when one of the men he shared the bunker with "went mad" and bit him.

Until he went to college, all of Mr. B.'s education was in Jewish parochial schools. He never enjoyed school. He remembered that on the first day of first grade he started crying, and that his parents had to come to school to pick him up. He had very few friends. He seemed to remember that, as a child, he knew several non-Jewish children. He inferred this because they had Christmas trees. A parent of one of these friends once took him to see Santa Claus, who asked him what he wanted for Christmas. This made him very sad because, since he was Jewish, he could not ask for anything. He also remembered going trick-or-treating on Halloween until his parents explained to him that it was not a Jewish holiday. In school, he always did very poorly, and also had trouble with his teachers. He wouldn't listen to them, and, as he got older, would avoid classes and get into conflicts with them over his activist involvements.

At the time of the interview, Mr. B. had friends but no especially close realtionships. Most of these friends were either from his Hebrew school and sympathetic to his political activities or were friends who were also involved in these activities. In high school, his major social interactions, when they did not revolve around politics, revolved around taking drugs. He belonged to a clique that regarded themselves as "heads." From the age of 15, he abused marijuana, hashish, opium, barbituates, and amphetamines. He has continued to use drugs but far less frequently because he felt that the drugs were damaging him physically and mentally. He was also afraid that, if his father found out, it would kill him.

Mr. B. was sent to camp for a month in seventh grade. This was the first time he had been away from home. In eighth grade, he spent the summer in Israel and enjoyed it so much that he didn't want to return home. He decided to go to a college near his home for financial reasons. He had no desire to move from his parents' home. However, he was eagerly anticipating going to Israel in the near future.

Identity and Beliefs

Mr. B.'s identity centered around a preoccupation with the Holocaust and with involvement in Jewish activist causes, particularly the oppression of Soviet Jewry which he saw as an extension of the Holocaust. He said of himself:

> I've been involved in Jewish political causes really for 10 years . . . and especially the problems of Soviet Jewry, I'll get into this a little later but the Holocaust was the prime moving force, it's been a major part, I guess you can say the Holocaust has been a major part of my life.

Mr. B.'s political involvement often led to legal difficulties, and he had been to court often. He also had gone to Moscow, where, with a number of others, he participated in a sit-in.

As early as the age of 10, he began circulating petitions to ban Nazi groups in America. In the fifth grade, he tried to write a history of World War II. Later, he wrote a column for a Jewish newspaper. He was also planning to write a book on the Jewish activist movement in America. The first chapter will detail his father's experiences during the Holocaust.

Mr. B.'s Jewish identity was cultural and nationalistic, and not religious. While affirming his lack of religion, he said:

> If you're wondering why I wear a yarmulka, I wear it basically for identification, and I see no reason why not to; it means a lot to my parents.... I grew up with the belief that being Jewish is wearing a yarmulka... it's not something I believe... it's just that I have a feeling for it... but I tell you, it's more than that, I have a feeling for the whole religion, it's not that I've rebelled against it 'cause it's too strict, it's at this point, I don't believe. [You don't believe in God?] I'm not saying that, I don't know... it's not important to me, really, because I'm not going to know and at this point in my life, it's only going to hold me back from things I want to do, and there's no point in dedicating myself to something like religion when I have no tremendous belief in it. You know, I do certain religious things out of feeling... and partly out of pleasing my parents... I don't mind doing it, I enjoy it and my father always tells me, when I get older, and have a family, I'll be religious because it's the only way to keep a good Jewish home, so maybe, it could be that I'll become religious again.

At the same time that he was not religious, he experienced a profound sense of the mystical in being Jewish. He said:

> I believe there is something very strange about the Jewish people, something very mystical, you know, and, at this point, the Jewish religion and the Jewish God are not ready to satisfy, uh, the interpretation of the Jewish people's experience, the Jewish religion at this point, as a real answer to why the Jewish people went through what they did, and how they survived, there's a mystical quality about the Jewish people.... [Can you tell me more about this mystical quality?] Yeah, I see the Jewish experience of revival, of rebirth, of destruction, the whole thing you know, as being a unique experience from any other people, and, and it's, and, I could see the concept of the Jews as let's say 'chosenness.' Let's say I could see the concept of chosenness in a mystical way that I don't understand... the whole thing about Judaism, I've found this in my own experience, in my, our own life, I've seen something, I don't know if you want to call it a miracle, I've, I can't really see it any other way, it's the whole question of Soviet Jewry, because I remember when we started out back in '64, '65, and everybody would tell us, Why are you wasting your time demonstrating?...and it was true...you know as someone who lived through it, lived through those days, and remembered how everybody who called themselves realists, called us dreamers, 'nothing's going to happen,' you know, and, and take a look at the whole experience of the Jewish people, as basically the dreamers were proven the realists, you can carry this through with Zionism, and you can carry this through with everything, the dreamers have been proven the realists and I really find this unique among the Jewish people, that, you know, against really ridiculous odds, you know, we just keep surviving.

For Mr. B., the definition of a good Jew was quite flexible. For example, since his last year of high school he had been eating nonkosher foods. At the same time, the Nazi attempt to exterminate the Jewish people has resulted in an imperative obligation that he felt he must shoulder, and which he felt he must allow to pervade his life. He said:

> I feel that no Jew after the Holocaust can, should be able to function while there are still Jewish problems in the world. In other words, if there are still Jewish problems in Russia, and this is after the Holocaust, then I, as a Jew, can't live in a self-centered life 'cause the Holocaust was such a profound, such a shattering experience, that more than shattering, more than profound, it has to overturn everything, everything has to start, you can't do anything as if there was no Holocaust. In other words, every part of your life has to be touched. . . . I think the experience has to touch every Jew in the kind of way where he doesn't just feel for it once a year, you know, it's an integral part of his life.

Mr. B. went on to make an explicit statement of his belief that his not having been in a concentration camp was merely an "accident of birth," and that, when he did a "good deed," it was merely to pay an obligation for "not having been born into different circumstances." Not only did he feel that "Jews owe other Jews," but he also felt guilty about doing things that were selfish, like spending money for luxuries, in the face of all the misery in the world.

Though Mr. B. was militantly Zionistic, Israel as a living nation posed conflicts for his sense of Jewish identity. He was distressed by what he saw as Israel's moving away from its "idealistic foundation" and by its "becoming another Western country." He has never doubted that Israel can withstand its foes militarily. For example, during the Six-Day War, though he took time off from school to collect money for Israel, his major concern was not for its survival, but for the exact time its forces would reach the Suez Canal. Nevertheless, he did feel that the future of Israel was jeopardized by internal strife. He was troubled by Israel's treatment of its Arab minority. On the one hand, he both felt that they were treated well, and also that "the hell with them, they declared war on us and have to suffer the consequences." On the other hand, he saw that the fact that the Jews were in a majority as an "experiment," of which he said that "If Israel becomes like South Africa, we can just close up . . . Israel has to be different because I believe Jews are different." While he saw Israel as a country whose promise was to produce a "new set of radical ideas," he was afraid that his children will lose this perspective. While he wanted them to grow up in Israel to have a strong Jewish identity, he did not want them to be like typical Israelis, who are "self-centered" and to whom "everything comes naturally." One sensed that he preferred the identity of the Jew of the diaspora, whom he saw as defined by "self-confrontation." He said, "It means something to be a Jew in the diaspora."

Mr. B.'s political involvement, though always motivated by what he saw as the lessons of the Holocaust, have not always been strictly limited to "Jewish issues." In high school, he had been very involved in leftist causes and even started a short-lived underground newspaper. Among the causes he had been involved with were demonstrating against the Vietnam war, the exploitation of migrant workers, and atrocities in Africa. These involvements were motivated by what he called his "Jewish consciousness." He said of his reasoning: "Here you're complaining that the whole world did nothing for the Jews, so what are you doing for Biafra." His disengagement from these causes came about as a consequence of a feeling that he could only stretch himself so thin, and "Jewish problems have to come first."

Mr. B. had spent much time thinking about the Holocaust and has well-articulated attitudes about it. These, in turn, also contained his more generalized view of the world. He was upset by comparisons of the Holocaust to any other event in history. He did, however, feel that it was justifiable to compare the Soviet treatment of Jews to the Holocaust. He said:

> Because... Soviet Jewry is the last remnant of European Jewry... it's a continuation of the Holocaust... I'm not saying it from any parochial point of view. I'm only saying it because this is the way I see it, and I think any genocide directed against Jews after Auschwitz is certainly at the level of Auschwitz simply because it's being done to the people who had gone through Auschwitz. You know, and you'd think that the world would already leave these people alone, any, anything that happens more is just staggering.

Mr. B.'s understanding of the Holocaust in the context of history emphasized his sense of the aloneness of the Jewish people in their suffering. He said:

> There was genocide in Biafra, and there was genocide in other places in the world which were certainly great tragedies, you know, but nothing, nothing can compare to Auschwitz, and I also think it's a measure of the full tragedy of Auschwitz that so little has been written on the subject and it strikes me, people consider Auschwitz a Jewish tragedy. They don't look upon it as a world tragedy whereas Biafra and Vietnam are looked upon as world tragedies. Everybody, you don't have to be Jewish to feel for Vietnam and Biafra. For some reason, you have to be Jewish to feel for what happened in Europe.

For Mr. B., one lesson of the Holocaust was that:

> After the Holocaust, I don't believe anything is impossible, there's no such thing as impossible. You can give all the reasons in the world, you can be speaking, you know, totally logical, but there's still room for the impossible to happen because it's already happened, which means anything can happen.

As a consequence of this orientation, he believed that Jews could easily be the victim of another attempt of mass extermination. He also believed that it could happen in the United States. However, he felt that he was not likely to be a victim because

I think that my type of orientation, from everything that I've learned from the Holocaust would be toward resistance, even if it meant futile resistance . . . even if it meant suicide. I couldn't see taking part in the Holocaust.

Mr. B. saw the most destructive element of the Holocaust as the attack on "dignity of individuals." More specifically, he said:

The Jews in Europe had the highest sexual and moral code . . . they had the highest sense of personal modesty, of sexual modesty, of, of, of, of, of living. Their code of living was a pure one, especially, especially in the *shtetl,* right, this is the way the Jewish code was, the Jewish way of living, and the fact that the Nazis put these people, put the Jews to the lowest form of degradation that I think has ever been deliberately meted out, I think is a tremendous irony. Here you had the most moral people in the world, the people who were most worried about purity, and personal cleanliness, and the rest of it, being put in this type of a situation, and I think it was the most destructive element of the Holocaust.

He saw the survival of victims of the concentration camps as a consequence of two things: luck, and also "the Jewish sense of survival that has been sharpened over 2,000 years." He also felt that survivors had to be affected by the experience for the rest of their lives.

While Mr. B. experienced a "violent rage" at the thought of Nazis, he felt that "American Jews were the real criminals of the Holocaust," because they were silent and did nothing to help their European brethren. If his feelings about these Jews were harsh, his thoughts about Nazis, Germans, and non-Jews in general, were even more severe. He said of those who committed the actual atrocities:

I think they were average, really average people. I think that anybody's capable of doing it, anybody, meaning in this question, it raises certain conflicts I have. On the one sense, I feel all men are brothers and it would be wonderful if we could have one big international community, no breakdowns, no nationalism, none of this you know. And, on the other hand, I feel that after the Holocaust there has to be a Jewish people, and there has to be a separate Jewish identity because we're better than they are, and you, so on the one hand, there's something telling me that everybody's equal, and on the other hand, there's something telling me that they're the *goyim,* you know, and we're Jews and the *goyim* are capable of doing this, and Jews aren't. Uh, I hope Jews aren't uh, I don't think that Jews as a whole are capable of doing something like that. I think the Christians are, you know, a pagan morality as far as I see it, I really think the rest of the world are pagans, especially after this experience, I could really see the Jews as being the only civilized people in the world.

And of Germans he said:

I view the whole German people, even those Germans born today, as criminals. The reason I do this is not because I believe they have the guilt of their fathers, but I believe if they, after what happened, they can still call themselves Germans, I know that if the Jews would do, would have done something like that . . . I couldn't call myself a Jew, I'd be too ashamed. And you have people talking about rebuilding Germany after that and, I mean Morgenthau . . . said that Germany should be plowed over, you know, and just laid desolate, it should not be allowed to be settled, and that's the way I feel and I feel that any German who would go and call himself a German, he's the same, he's a Nazi because he's not repudiating his past, he's accepting it, to a German who ran off, who wants nothing more to do with the German people, who doesn't feel part of it, I feel I could establish some sort of personal dialogue with, but to no one else.

Another conclusion that Mr. B. drew from the Holocaust was that Jews must turn to each other for justice. He felt, for example, that the Nuremberg War Crimes trial reflected what he called "the Christian sense of justice" which he feels was "really based on tokenism." He contrasted it to the Eichmann trial, saying:

That [was] the real significant trial . . . because that was Jewish justice, and it was justice that was done against the wishes of the whole world. Jews, the Israelis, went into Argentina and kidnapped him in violation of international law, and put him on trial in Jerusalem and I think that put the whole thing in its proper perspective, because it put the Holocaust above international law, it put the Jewish experience, and it put the Jewish people above international law.

He went on to say:

I don't think we're bound by international law anymore, this is the way I feel, we're not bound by international law when it comes down to our own suffering, if there are Jews suffering in Russia then there are no laws which should be respected. If there are Nazi war criminals on the loose, there are no such things as laws, and, uh, I think . . . Germany proved that most of all because everything they did was legal, everything they did to the Jews was done legally. . . .

Mr. B. was named after his grandfather. He saw in this a symbolic representation of the continuity of the Jewish people. Nevertheless, he was less sanguine about the continuity of the human race. He doubted that "there is enough wisdom around to check the power" that man has to destroy the world. He felt that "there won't be too many generations after this." If the world does survive to the year 2,000, he felt it would be a "frightening society."

Mr. B.'s ideal vision of his own personal future was to be able to travel and to write. He had difficulty seeing himself as being able to fulfill this aim, because to do so would mean having the freedom afforded by money. He felt that he would be psychologically unable to pursue any occupation that would be financially rewarding. This, he felt, was because he could not tolerate the regimentation required for such a job. He would like to live in Israel, but anticipated difficulties, again because he would have difficulty with the regimentation required by kibbutz living. Nevertheless he did not consider not living on a kibbutz.

Dreams, Fantasies, and Associations

Mr. B.'s unconscious life was characterized by Holocaust imagery. He remembered that the dreams he had as a child had to do with Nazis and concentration camps. He related the following dream which he had had at an age which he said was too young for him to remember:

> I was at Coney Island. I was with my parents on the boardwalk, and all of a sudden Hitler came, you know. He was leading a kind of invasion, and the thing that I remember very clearly, very clearly, was that there was like a war going on, you know, and everybody was just walking around. This happens in dreams, you know, where something is happening to you and everybody is just walking around, business as usual, and, uh, I might have been killed in that one.

The only comments Mr. B. was able to make about this dream were that he felt very anxious in it, as if he were being chased. He said he could not remember any more recent dreams.

Mr. B. also said that between the age of five years and the present he has had many fantasies of himself being in a concentration camp. He described one as follows: "I've felt myself a lot of times as if I were in a concentration camp, and I could just see myself like throwing myself on the barbed wire, or something, just committing suicide." Another typical fantasy, which continued through the present, involved variations on the theme of discovering that Nazi war criminals were hiding somewhere and going with friends to hunt them down. One variation of this fantasy was: "I've had fantasies about meeting up with Nazis and just *not* strangling them or anything. . . . " The emotion he experienced toward the subject of Nazis was expressed as follows: "Always, always, always, I used to feel a violence toward it, an insane violence, an uncontrollable violence. . . . "

In answer to the question: What's the first thing that comes into your mind when you think about Nazis?", Mr. B. said:

> Well, the first thing that comes into my mind is the rallies, the rallies that, but I don't know if I identify Nazism with that. [What then?] I've often had the fantasy of seeing myself in one of those rallies and just standing there and watching. And, and all around me people just going hysterical, like in some religious revival, you know, everybody just *sieg heiling*. I've had this many times. [What are you doing?] Just trying to run away, or scream, or something, you know. [Where are you?] I'm in the middle of it, you, there's like no pushing out of the crowd, trying to get out. [What are you feeling?] I'm feeling like I'm just losing my mind, like there's no sanity anymore, you know, it's insane. And, uh, you know, just get me out of here. I think that's the way I would have felt in the camps also. I would have just lost my mind, I think.

In answer to the question: What's the worst thing that could happen to you?", Mr. B. said, without hesitation, that it was being the subject of a Nazi experiment. As a child he had read in a Classics Comic Book of an experiment performed by Nazi doctors in which a man was suspended in a block of ice, to see how long it would take him to die. He has often imagined himself as a victim of that experiment.

At this point, it is also worthwhile to quote Mr. B.'s descriptions of the associations and thoughts he experienced during the sit-in in the Soviet Union alluded to earlier:

It was a tremendous experience. We were held for eight hours and then released and they allowed us back on the tour. They didn't even deport us because they wanted to downplay the whole thing. You know, uh, but uh, it was too late because it was all over the press, they couldn't stop it. Afterwards we met with Soviet Jews. . . . We got into very close relationships with a few of the Jews there, you know, personal-type relationships and we call them up every week on the phone and we write to each other. You know, the whole Soviet Jewry question for me, it never was a statistical type of thing, it was always very emotional, very real to me, but it lacked that one dimension of personal contact which I now have with the problem, it's my personal friends who are there now, it's much more clear to me now, the Soviet Jewry thing.

[How did you feel when you were there?] You know, I didn't realize how I felt until a few weeks ago, uh, everytime I thought of being there with those Jews and talking to them and being on the steps of the synagogue, and just mingling with them, everytime I thought about it, I just got like a tremendous chill, you know, I'd get terribly depressed, you know, I couldn't put my finger on it. Why? Because it really wasn't . . . that much of a unique experience talking to these Jews because I knew what they would say, I'd read it before, I'd spoken to people who had gone there, I was, I'd say I was totally prepared for the emotional experience of meeting them, I might say, I might have even exaggerated what would happen because you know, you read reports, you live with this thing, you really know what the standard lines are, what the standard thing is, they approach you, what they're going to say to you, you know, but I really couldn't understand why I felt so emotionally touched by the whole thing. But it occurred to me a few weeks ago that I really felt that I really felt that, that, we were standing, standing among Jews, it was as if like 1939, you know, we were standing with Polish Jews about to be sent to the gas chambers and it was this type, a tremendously personal type of a relationship to the Holocaust. I really think that was what it was, it brought the Holocaust into much clearer meaning because here were the people who were about to be sent away, the you know, these are the Jews you're meeting, six million Jews, that's the way I felt, I didn't look upon them, I didn't look upon it as being 1972, I really felt this was like pre-Auschwitz, you know, and, and, I think that's that's that's really really says it all, you know.

[How did you feel during the sit-in] Oh, oh, well, uh, the way I felt, I felt also in the sense that we, we got beaten up in the office, by the by Soviet police, and so I guess we felt [laughs] but emotionally the way we felt, in a lot of ways they had taken on the the Gestapo, the appearance of the S.S. and the Gestapo to me, and it really seemed as if they were shouting at us in, you know they were calling us Kikes in Russian, you know and it really seemed to me like here we were again, you know, that's the way it seemed, the whole trip.

[Were you afraid?] It was beyond that, we were afraid until we got in, when we got in, when I got in, I was just tremendously exhausted anyway, I really just exhausted myself emotionally. And from fear, it wasn't. I couldn't any more because there had been so much before, you know, I just didn't feel anything, I really felt like I was numb, I walked into that office, I was depersonalized, and I was just so tired I really wanted to leave, and go to sleep, you know, we went through the motions of taking it over, didn't feel too much, and I think also, I think the emotional experience could have been much more with the Jews there had I not been so tired and run-down and hungry, we were on a hunger strike at the time and all the rest of it, you know, uh, the physical, physical condition we were in at the time, we were just so run-down, that I think, you know, a lot of the emotional experiences were lost.

Problems in Living

Mr. B. had been in psychotherapy for one year. He entered because he experienced difficulty becoming close to others. He said that whenever he became intimate with someone, a "love-hate relationship" developed. He also imagined that other people thought badly of him and was sensitive to social slights of any kind.

Mr. B. described himself as often depressed. Associated with depression was considerable difficulty falling asleep at night. Suicidal ideation was also manifest, although he did not consider it to be a problem. He said that he was "ambivalent" about dying and that "it wouldn't mean a lot to me if I died." He has thought about taking his life with either pills or poison. Mr. B. thought about death a great deal. He said, "Sometimes I project myself into situations where I'm going to die in a few minutes or a few days."

He also described three phobias. He was afraid of high places, and often had the thought that he might be pushed off such places. He was also afraid of dogs, particularly stray dogs, and of being bitten by them and getting rabies. Finally, he was afraid of snakes. He described a fear of being "overwhelmed" by snakes. He sometimes had the fantasy of an "army of snakes" attacking him. At times, when he was sitting by himself, he got the idea that "there are snakes everywhere and there's no place you can escape to."

Discussion

Central to the analysis of Mr. B.'s character was the observation that the dual themes of concentration camps and Nazis pervaded his conscious and unconscious life. The meaning of an obsession of such magnitude must, whatever else it signifies, have a reference to the individuals' family experience.

An important contradiction emerged as Mr. B. described his home life. He described it in abstract, idealized terms, as a haven of warmth, intimacy, and security. However, he also provided more concrete descriptions of events and interactions, including a description of his lifelong inability to discuss his feelings with his parents, which suggested a chaotic and unstable situation characterized by the emotional unavailability of both parents and the free-floating rage of the father. Mr. B.'s constant reiteration of his parents' involvement with him represented his need to deny his experience of emotional alienation.

At the same time, Mr. B.'s life mirrored his father's life. His father had been a militant Zionist in his youth, as was Mr. B. His father was considered by his community to be a "crazy radical," as was Mr. B. The extent of Mr. B.'s recapitulation of his father's life included retracing his footsteps in space (he journeyed to the Soviet Union) and in time (Mr. B.'s associations, while in the Soviet Union, took him back to the Nazi era). Mr. B. even had a fear of rabid (that is, "mad") dogs, which recalled his father's having been bitten in the neck by a man who went mad.

The distortions implicit in Mr. B.'s conscious representation of his family, and his primitive incorporation of his father, suggest that two simultaneous conditions existed in his family. On the one hand, Mr. B. received a message that his parents were unable to provide him with the emotional supplies that he needed. On the other hand, he received a message that they desperately needed him. The father, whose life had been "shattered" by the Holocaust, turned to the son to live out his own unfulfilled desires and aspirations. These two conditions, bolstered by the child's knowledge of what his father had endured, perpetuated a symbiotic relationship. Any attempt to individuate, normally accompanied by stress, was rendered even more difficult by the fact that it constituted further injury to a man who has already suffered so greatly.

The incidents of Mr. B.'s going trick-or-treating and his meeting Santa Claus were particularly significant. Both of these incidents represented prohibitions, at first parental and subsequently internalized, of participating in any aspect of life outside of the family's rigidly defined boundaries. The situation in which Mr. B. found himself was that of being stranded in the world of survivorhood. He could consider going to Israel because the land to the Jews represented an extension of his family. Although negative feelings about his family were forbidden, he had to deal somehow with the rage he felt toward them.

Historical reality, made more immediate by his father's personal history, provided Mr. B. with a system of symbols through which he expressed his predicament. The three major symbols that he had were *Christians, Nazis,* and *Jews.* Each of these symbols was essentially ambivalent. Before detailing the complex representations of these symbols, their microgenesis must be described.

Probably motivated by a conscious desire to bring up his son the best way he knew how, Mr. B.'s father told his child "bedtime" stories about the Holocaust from at least the age of five. On the basis of what is known about the father's explosive temper, and on the basis of what may be assumed to have been the rage emerging from its having been repressed during his years of persecution, it may be speculated that these stories were also motivated by unconscious and displaced sadistic impulses. The child's having had nightmares of being attacked by Hitler suggests that these stories were an early assault on his ego.

As a consequence, these stories were integrated by the child not only as representations of historical events, but as personal symbols having immediate significance. As the child developed through successive stages of character formation, these symbols became more and more elaborated as representations of immediate intrapsychic concerns.

Christians seem to have been the least pervasive of the three symbols. (A clinical "hunch" of the investigator, unfortunately unsubstantiated by available evidence, is that it was the most cathected symbol.) Mr. B. saw Christians as people who were not as good as Jews because they allowed Jews to be persecuted. To some extent, they recall the American Jews (with whom Mr. B. may have associated his mother, who came to America in 1938), "the real criminals of the Holocaust," who failed to come to the aid of the victims. Christians, Mr. B. said, had a "pagan morality" characterized by "tokenism" because they failed to adequately punish the Germans. However, Mr. B.'s images of Christianity were also images of oral nurturance, specifically oral nurturance that had to be denied. (For example, Mr. B. had to stop going trick-or-treating on Halloween, and he was not able to ask Santa Claus for a Christmas present.)

It must be remembered that Mr. B.'s mother, who was so conspicuously vague in his descriptions of his family, had the role in the home of protecting him from his father's rages. It may be assumed that she was probably not entirely successful. It is also likely that she, like the father, was limited in her capacity to respond to his emotional needs. In addition, Mr. B.'s relationships with others to whom he felt close, which he said were characterized by "love-hate," were probably modeled on his relationship to his mother. The correspondence between Mr. B.'s unconscious experience of his mother and his representations of Christians is clear. He had to reject angrily everything Christian, because he could not be conscious of his wish to reject his mother.

The symbol *Nazis* was extremely complex and existed in relationship to the symbol *Jews.* Not only must the child have been frightened when his father first told him about Nazis, he must also have been confused. Who were these people who hated his father? The answer was supplied through the unconscious formulation:

The Nazis hated my father.
I hate my father.
I am a Nazi.

The symbol was further complicated when Mr. B. learned that Nazis hated Jews and that he was a Jew. As Mr. B. experienced his father's aggression and his own fear of his father, he completed, in the shorthand of the unconscious, the following formulation:

My father hates me.
I am a Jew.
Nazis hate Jews.
My father is a Nazi.

As a consequence, Mr. B. turned all of his conscious hatred and fear to the Nazis who stood for his father. At the same time, he also hated himself, as was manifested by his severe depression, because he too was a Nazi.

While in no way invalidating the justification for Mr. B.'s consuming political activity on the level of conscious reality, this activity also portrayed familial and intrapsychic conflicts. Further, Mr. B.'s activity also provided him with a solution to these conflicts.

The anxiety which threatened Mr. B.'s psychic balance was, to some extent, neutralized by the defense mechanism of projection. In his case, projection was so bolstered by reality that, given the intensity of the conflicts, it was especially effective.

However, there is an additional factor that must be discussed. The father's sadism, as frightening as it was, was also a prime avenue of interaction between parent and child. As such, it became gratifying, if not sexualized. Thus, Mr. B.'s first association to Nazism, being in a crowd that gave expression to its instinctual impulses, represented a portrayal of himself being caught up in the swirl of his own impulses. In the association, he was desperate to escape from the demands of his own libido. Similarly, his fantasy of an army of snakes attacking him was a dual representation of his being attacked by his own sinful impulses and also his father's rage, which also provided masochistic gratification. He said, however, that there was no escape. Yet another prominent aspect of his fantasy life reveals where he did, in fact, escape to (that is, the concentration camp). In his fantasy of being incarcerated, he gratified the masochistic aim of his instinctual life, punished himself for his objectionable thoughts, and finally—through his being rendered helpless—protected his family from his own destructive and sadistic impulses.

The symbolic significance of *Jews* now becomes more apparent. At one level, Mr. B. continually had to prove that he was a Jew in order to prove that he was not a Nazi. At another level, Mr. B.'s immersion into his Jewishness, for example, his wearing a yarmulka for "identification," was a counterphobic defense against the vulnerability he felt in being Jewish. This vulnerability was certainly related to the actual physical vulnerability of Jews during the Holocaust. However, this physical vulnerability also represented the symbolic castration of the father as he was rendered helpless by the Nazis, which in turn became part of Mr. B.'s own unconscious through his identification with his father. Hence, Mr. B.'s activities in the service of Jews can also be seen as a struggle against the narcissistic mortification he endured in being Jewish.

At a third level, being Jewish represented the grandiose, infantile, omnipotent aspect of Mr. B.'s character. At a very early age, he hallucinated angels annointing him with their music. That he felt so singled-out is not surprising, given the special role he was chosen to fulfill *vis-à-vis* his parents. His rage at his sister resulted from her threatening his special position. He regained his position as he experienced the special mystical quality he attributed to being Jewish. The role of the Holocaust here becomes apparent when it is recalled that the special position of the Jew was announced to Mr. B. through their suffering. And it is also suffering which puts Jews above international law, which in the language of Mr. B.'s unconscious, was his own harsh superego. Thus, when Mr. B. penned crude Jewish stars on his clothing, he was symbolically and paradoxically wearing the yellow star Jews in Europe were forced to wear as a mark of shame. As he lived through the concentration camps in his fantasy life, he was also affirming his own special place and his own special power in the world. Israel posed a special problem for him, because it represented Jews as victors rather than victims.

It is not the intention of this study to imply that Mr. B. would not let go of the Holocaust (as he affirmed its continuation in the form of the persecution of Russian Jewry) only because of the vicissitudes of his unconscious life. His statements that the Holocaust's impact on his life had been to make him more sensitive to the problems of human suffering and tyranny, are of profound importance—ultimately more important and more hopeful than the dynamics detailed in the preceding analysis.

9

Case Study 3: A Jewish American Princess

Our arms and legs are full of sleeping memories of the past.

[Proust, 1959, p. 2.]

Miss E. was a 19-year-old freshman majoring in education. She lived with her parents in an upper-middle-class suburban community. Miss E. was attractive, quite tall, and slightly plump. She wore heavy make-up, particularly around the eyes, and had a deep, cultivated suntan.

Her mother was a 48-year-old housewife who had emigrated to the U.S. in infancy. Her father was 53 years old and was born in Hungary. After his liberation from a concentration camp, he wandered through Europe, supporting himself by trading on the black market. He came to the United States in 1951 and became a building contractor. Miss E. had one brother, who was three years her junior.

Interview Behavior

Miss E. was invited to participate in the study by a colleague of the interviewer who knew her casually. At first she refused; however, she later approached her saying that she wanted to participate. When initially contacted by the interviewer, Miss E. insisted that he conduct the interview in her home.

Miss E. greeted the interviewer at her door wearing a bikini. She asked that the interview be conducted in her garden so that she could sunbathe during it. The interviewer stated his preference for remaining indoors. It might be noted that the interviewer did not experience Miss E.'s behavior as sexual. His theory, which grew stronger during the course of the 70-minute interview, was that, by consenting to participate in the study and by greeting the interviewer as she did, Miss E. was living out her fantasy of her own importance; that is, that someone would travel a long distance to talk to her.

The interviewer felt that Miss E. was extremely invested in communicating a particular image of herself. At the same time, she was quite unproductive. The process of the interview was characterized by the interviewer's asking questions that Miss E. would briefly answer. There was little spontaneity. At times the interviewer felt that Miss E. was quite contemptuous and that her manner communicated the attitude, "What a stupid question."

Relationship to Parents

Miss E.'s description of her parents was vague and diffuse. The following interchange illustrates the difficulty encountered in trying to obtain a picture of them:

> Interviewer: Can you tell me what kind of people your parents are?
> Miss E.: What do you mean?
> Interviewer: Well—
> Miss E. [interrupting]: I get along with them, that's it, they're nice.

A few details about her parents did emerge during the interview. For example, she said of her father:

> My father works very hard, he does, even if he's off, he finds something to do, and they don't travel because they don't have time to travel, he's nervous about certain things, clean, keeping the house clean, things like that.

He also apparently had an obsession abut food. He refused to eat food not prepared at home, because he believed it would be contaminated either by dirt or by unhealthy additives. He was also described as being prejudiced against black and Puerto Rican people.

Miss E.'s mother was described as having no interests besides shopping and taking care of the house. While her husband had a few friends from Europe and she had one close friend, they rarely socialized with them or visited any of the mother's cousins who were the only living relatives of either parent.

Miss E. could only say about her parents' relationship with each other, "It's not a great relationship, they're just married." She also revealed that her parents occasionally argued about "silly petty things," such as the house not being clean, the food "not right," and the mother wanting "more money." Miss E.'s portrayal of her relationship with her parents had an arrogantly defensive quality. For example, in response to a direct question about it, she said: "They're my mother and father. I don't understand what you mean. Is my mother my friend? Do you mean something like that? No! She's my mother."

Although she lived in her parents' home, and had never been away for more than two weeks, she "never really spent time with them." No conversation with them stood out in her mind. She explained, "I never did anything wrong so

I never had to talk to them." When encouraged to remember some interaction with them, she said: "They're really not like that, not always giving me lectures like, 'You do this' or 'You do this.' So there's nothing really that would stick in my mind."

The impression that her parents exerted so little control over her was belied by her somewhat tangential response to the request that she describe her parents' attitudes about her: "I listen to what they tell me about what they think is right, and like most of the time, I follow it because I agree with them. I really don't have any problems with that." Miss E., for all her denial of the role of her parents in her life, seemed to have been extremely compliant to their wishes. For example, she described herself as a child as follows: "Good, I never did anything wrong. I used to do anything anybody told me. [What do you mean?] If you told me to sit on the chair and don't move, I'd sit on the chair and not move." When her own wishes were in conflict with her parents' wishes for her, her solution seemed to be to accept their wishes as if they were her own. For example, she said of her choice of college: "Well, I originally wanted to go away to school. My parents didn't want me to go and then I decided I didn't care because it was a lot of money."

Throughout the interview, Miss E. insisted that she never disagreed with her parents. however, at one point, she did admit that there were "just minor fights when they don't want me to go anywhere." Her adaptation to their concern for her safety was not to have time to give them worry. She said: "The only thing they're worried about is me being safe. I don't have time to get in trouble, even if I wanted to, because I work and I go to school, and I have my friends, you know, my time is full."

It seemed to the interviewer that it was very important to Miss E. to let him know that she was not "spoiled." One of her few spontaneous statements was:

> There's nothing that I really ask them [her parents] for because I have money to buy them. [What do you mean?] Whatever I want materialwise. [How about before you started working?] I'd never really asked them for much. I didn't need more than I had, and I never asked them for more.

Miss E. could not describe any expectations her parents had of her. She also could not describe anything for which her parents were critical of her. To the question, "What about you are they most pleased with?", she responded:

> Everything, I'm just wonderful, I'm just kidding. I think they're pleased that I'm happy, I always was, really. But you know, they see other people's kids are unhappy, or into drugs, or what not, and I'm not, you know, they're happy that I'm happy.

Developmental History and Character

Miss E.'s earliest memory was:

> I was three years old, and we were up in the country, and I just remember my aunt's car got stuck, and we had to push it down the road, I remember that. [Who was with you?] Yeah, my mother, my father, my aunt, my uncle, and my three cousins. It was a new car. [How were you feeling?] It was fun because I was with my cousins.

Very few other memories from childhood were accessible to Miss E. When asked what her favorite fairy tale was as a child, she said that she did not remember, but that her mother "knew." When asked about her dreams as a child, she said that she once had a nightmare about a cat. Although she could not remember it, she said that her mother "knew" what the dream was. Similarly, she could not remember her feelings about her younger brother. However, her mother has told her that she was jealous when he was born.

Miss E. could not remember ever having been angry at anyone as a child. When asked to describe her "first fight," she said, "I never fought with anybody." However, she did express anger in the present, but was confused by it. She said, "I get angry but I don't know why."

Miss E. gave two other examples to illustrate her angry feelings. Both concerned her brother. The first was that she became angry at him for throwing away a book of matches she had been planning to save. She explained, "I save everything."

Miss E. was "shy" as a child but changed to an "outgoing, friendly" person around the age of 13. She said that she had many friends. Her attraction to people has always been based on "their looks," that is, their physical beauty. When asked if she ever talked about problems with her friends, she responded that she would consider doing so but had never done so because "I don't have any problems." To support her claim, she reported that she had taken a test in school that "showed that I was a pretty self-actualizing person."

Although she could not remember any of her childhood friends, she was able to describe her relationship to a number of people whom she has known for some time. Miss E. explained that her best friend, Judy, was important to her because "We've really decided that people really use each other a lot and we don't." She went on to say that Judy was very similar to herself. For example, both she and Judy have been "spoiled" by the boys they dated. In addition, she reported that they often refused to go out on dates with boys unless the other one came along.

Miss E. began dating when she was 13 years old. Her relationships with boys seemed to be characterized by her contempt for them. She described several of the boys she had dated as "idiots." She said that most of the boys she dated "make me sick." Miss E. said that while she would go steady with boys for a period of time, she would always date others while her "steady" dated her exclusively. She added that it was always she who broke off the relationship. She described ending a relationship with a boy she had dated for a year:

> Well, I broke up with him because I got sick of him. Nothing ever affected me when I broke up with anyone because I never used to like the boys I went out with, 'cause I really didn't care. It was bad, I felt bad, because it was my best friend's cousin, but she didn't care, I mean it didn't affect our relationship, but I felt bad because it really destroyed him. People say that he was never the same since I, he went out with me, and he still calls me, and every time I see him, but I don't have any feelings about it.

Miss E. had been dating her present boyfriend for two years. She described his appeal to her by contrasting him to the other boys she had dated:

> He's nice to me but he doesn't let me walk all over him like all the other boys. I hated them, like if I said 'jump off the roof,' they'd jump off the roof, and I couldn't stand that, that's why I'd never like a guy, because he was like that, he'd take me anywhere I'd want to go, and he would buy me anything I wanted, and I don't like that.

Although her present boyfriend did set limits, she continued to test him. She said, "I like to start a fight with him all the time." For example, she said that she was "always late," although she knew that it annoyed him. At the same time, if he were "even one minute late," she would snap at him.

It was difficult to gain access to Miss E.'s primary process ideation. When asked about her daydreams, she said, "I don't daydream." The only recent dream she could remember was "Something about buying souvenirs and going through customs. I don't remember what I did. [How were you feeling?] Probably good, I don't remember anything else." Her subsequent association to the dream was that she was returning home from Europe. When asked if she had ever dreamt about Nazis, she said: "I once had a dream about war but not about Nazis. I looked out my window and I just saw warplanes flying across the sky, but I think that they must have been our planes." The above dream occurred during her ninth year.

It seemed extremely important Miss E. to be able to convince the interviewer that she was an independent person. She was very proud of being able to maintain her job as a salesgirl in a department store which specialized in women's clothing. In a boasting tone, she described having been offered an "executive position" by the president of the company. The reasons she rejected the offer were not clear, nor was the reality of it. However, it was clear that she regarded the job as proof of her autonomy.

It also seemed important to Miss E. to portray herself as an extremely busy person. Although she enjoyed horseback riding and swimming, and intended to learn to play tennis and ski, she also said that she did not have the time to enjoy her hobbies. When asked what she did during her spare time, she said, "I don't have spare time, I work, and I go to school, and I go out [that is, on dates with boys]." On the basis of the context in which she described "going out," it seemed to the interviewer that going out was a special kind of chore.

Miss E.'s career choice was teaching. She explained her motivation to become a teacher: "I don't know, when I was little, I guess I loved my kindergarten teacher, and ever since then, I used to love school." She added that she always enjoyed helping her teachers grade papers and tests. Miss E. went on to say that if she did not get placed in a "good neighborhood," she would not teach. Further, her fantasy was that after several years she would stop teaching and open a boutique with her friend, Judy.

Ideas, Beliefs, and Affiliations

Miss E.'s involvement in the issues which concerned the world outside her home was minimal. She never read newspapers, she walked out of the room when television news reports appeared, and said of politics, "I don't really care about it." She also said that no issue in American life was important to her. When asked what social issues concerned other people, she said, "I don't know, money." Miss E. was asked if she would ever consider moving to another country. She said, "I'll see if I like it better."

When asked about her thoughts about minority groups in the United States, Miss E. said: "Sometimes I feel bad for them, other times I don't. You know, because they don't have much of a chance, but I'm a minority group also."

Although Miss E. was Bas Mitzvahed at age 13, the extent of her observance of Jewish tradition and ritual was to go to services with her father on the Jewish High Holy Days. Nevertheless, she did indicate having Zionistic feelings. For example, she said of her reaction to the "Six Day War": "I felt happy when they won, also nationalistic even though it's not my country, but I guess it is, because everyone who's Jewish can be a citizen there."

Miss E. did not believe in the Jewish conception of God. She explained:

> I believe in something up there but I don't know what it is. I believe in fate, I'm a fatalist. [What do you mean?] If your time to go is coming, you're going to go no matter where you are, and I believe things happen because they were fated to be that way, where you go, whether you meet people, what you're going to do in life, if you're going to be happy or sad.

Her belief in fate began in high school where she studied Greek tragedy. She said:

> Because the people they write about in plays are very much like the people who are living, you know, you and me and everybody else, and fate always has some kind of turn in the play, so fate must play a part in our lives, also.

With the possible exception of her feelings about Israel, Miss E. seemed particularly uninvested in any of her attitudes and beliefs. As has been noted, even her ambition to become a teacher did not have any compelling force for her. She did, however, describe one thing that was very important to her. She said:

> I'm very materialistic, in case you didn't realize that by now. I'm very materialistic, I like a nice car, I'd like a big house, I like jewelry, I like to go out, I like to travel, you need money to do those things.

Relationship to the Past

Miss E. would not allow information about her father's past experiences into her consciousness. For example, she had "forgotten" the names of the concentration camps her father had been in.

Her father apparently talked about his experiences "a lot." However, Miss E. "doesn't like to listen to it." She was asked to describe what he said. She responded:

> Nothing he says, how, he just tells how, what they did, not really. They didn't do anything to him like they did to, he was like a strong, he was a young boy, so he was able to work, so they didn't do anything to him. But you know, like they didn't feed him and I can't listen to things like that.

When asked if she ever asked her father about his experiences, she said: "I wouldn't want to know anything so I haven't asked him. You know, people here, they ask him about it and I listen but I really don't listen, I hear it but I don't listen to it."

Miss E. was slightly more cordial to learning about her father's life before the Holocaust. However, even here, her knowledge was limited: "He just told us about the farm he lived on and how everything was so wonderful there because it was natural, you know, not all poisoned food and stuff like that." It is important to note that Miss E. was planning a trip to Europe. While she was excited about the idea of her trip, her major concern was the availability of edible food and clean lodging.

Miss E.'s thoughts about the impact of her father's experiences on his later life were contradictory. She said: "I think it affected him a great deal because otherwise he wouldn't be so nervous today, but that's really all, he doesn't show any other signs like being afraid of things." With regard to the impact of his experiences on how he saw the world, she said:

> Yeah, I guess it does probably, but it's hard to say, you don't know what would have happened if he was never in a concentration camp, he could have turned out the same way, and you know, I think it is, basically, it didn't affect him that much.

Miss E. did admit that her knowledge of her father's experiences has affected her feelings about him. She said, "I sometimes think that he had such a hard life that I wouldn't do things to make it worse for him now."

Thoughts about the Holocaust

Miss E. expressed her general attitude about the Holocaust as follows: "I think it could have been avoided . . . it's just a bad part of history." At the same time, she seemed to believe that the Holocaust stood out in its enormity. When asked if she thought the Holocaust was a unique event in history, she said: "I'm sure all through history people were tortured and for many different reasons, but this was outrageous because there were six million people who were tortured." Miss E. was asked if she thought "something like the concentration camps could happen again." Her response was contradictory: "I don't think so but that's what people thought then, that this could never happen, I don't believe it could happen." When asked it "it could happen somewhere else" she replied, "Oh yeah, I believe it could, people are crazy."

Miss E. felt that the most destructive aspect of the concentration camp experience was "being around people who were tortured and being treated like an animal is pretty destructive, and seeing your relatives being killed, that could be pretty destructive." She said of people's being able to survive the camps:

> I think it had to do with whether, if they were young, and strong, and could work, and wouldn't have to be killed, or also, they had hope it would end, so, even during the concentration camp, a lot of people didn't believe it was really happening, what was happening.

Her thoughts about the consequences of the camp experiences for the survivors were: "I'm sure it's like something in their minds that they'll always remember . . . some people could have put it outside of their minds, altogether."

When asked about her thoughts about the motivation of those who perpetrated the crimes of the Holocaust, she said:

> A lot of it, it said was an order from the state, and they thought it would benefit their country, I don't know why else they would have done it. They could have been sick also, I mean the only person who was really sick was Hitler, I don't think a lot of the other Germans were sick also.

Miss E. did not believe that German citizens in general were unaware of what took place inside the concentration camps. If she had been in their place, she thought that she might have fled the country. At the same time, she said:

But I don't know, if I were a German, how do you know I would think they were wrong... I don't know, if I were a German, I probably would have been led to believe that these people were taking away something from me and if somebody's taking something from you, you'd probably do anything to them.

Miss E. first association to Nazis was the following:

Blond hair and blue eyes, a fair-skinned person with blond hair and blue eyes. [What else comes to your mind?] Stern, like their language is so gutteral that I can't, it's just not a nice language. [Is blond hair pleasing or displeasing?] Well, blond hair and blue eyes and dark skin is very pleasing, but blond hair and blue eyes and fair skin isn't, I mean I have nothing against, but they're not attractive to me. I like dark skin.

Miss E. explicitly rejected any identification of herself with survivorhood. When asked if having been a child of a survivor had affected who she was, she responded "No." She did say, however, that she would tell her own children that her father had been in a concentration camp. She explained, "Because you should know about your grandparents, you have to tell them a little bit."

Before the time of the interview, Miss E. had never had a conversation about the Holocaust with anyone. Not only had she never sought out books and movies about the Holocaust, she had consciously avoided them. For example, she said, "Isn't there a movie out now about Hitler? [Yes] I wouldn't see it."

Miss E. reported that she had never had, even during her childhood, any thoughts about Nazis or concentration camps. However, she was named after her father's mother. When asked if she had ever thought about the relatives her father had lost, she said: "Yeah, of course, I wonder what they would have been like and where they would live, and I feel awful because it's terrible when you lose somebody that's close to you."

Miss E. was asked if she thought that she would have survived incarceration in a concentration camp. In responding to the question, she indicated an identification of herself that seemed antithetical to the identity of being a child of a survivor. She said:

Oh, I wouldn't have. I can't live without every little thing being perfect. [What do you mean?] Well, I need all the comforts and conveniences. I couldn't survive without eating, without bathrooms.... I'm a J.A.P. [i.e., Jewish American Princess]. You know what a J.A.P. is? [Yeah] Well that's what I am. [What does that term mean to you?] Well, it means I'm a princess, and I need all the conveniences a princess needs.

Discussion

The data provided by Miss E. were more fragmentary than those provided by either Miss A. or Mr. B. Where they participated in the task of exploration, she persistently avoided it. The problem of understanding the lives of Miss A. and Mr. B. involved understanding the clinical material they provided. The problem of understanding Miss E.'s life required understanding her spontaneous denials.

Miss E. described a distant relationship to her parents. However, in her very denial of an intimate relationship with them was the clue to a symbiotic relationship with them. Her self-object differentiation was so limited that she was not able to describe, or perhaps even experience, her parents' characters. Evidence of the symbiotic bond between her and her mother was her repeated attribution to her mother of knowledge of early childhood memories that she herself did not have. It was as if the fact that her mother "knew" made it unnecessary for her to find out or remember. Miss E. seemed to be at least somewhat aware that her concern about food (which will be discussed below in another context) and cleanliness resembled her father's concerns. However, she was not at all aware that her portrayal of herself as always "busy" mirrored her father's portrayal of himself. Aspects of Miss E.'s relationship with her parents may have been replicated in her symbiotic bond to her friend, Judy, which was cemented by their common distrust of the rest of the world.

Miss E.'s spontaneous denial that, in their relationship with her, her parents manifested intrusion, anger, criticism, or control raises the hypotheses that they controlled her to the extent that she was not allowed to call attention to it. Her picture of herself as the daughter who was always "good" and obedient to parents who never demanded obedience suggests that her adaptation to their control was through symbiotic compliance. That is, she took on her parents' wishes as if they were her own. Her decision to attend a local college was one example of her symbiotic compliance.

Implicit in Miss E.'s denial of her parents' aggressive impulses toward her was the denial of her aggressive impulses toward them. The depth of Miss E.'s aggressive impulses was revealed by two characteristics of her relationship to men. These must be regarded as transferential. First, she was exceedingly contemptuous and abusive toward them. Her idea that a boyfriend she had broken up with was "never the same afterwards" contains her fantasy of her own destructiveness. Second, her positive experience of her present boyfriend was based on the fact that, although she tested him, he did not allow her to abuse him. That is, her attraction to him was based on his ability to set limits on her aggression.

There is also evidence that Miss E. identified with Nazi aggression. For example, when asked to put herself in the position of German citizens, she justified Nazi activity. She said that "if somebody's taking something from you, you'd probably do anything to them." In addition, her first association to Nazism suggested an ambivalent attraction to the physical characteristics, the "blond hair and blue eyes," of Nazis. Further, her calling herself a J.A.P.

involves an unconscious pun on *Jap,* which is a derogatory term for the Japanese who were allies of the Germans.

In this context, Miss E.'s extreme need to avoid knowledge of her father's persecution becomes understandable. Although she might have consciously denied it, it was clear by the way she described it that she enjoyed her fantasy of having been so destructive to her former boyfriend. That is, she enjoyed being a Nazi to someone who represented her father. Thus, Miss E.'s inability to listen to her father describe what the Nazis did to him was in the service of denying her own identification with Nazi aggression.

Concomitant to Miss E.'s phobic response to her father's communications about his concentration camp experiences was her need to consciously deny the importance to her identity of the European past. It nevertheless hovered over her like the warplane in the sky of her dream from her ninth year. One may speculate that Miss E.'s earliest memory, of being in a new car which was "stuck," symbolized the predicament of having to make the transition from the past to the new world. The fact that she remembered the experience as "fun" was a manifestation of her most typical defense. The same is true of the positive feelings she avowed in her dream of bringing something through customs. It was significant that her one association to the dream was of returning from Europe. Although she could not remember what she was bringing through customs, one implication of going through customs is having something to hide and being fearful of discovery. The final vestige of affiliation to the past in Miss E.'s life was her habit of "saving everything." One possible interpretation of this habit is that it represented a wish, opposed by an intense need to deny the wish, of keeping the past alive.

Another interpretation of Miss E.'s habit of saving things was that it reflected her profound feelings of deprivation and her need to guard all of her supplies. Some indication of her neediness was suggested by her having decided to become a teacher on the basis of her love for her kindergarten teacher. The persistence of the memory of that teacher over so many years, in a person whose memory for her past was so limited, is sad evidence to the fact that she loved and felt loved by few people in her life. It is therefore not surprising that a thread of food imagery ran through the interview. Miss E. described her father's preoccupation that food was tainted and his comparison of American food to the pure food of his European childhood. She also indicated that she shared his beliefs about food prepared outside the home. She reported her inability to listen to her father describe having been deprived of food and her own concern with the quality of the food she would eat when she visited Europe. The concern with food she manifested, while also an identification with her father, betrayed her own profound oral deprivation. Her inability to experience consciously her own deprivation was reflected in her inability to acknowledge the extent of her father's suffering.

One must ask the question: Why did a girl who felt so deprived adopt for herself the conscious identity of a Jewish American Princess? At one level, Miss E.'s identity as a princess was clearly an attempt to compensate for her feelings of deprivation. At the same time, one must note her comment that she had no free time because, among other things, she was busy "going out" on dates. One inference that may be drawn is that "going out," while congruent with the behavior of a princess, was quite a burden on her. If it is remembered that the only desire Miss E.'s parents had for her was that she be happy, and that throughout the course of the interview, she attempted to prove that she was happy and "self-actualized," it becomes evident that Miss E. had to be a princess. That is, being a Jewish American Princess represented her fulfillment of a symbiotic parental demand to experience her happiness vicariously.

Part of being a princess involves adorning oneself with clothes and admiring one's body. One core dynamic of Miss E.'s character was her body narcissism. Her cathexis of her body was revealed by her greeting the interviewer in a bikini, her heavy use of make-up and concern for clothes, and finally her attraction to others solely on the basis of their physical beauty.

The explanation that Miss E. maintained of her father's survival was that he had had the youth and the physical strength to endure. That is, he survived because his body was intact before he entered the camp. It may be inferred that Miss E.'s body narcissism, which in part was determined by her perception of her father's survival, also was fostered by her explanation of his survivorhood. Miss E.'s construction of her father's survivorhood led her to the identity of a princess which constituted her own strategy for survivorhood in her world.

Miss E.'s idea that she could not have survived the concentration camps because she was a princess whose survival was dependent on being pampered was her way of denying her fear of being persecuted as was her father. Although she consciously denied any identification with the events of her father's past, the basis of her identity as a Jewish American Princess was an adaptation to that past. It further constituted a survival strategy for the present based on the images of the past. Her views of people and the world were also framed by issues of survivorhood. For example, she believed that people exploited each other and were capable of creating another Holocaust because they were "crazy." Concomitantly, she betrayed a lack of allegiance to any idea or institution. Like a homeless survivor, she had no ties to the country in which she found herself, and was willing to emigrate to anywhere that suited her better. Her own perceived status as a member of a "minority" left her without resources to empathize with the suffering of other groups of people. Further, she believed that the world was governed by fate. Although justified by autistic logic, her belief in the power of fate reflected her feelings of helplessness in the face of indifferently malign and overwhelming forces.

Miss E. was a survivor of traumatic images from the past as well as from her family's dynamics. When asked about the subsequent effects of concentration camp experience on survivors, she said, "Some people could put it out of their minds." Her statement recalls her driven "happiness" and her primary defense of denial. That is, Miss E. attributed to survivors and adopted for herself the same strategy for continued psychological survival.

10

Discussion

So in this new event we see
New forms of terror working through the blind,
Or else inscrutable destiny.
I am not one to say 'This is vain'
Of anything allotted to mankind.
Though some must fall, or fall to rise again,
Time watches all things steadily—

[Sophocles, *Oedipus at Colonus*]

In considering the data generated during the course of this inquiry, it must be remembered that none of the 20 interviews took place in an emotionally neutral situation. On the contrary, it may be inferred that each subject consented to participate in the study in order to satisfy some personal need. For some subjects, the interview represented an opportunity to support their already established defensive structure. For others, the interview represented an opportunity for self-discovery and expression of highly charged feelings. The investigator, throughout the course of the study, was aware of his role as a participant-observer and the needs he brought to the study as well as the intense emotions he experienced as he conducted it.

Summary of Findings

All subjects had known of their parents' survivorhood for as long as they could remember. Not one subject could remember a time he did not have at least a dim awareness of his parents' experiences of persecution. Although a few subjects had learned the exact chronology of their parents' lives, most subjects had only fragmentary knowledge of isolated details. There were a few subjects who did not know anything about their parents' experiences beyond the fact that they had been in a Nazi concentration or slave labor camp. Not one subject's description of his parents' experiences approached the horrifying portrayals which are readily available in the literature that has arisen out of the Holocaust.

The quality and range of parents' communications about their lives before migrating to the United States, as reported by subjects, was extremely varied and broad. Some parents had withheld all information about their experiences in the past, while others had constantly harangued their children with accounts of their past from very early in their children's lives. However, even those parents who very extensively communicated to their children about the past tended to repeat the same stories; and very few parents provided their children with a coherent picture of their lives before and during the Holocaust. In some cases, children accidently learned critical information, such as the fact that a parent had been previously married, or that their real mother had died in childbirth, at which time the father had immediately remarried. The emotions accompanying parents' accounts ranged from emotionlessness to agitation, and from obsessive involvement with particular detail to clear discomfort with the process of communicating. Parents also found indirect means of communicating their experiences to their children. These included speaking to visitors about the past in the presence of the children and leaving mementos and documents where the children could find them.

Different parents' accounts of the past centered around different themes. The general themes of these accounts included the following: (1) the world they had lost; (2) denial of any culpability and affirmation of their personal virtue while they were camp inmates; (3) the suffering and deprivation which they endured; (4) descriptions of their escapes from death and their modes of survival; and (5) the general capriciousness of life. In addition to their parents' accounts, subjects had access to the events of the Holocaust through different cultural media such as television, movies and documentaries, novels, and even comic books. In later life, a few children of survivors visited the sites of actual concentration camps.

Subjects' immediate responses to their parents' accounts included isolation of affect, denial, horror, guilt, anger at the world, and anger at their parents for subjecting them to the horrors of the past. Some subjects reported that their parents' accounts had precipitated various kinds of fantasies in them. It was not possible to determine if fantasies had been precipitated and then repressed in the other subjects. Almost all subjects indicated a desire to learn more about the Holocaust in general or the details of the parents' past lives in particular. Some subjects were concerned about specific aspects of their parents' experiences, such as crimes parents may have committed in concentration camps and specific abuses inflicted on them. Most subjects were extremely hesitant to question their parents directly and seemed to feel that to do so might cause their parents pain.

A final response to parents' accounts of their experiences involved altered reactions to and perceptions of parents. Some subjects reported that knowledge of their parents' suffering was very painful for them and produced in them a need to distance themselves. Many subjects indicated that they felt sympathetic to their parents and tolerant of their parents' faults, and also obligated to their parents because of their knowledge of their parents' hardships. At the same time that many subjects were in awe of their parents' ability to endure in the face of the seeming overwhelming conditions of the concentration camps, subtle evidence existed that some subjects' knowledge of their parents' survivorhood produced negative feelings about their parents. Such feelings seemed to be a product of unconscious fantasies of shameful acts committed by parents during their incarceration.

Although the manner in which subjects described their parents ranged from idealized portrayals to almost total condemnations (with most subjects tending toward denying negative feelings and perceptions of their parents), certain themes emerged as characteristic of parent-child relationships. These themes were the unavailability of parents for their children's emotional needs, the extremely controlling and overprotective behavior of parents, the induction of guilt feelings in children, and extreme—though denied— aggressive feelings of parents toward their children. Each of these themes was emphasized to different extents in subjects' descriptions of their relationships to their parents and reports of interactions with their parents.

The most outstanding feature of all subjects' reports was the parents' inhibition of their children's separation. Parents inhibited separation by cueing for symbiosis, communicating the idea that the only thing of value left in their lives was the children, living vicariously through the children, and imposing their own attitudes and beliefs about the world on the children. The positive aspects of the parent-child relationships were that no subject doubted his parents' love and that all subjects saw their parents as consciously having their best interests in mind.

Subjects' conscious beliefs about the impact of having been children of survivors on their lives ranged from those who felt that it had had a shaping influence on them to those who denied that it had had any impact at all. However, the importance of the Holocaust to all subjects was manifested by thoughts and behaviors. The Holocaust also clearly provided a source of unconscious symbolism for many subjects. In addition, although subjects' political and social attitudes were quite diverse, the influence of the Holocaust on them could be identified. The most important finding was that the imagery of the past (integrated differently by each individual) provided a central organizing principle for the present interactions with the world of children of survivors.

No character type emerged which could be described as typical of children of survivors. On the contrary, subjects were quite different from one another, and the diagnostic range encompassed by subjects was from exceptionally well-functioning individuals to those with serious problems in living. Nevertheless, certain dynamic themes may be identified as characteristic of the sample. All subjects had extreme difficulties in achieving separation and individuation. Many subjects had profound interpersonal difficulties which were manifested by their isolation from others, basic mistrust, and fears of mergence. Other themes which were prominent in many subjects were conflicts over anger, the need to be in control and fear of losing control, shame, grandiosity, sibling rivalry, inhibition of gratification of impulses, guilt, fearfulness, and representation of self as victim. The most prevalent symptom reported was depression.

Two Frameworks for Understanding the Data

Two alternative approaches can be used as frameworks for understanding the lives of children of survivors. The first is an approach based on constructing the reality of children of survivors in terms of causes and effects. This approach attempts to isolate the unique characteristics of children of survivors and then to define the specific factors which produced them. The advantage of this approach is that it allows the identification of the critical influences, if any, in the lives of children of survivors. It also allows the assignment of relative weights to the different influences observed. This approach also insists that the unique characteristics, that is, effects, of having been subject to these influences, be defined. Other investigators (e.g., Aleksandrowicz, 1973; Sigal et al., 1973; Rustin, 1968) using this approach have had difficulty establishing the differences of children of survivors from control groups. The disadvantage of this approach is that, when consistent correlations between specified causes and hypothesized effects fail to appear, it may be assumed that no relationship exists when, in fact, a compelling but exceedingly complex relationship exists.

The second approach to understanding the lives of children of survivors involves describing influences in their lives and the outcomes of these influences in terms of "a mutual, reverberating process occurring in a system of relations" [Spiegel, 1971, p. 29]. Using the model proposed by Spiegel, children of survivors can be studied from the point of view of a transactional field in which, in place of the attempt to isolate factors, all factors are considered to be interdependent. Because they exist "in functional relation to all others in an inclusive system of relationships" [p. 41], no factor may be omitted without destroying the whole field. Spiegel identified what he termed the "foci" of a transactional field. These are: universe, culture, society, group, psyche, and soma. The advantages of the transactional approach are: (1) that the complexity of the lives of children of survivors is maintained rather than simplified and thus distorted; (2) that in choosing to focus attention on any part of the field, an awareness is maintained of its interaction with other foci; (3) that artificial distinctions between the intersection of the experience of children of survivors with others are avoided; and (4) that the lives of children of survivors may be examined in terms of an ongoing process rather than as a static entity.

Influences

Five influences in the lives of children of survivors will be discussed. These are the children's knowledge of their parents' experiences, the quality of the parent-child relationships in survivor families, the heritage of Jewish tradition, the disruption of the cycle of generations and the position of children of survivors as they are caught between the forms of their parents' European past and their own present American reality, and the existential framework imposed by the Holocaust.

The Influence of Knowledge of Parents' Experiences

The knowledge that their parents had survived the Holocaust is the first influence to be considered in the lives of children of survivors. However, although all children of survivors shared this knowledge from as early an age as they could remember, the specific details they knew and their comprehension of the range of parental experiences entailed by having survived varied greatly. Indeed, it would be as accurate to say that children of survivors shared a wondering about the mysteries of suffering during the Holocaust rather than to say they shared knowledge of it. One may speculate that the importance of that wonder to their later development was equal to the importance that has been attributed to children's wondering about the consequences of touching "forbidden" areas of their bodies, and why boys are different from girls, and what goes on in their parents' bedroom after the doors are closed.

In considering the impact of the knowledge and wonder about the concentration camps, it must be remembered that parents' styles of communicating to their children were very different. Some children pursued their interest in their parents' experience, and others denied it, as parental attitudes toward that wonder ranged from overt attempts to encourage it to expressed desires that the children suppress it. In spite of the modes of communication and the emotions accompanying them which were used by parents, it is clear that all parents were deeply ambivalent about allowing their children to participate in the knowledge of their past lives. On the one hand, sharing the past meant re-evoking painful memories. On the other hand, it may be assumed that parents desperately needed to share their suffering and insure the continuity of their own lives by making their children privy to the events which so changed them and from which some dated the beginning of their lives. No matter which side of the ambivalence a parent favored or the intensity of the double messages a parent communicated, the family functioned in the aura of the historical past.

In being exposed to the Holocaust, children of survivors were exposed to nothing less than the stress of having to confront a cataclysm. In contrasting the Holocaust to other destructive events of great magnitude, Luchterhand (1971) wrote that "as the source of stress shifts from indiscriminate violence by nature to the discriminate oppression by man, the damage to human personality becomes less remediable" [p. 47].

Any one of the details of persecution, the uprooting in space and time, the loss of loved ones, the physical hardships and brutalities, the assault on human dignity, is so intrinsically horrifying that even the adult ego of those removed from the event must mobilize all of its resources to protect itself. Any of the many questions which are provoked by the details which have been omitted is sufficient to generate nightmarish fantasies in anyone. For these children, whose parents were still living with the scars of the Holocaust, the knowledge of the past must be considered to have been traumatic. For some of them (for example, the subject who discovered photographs of emaciated bodies in an album of her baby pictures) the trauma was as direct as the "acute shock trauma" [Niederland, 1971, p. 3] of a child who has witnessed a "primal scene" or who has been abused by a trusted adult. However, all of them were subject to what may be called "cumulative" [Niederland, 1971, p. 4] or chronic "strain trauma" [Sandler, 1967, p. 168]. In other words, the constant, stressful presence of concentration camp imagery and evidence of their parents' past suffering constituted a prolonged, day-by-day exposure to a series of experiences, none of which in itself may have been traumatic but which combined to produce a traumatic effect.

An additional aspect of the children's traumatization was their exposure to their parents' state of having been traumatized. Greenacre (1967) wrote:

> Severe trauma, either as acute occurrences or as chronic states in those close to the child,...may be experienced directly almost as though happening to him....Conditions in later life that re-arouse these demonic repetitions,...sometimes may be of a slight and fortuitously experienced variety, but not infrequently they may consist in the occurrence of events that directly stimulate fear for survival of those close to the individual, even though he himself may be personally exempt from danger. But perhaps most common of all is the situation in which the healing over of the original disturbance has not furnished even fairly good protection and there is marked repetition in which the demon is...constantly active...[p. 151].

That is to say, exposure to their parents' state of having been traumatized was, for at least some children of survivors, psychologically close to their having been in a concentration camp themselves.

A further aspect of survivors' children's traumatization is that the imagery of the Holocaust which derived from real events may be also regarded as a point of intersection between reality and the primary process. That is to say, the imagery of the Holocaust existed in the unconscious before the occurrence of the Holocaust. For example, the image of the end of the world, whether by cataclysm or destruction of every reference point of a way of life, is common to many psychotics. The terror of complete helplessness is symbolized by the image of the concentration camp inmate, as is the position of being totally abandoned and alone in an implacably hostile world. And what better representation than a concentration camp of the ancient Biblical vision of being doomed to hell in punishment for real and imagined sins? Thus, one can regard the imagery of the Holocaust as a confirmation, in reality, of primitive, dreaded themes of unconscious life.

It may be speculated that second-generation concentration camp traumatization had an impact on different areas of character development. In considering the impact of trauma on development, it must be remembered that trauma may influence phase-specific issues as its occurrence coincides with the times those issues first appear. Or, if the trauma appears in the life of the child at a time subsequent to the end of a particular phase, it may revive the issues of that stage.

Several examples of the impact of second-generation concentration camp traumatization on development will be given. Basic trust, as it emerges or is impaired during infancy, is certainly influenced by the sequelae of massive trauma in the mother, as her capacity for childrearing is affected and her anxiety is communicated to the infant. As basic trust is elaborated in subsequent stages of development, it is vulnerable to the images of a seemingly stable world which, for no understandable reason, was invaded by Nazi demons and then destroyed. The second stage, to which Erikson (1963) attributed the conflict of autonomy versus shame and doubt, is vulnerable as the institutional expression of that stage, namely law and order (Erikson, 1963), is seen to have been overwhelmed by chaos and sadistic caprice. Similarly, the vicissitudes of the Oedipal period, with its residual sadistic and masochistic features, are also vulnerable to the unconscious referents of the Holocaust. On the one hand, the fact that the parent has already been so devastated gives the child the fantasy of too easy a victory in the Oedipal competition. On the other hand, it may prevent him from competing by restricting his aggression.

The whole area of aggression is made more conflictual for children of survivors. Their aggressive impulses toward their parents are too easily confused with the deeds of the Nazi aggressors, and thereby the guilt associated with aggression is potentiated. Similarly, the range of punishments that may be anticipated include not only castration but also incarceration in a concentration camp. Finally, according to Jacobson (1964), the child needs the image of a strong parent who can protect him from his frightening aggressive wishes. The survivor parent confronts his child with the confirmation of the child's worst fantasies of the consequences of aggression. In reaction, the child may turn his aggressive wishes toward the parent against himself.

On the one hand, the child's identification with a survivor parent may reinforce infantile omnipotence as the child perceives those awe-inspiring qualities which allowed the parent to survive. If such an identification proceeds in the context of a parent-child relationship in which individuation is encouraged, self-esteem is fostered. However, if such identification proceeds in the context of a relationship in which the child is singled out for a special role in the life of his parents, grandiose strivings may occur. On the other hand, the child may identify with his parent as a victim. During the course of normal development, a process of devaluation of parents occurs. Jacobson (1964) wrote of the late pregenital period, "Oral, anal and genital forms of aggressive devaluation combine, and the child may experience his degraded love objects either as weak and empty, or as dirty and disgusting, or as destroyed and castrated" [p. 105]. According to Jacobson, the disillusionment of the child, because it stimulates reactive libidinal strivings, provides the incentive for the child's increasing idealization of his parents. The images of a parent's debasement and powerlessness during the Holocaust, which increasingly become more available as the child is exposed to various media, increasingly constitutes a component of the representation of the parent, and may make it more difficult to fight the devaluation of the parent with the support of idealizations. Thus it is not surprising to discover in survivors' children either excessive and inappropriate idealizations of their parents in later life or the maintenance in a few of them of an image of a totally worthless parent. However, the two main consequences of the devaluation of the object are the self's own narcissistic mortification and its cynicism about the world as, through the mechanism of successive incorporations and projections, the child's self-image assumes the characteristics of the object image and the object image assumes the characteristic of the self-image.

The Influence of Family Relationships

In chapter 4 the outstanding themes of parent-child relationships in survivor families were presented. The importance of parent-child relationship to personality is axiomatic: nothing less than basic character evolves from it. Two questions are raised immediately. The first is: To what extent are the themes of parent-child relationships in survivor families a result of the parents' experience of survivorhood? The second is: In what ways do the particular themes that were observed direct the development of children of survivors?

The survivor brought to his family not only the sequelae of persecution but also the remnants of the adaptation he had achieved prior to his incarceration. Even though all of the survivor parents represented in the sample did not come from the Eastern European *shtetl,* the family norms of the *shtetl* provide some basis for comparison to the patterns of interaction observed between survivor parents and their children. In their study of the *shtetl,* Zborowski and Herzog (1972) were able to reconstruct some of these family norms. They found that the foundation of the *shtetl* family was the unshakable conviction in the love and devotion of parents for their children. A mother's love was manifested by unremitting solicitude about every aspect of the child's welfare. Such love necessitated her intrusion into every aspect of the child's life. Parental love was also expressed by parents' unqualified willingness to sacrifice for the children. However, such sacrifice was "not shrouded in silence" [p. 294]. Rather, the children were constantly reminded of all the parents had sacrificed in their behalf as well as their willingness to give up their own lives for the children. A typical expression of parents, when any misfortune, no matter how great or small, befell the child, was, "O, it should have happened to me" [p. 294]. At the same time, the parents' vulnerability to pain caused by the children's actions was often used as a weapon. Children had rigidly defined obligations which proceeded directly from their role as extensions of the parents, and there was a strict prescription of their activities. Corporal punishment was an accepted mode of parental retaliation for children's misdeeds. Although babies were doted upon, children were rarely praised openly. Finally, the strength of family bonds was an unstated but defining assumption of family life; and a three generation household was the expectable family group.

The similarities between the patterns of the *shtetl* family and many of the themes observed in survivor families are striking. The most noteworthy of these are the inhibition of separation by direct pressure, the cueing for symbiosis, and the insistence on the child's obligations to parents. The features of parental intrusion, overprotectiveness, control, sacrifice, guilt induction, physical aggression, and withholding of praise are also quite similar. Even survivors' reticence to reveal their experiences of persecution recalls that in the *shtetl* children were almost grown before they discovered that brothers and sisters who had come before them had died in infancy.

However, there are significant contrasts. The first of these is that family life in the *shtetl* took place in the context of a closely knit community. The family life of survivor families, even those families which had resettled in exclusively Jewish-American communities, took place in the context of the families' isolation from others in everyday affairs. The extension of this contrast is that the *shtetl* family socialized its children for participation in a community, while the survivor family raised its children regardless of and often in opposition to the demands of the outside community.

In addition, on closer examination, many of the points of overlap between *shtetl* family norms and survivor family norms are misleading. For example, in the *shtetl*, the inhibition of separation was balanced by concomitant pressures for individuation in that even the very smallest child, sometimes children as young as five years, were expected to be responsible for themselves and to demonstrate competency in doing their part to support the family.

Finally, there are dramatic contrasts between the *shtetl* families and the families of children of survivors. For example, the parental education of children to the nature of the world, with its exclusive emphasis on the dangers and evils of the world and the parents' exhortations that the children guard all of their resources lest they be stolen, are in marked contrast to the *shtetl* values of generosity and charity. While all 20 subjects shared the implicit assumption of parental devotion, many survivor parents were restricted in their sensitivity to their childrens' emotional needs.

In attempting to define the impact of the Holocaust on the later relationships of its survivors to their children (granting the possibilities of predispositions in the parents' character), it is possible to identify some features of the parent-child relationships which are directly attributable to the impact of the Holocaust. For example, the free-floating rage which existed in survivor families is likely to have been directly derivative of the parents' trauma of persecution. However, other features of the parent-child relationships need to be understood in the context of having been built on the norms of the culture which existed before the Holocaust and on which the experience of persecution left an indelible mark.

Attempting to define the directions in which the themes that were observed in survivor families might be expected to shape the child is an exceedingly complex task. To do justice to it would require a separate study for each one of the themes which were identified. A more limited goal is to state the essential problems of survivor children in relation to their parents. That is, the parents had difficulty allowing the children to be separated from them because the children represented the parents' renewal of involvement in life. Thus the relationship between parents and children was predetermined by the parents' need to impose on the children the burden of restoring all that had been lost— relatives, aspirations, and a way of life—so that the parents could experience the possibility of a future for themselves.

At the same time, the parents themselves, because of the massive trauma that marked their existence, were left depleted and had difficulty satisfying the emotional needs of their children. Thus the position of children of survivors, as they proceeded through the normal stages of development, was to confront the burden of having to provide a vicarious existence for their parents at the same time that they adapted to their own deprivations. It is, therefore, no surprise that so many children of survivors found careers in the helping professions.

The Heritage of Jewish Culture

One cannot consider the impact of the Holocaust on children of survivors without looking at its context in Jewish culture. Although the values of their parents had been diluted by the destruction of their European referents and by their transplantation to the United States, the values still existed. Wolferstein (1957) points out that response to disaster is in part determined by cultural norms. Thus, in their very exposure to their parents' response to traumatization, children of survivors were also exposed to the culture of the past.

The central relevant dimension of Jewish cultural tradition in setting the background to children of survivors' response to the Holocaust was that it was consistent with 2,000 years of Jewish history. That is, Jewish culture evolved in the shadow of threat and persecution (Dimont, 1971; Grayzel, 1968). Several adaptations to this history of persecution are evident. The first is that the Jewish response to suffering has been to understand it as part of their special covenant with God (Wolferstein, 1957). The emphasis in Judaism has been on God's punishment of his "chosen people" for their sins (Frankenheim, 1970; Weisel, 1973; Zborowski & Herzog, 1972). Indeed, the intimate relationship between God and the suffering of the Jews is reflected in the traditional Hasidic song about the "law suit" initiated by the Rabbi Levi-Yitschok of Berditchev against God for having unjustly punished His people:

> Good morning to you, Lord of the Universe!
> I, Levi-Yitschok, son of Sarah, of Berditchev,
> Have come to You in a law suit
> On behalf of Your people Israel.
> What have You against Your people Israel?
> And why do You oppress Your people Israel?
> ....
> And I, Levi-Yitschok, son of Sarah, of Berditchev, say:
> ....I will not stir from here!
> An end there must be to this—it must all stop!
>
> [Zborowski & Herzog, 1972, p. 237.]

The second adaptation to the history of persecution derives from the perception of persecution as evidence of God's covenant with Israel. That is, pride and self-esteem for being among the chosen was mobilized as a means of coping with suffering. A consequent cathexis of suffering is also a possibility. In considering the context of children of survivors' adaptation to the Holocaust, Devereaux's (1970) comment is relevant:

> "Cultural materials" implements and reinforces psychological defenses. Culture also establishes a preferential hierarchy of the defenses and patterns them; the chief product of this process is the ethnic personality [p. 121].

One may speculate about an additional adaptation to the history of suffering. That is, the cohesiveness of individual Jewish communities and the universal adherence to the tenets of the Talmud (which prescribed in detail everyday behaviors) by communities spread all over the world by the diaspora was an adaptation to oppression. Taking the thought to its conclusion, one may speculate that the survival of Judaism, from the time of the destruction of the second temple, was enabled by the common suffering of the Jewish people. Thus, it is not surprising that several subjects mentioned in passing that the only reason they maintained an affiliation to Judaism was because of the Holocaust.

The Disruption of the Cycle of Generations

A fourth source of influence in the lives of children of survivors is the disruption of the cycle of generations. Y Gasset (1960) wrote:

> The son's generation is always a bit different from his father's: it represents a new level from which to savor existence. Ordinarily the difference between sons and fathers is small, so that what predominates is the common nucleus in which they coincide, and the sons can see themselves as containing and perfecting the type of life which their fathers led. But at times the distance between them is enormous: the new generation finds hardly any community of interest with the past. Then one speaks of a crisis in history [pp. 37-38].

The result of the Holocaust was to disrupt the generational continuity of Jewish culture, as one entire generation was wiped out and the survivors were uprooted. Erikson (1964) alludes to the consequences for children of survivors:

> The danger of any period of large-scale uprooting and transmigration is that exterior crises will, in too many individuals and generations, upset the hierarchy of developmental crises and their built-in correctives; and that man will lose those roots that must be planted firmly in meaningful life cycles [p. 96].

Before the Holocaust, Jewish culture was essentially what Mead (1970) called "postfigurative." That is, the survivors came from a world indelibly stamped with the cultural form of the absence of the realization of change. The postfigurative culture depends on the actual presence of three generations, the older ones providing a model for the way of life the younger ones could expect to lead. Mead (1966) wrote:

> As relevant characteristics of personality development in homogenous and slowly changing societies, we may identify: the sequential consistency between the experience of a growing child at one period and at another; the *summation* or total expression of the gamut of cultural experience in the behavior of the adult members of the society; the prefiguring of the future experience as the child sees others go through sequences through which he will later

go; the *consolidation* of past experiences as the growing individual sees younger individuals go through sequences culturally identical with those he has passed; and the increasing *automaticity* of behavior and the consequent increasing *sureness* which accompany maturation [p. 90].

Although there are other dynamic explanations, it is possible to understand, in this context, why so many subjects spontaneously spoke of having missed not having had grandparents.

One result of parents' transplantation to the United States was that they and their children were confronted by a culture that was essentially different. That is, in the United States, with its cofigurative elements, one finds "the prevailing model for members of society is the behavior of their contemporaries" [Mead, 1970, p. 25]. The position of survivors' children was to be caught between the simultaneous impacts of parents attempting to impose the old ways and the new demands of the world around them. The dilemma of survivors' children was the following: on the one hand, their parents' demands and prescriptions were inappropriate in the new world; on the other hand, adherence to the demands of the new culture precipitated the displeasure and condemnation of parents. Thus, caught between the two worlds, the children had difficulty giving their fidelity to either. The consequences are suggested by Erikson's (1964) comment: "To be a person, identical with oneself, presupposes a basic trust in one's origins—and the courage to emerge from them" [p. 95].

Existential Influences

A final source of influence in the lives of children of survivors may be termed existential. That is, in the intimate relationship of children of survivors to the Holocaust, the imagery of the Holocaust comes to provide visions of what is possible in human life. These range from the vision of the violation of the human order by human evil to the visions of courage, triumph, and the capacity for man's survival. In turn, those visions provide a framework for acting in the world. Those actions range from attempts to avoid confrontation with those visions, to the adoption of those visions as a justification for withdrawal of involvement with the world, to attempts to engage life with those affirmations of human worth which also have their place in the imagery of the Holocaust.

Consequences

After having defined the wide range of influences in the lives of children of survivors, it becomes necessary to consider their consequences. From the transactional point of view, each of the influences may be seen to have combined to shape the lives of the subjects. However, one must still wonder about these influences in terms of a coherent set of observations about their outcomes. Can such a set of observations be established? Can any observation be causally linked to specified influences? And can relative importance be assigned to influences, in terms of either their magnitude or contribution to the genesis of any observed characteristic? Three sets of observations will be discussed in terms of the influences which produced them. These are the diversity of the sample, the process of adaptation, and the use of metaphors and symbols from the past to reconstruct present reality (thus organizing personal identity).

Diversity

The first observation of the sample was the diversity of the individuals who comprised it. Although there were many observations which could logically be outcomes of the influences described, these observations do not form a coherent set. Rather, they cover a broad range and variety of characteristics.

Perhaps most surprisingly, not all subjects consciously experienced that having been children of survivors had affected them. Subjects varied greatly in the degree to which they experienced their status as children of survivors as being central to their conscious identity. Their reported reactions to their parents' accounts of their experiences varied. Similarly, although all subjects reported an alteration of their perception and of their relationship to their parents due to their background, these, too, encompassed a broad range.

Subjects' beliefs and attitudes about the events of the Holocaust also varied. Some described those beliefs in the context of their being ignorant about the Holocaust as a historical event while other subjects were "experts" on the Holocaust. Similarly, subjects varied along the dimension of immersion into Holocaust imagery and numbness to it. At one extreme, subjects reported frequent dreams and daytime fantasies about the Holocaust, while at the other extreme there were subjects who had clearly guarded against the intrusion of any Holocaust image into their consciousness or perceptual field. Some subjects clearly manifested thoughts and feelings which could be interpreted as second-generation survival guilt. No evidence of such guilt coud be observed in other subjects.

It might reasonably be expected that subjects would manifest sympathy, or at least a feeling of commonality, with other persecuted minority groups. In fact, though there were subjects for whom commitment to social justice was important to their identity, there were also subjects who explicitly stated that they could empathize only with other Jews. Similar diversity characterized subjects' general social beliefs and attitudes.

It might also be expected that subjects would, because of the stresses in their backgrounds, be vulnerable to psychiatric symptomatology. In fact, the diagnostic range of subjects was broad and, while there were subjects who suffered marked problems in living, there were also those who functioned at extremely high levels. Certain psychological conflicts and characterological themes are also expectable on the basis of the influences in the lives of children of survivors. Among these are (1) extreme difficulties with separation, based in part on the symbiotic demands of survivor parents; (2) exacerbated sibling rivalry, based in part on competition for the gratification deriving from the special importance of children to their parents; (3) exacerbated conflicts over anger and aggression, based in part on parents' vulnerability and the traumatic images of the consequences of aggression; (4) extreme mistrust of the world and others, based in part on the images of human evil implicit in the Holocaust and in part on early parental inconsistency deriving from the trauma of persecution; (5) a need for control, based in part on images of a world gone crazy; (6) inhibition of gratification and cathexis of suffering, based in part on identification with parents who suffered; and (7) grandiosity, based in part on identification with parents who portrayed awe-inspiring strength. However, none of these conflicts and themes is restricted to children of survivors; and not all of these themes were observed to be prominent in the lives of all subjects. Nor has it been demonstrated that any of these characteristics occur with greater frequency in children of survivors than they do in the general population. Indeed, it can be argued that all of the psychological issues observed in children of survivors are attributable to other causes.

What, then, can be made of these findings? First, it must be pointed out that the methodology used in this study did not allow for fine discriminations of causal connections: subjects were not strictly comparable on many influences. For example, it is possible only to speculate about differences in survivor children due to level of parents' pathology, the actual range of parents' experiences, survivorhood in both parents as compared to just the mother or just the father, parents' style of communication about their experiences, actual age a child was first confronted with traumatic imagery, the ratio of actual information known to a child to fantasies generated in him by unresolved questions, degree of involvement allowed to a child with outside influences, and a host of other significant formative experiences. Each of these variables is likely to have had significant impact on the lives of children of survivors. In addition, given the scope of this study, the use of control groups to isolate the impact of the five influences discussed was not feasible.

Second, it may be argued that the specific influences in the lives of children of survivors, which through the study of individual case histories may be demonstrated to have had a powerful effect, do not necessarily, and indeed would not be expected to, lead to the same outcomes in all persons. For example, Waelder (1967) pointed out that trauma may lead either to an autoplastic or an alloplastic adaptation. For Freud (Furst, 1967b) the traumatic potential of an event depended on constitutional predisposition, the state of the psychic apparatus, and the degree of relatedness to drive-cathected wishes and conflicts. Thus Furst (1967b) wrote, "A given stimulus may be traumatic for one individual but not for another; further, for a given individual, a stimulus that is traumatic at one time may be assimilated without being overwhelming at another" [p. 37]. Krystal (1971) wrote that trauma was always "initiated by the *psychic reality* [author's italics]—that is, the individual experience, interpreted, as it were, by the associations it provokes" [p. 11]. And Anna Freud (1965) wrote:

> Traumatic events should not be taken at their face value but should be translated into their specific meaning for the given child. Attributes such as heroism or cowardice, generosity or greed, rationality or irrationality have to be understood differently in different individuals, and judged in the light of their genetic roots, their phase and age adequateness, etc. Thus any of the elicited elements, although identical in name, may be totally different in significance in a different personality setting. [p. 139].

From another time perspective, Kris's (1950) observation that the significance of the traumatic event is determined by the further course in life is both consistent with the results of this study and pertinent to changes in observed traits over the course of an individual's life history.

Finally, in considering diversity as a characteristic of children of survivors as a group, it becomes clear that diversity in itself is a direct consequence of the influences in their lives. That is one might expect heterogeneity to characterize the sample precisely because of the nature of the influences described.

First and most obviously, the position of children of survivors in the cycle of generations (that is, being the first generation in a new world at the same time the parents try to pull them back into a world that has been murdered) imposes upon them conflicts and confusion. On the one hand, the diversity observed results from the interruption of historical continuity and the fragmentation of identity suffered by subjects who had been cut off from their moorings in the past and cast adrift. On the other hand, the consequences of contact with a new culture is that, according to Mead (1966) the outer world is reduced into "atomized meaningless units" [p. 97], and the child develops an approach to life which Mead called "situational" [p. 95].

Second, the Holocaust itself is an event of such magnitude that it does not have any common signification. That is, the diversity of consequences produced by the imagery of the Holocaust derives from the wide range of meanings implicit in that imagery. However, one image of the Holocaust may be selected for special attention. For example, one Holocaust theme is that human life takes place within a universe where anything is possible. In the words of one subject, "If the bomb fell tomorrow, I'd say, 'Yep, I knew it.' If the bombs didn't fall tomorrow, I'd say, 'Yep, I knew it.'"

One implication for identity may be found in Erikson's (1964) definition of identity formation:

> Identity formation... is a process based on a heightened cognition and emotional capacity to let oneself be identified as a circumscribed individual in relation to a predictable universe which transcends the circumstances of childhood. [p. 90].

That is, in the background of children of survivors, one of the criteria for the development of a stable identity—a predictable universe—is not met. However, from another point of view, Lifton (1971) has suggested that

> it is quite possible that even the image of personal identity, in so far as it suggests inner stability and sameness, is derived from a vision of traditional culture in which man's relationships to his institutions and symbols are still relatively intact—which is hardly the case today [p. 316].

Lifton went on to suggest the image of "Protean man" (who is constantly in a state of change) as a model for identity in an unpredictable universe. In these terms, the diversity manifested in the sample can be understood in terms of the flow of children of survivors in a state of continuous adaptation to the images of the Holocaust and the world around them. For example, the case of Miss A. portrayed her changing ideas about the Holocaust as well as a shifting cathexis of suffering as the Holocaust failed to be as adaptive for her as it once was.

The third source of diversity in the lives of children of survivors derives from the complexity of their relationships to their parents. While the Holocaust had a decisive impact on the family, the form taken by such impact varied. Further, themes common to families were integrated differently in each family. For example, the notion that it was up to the children to replace the losses parents endured by providing opportunities for vicarious fulfillment could be found to varying degrees in each family. Similarly, different families gave more of less latitude in the ways the child was required to compensate for hardships suffered by their parents.

The Process of Adaptation

In attempting to answer the questions about the relationships of children of survivors to the influences in their lives, the outcomes observed have to be considered in the context of their representing a process of adaptation. Put more strongly, the consequences of second-generation survivorhood are not specific traits or characteristics but the necessity of having to confront and resolve issues and conflicts. As an example the process of adaptation to traumatic imagery will be considered.

According to Sandler (1967), the traumatized ego "undertakes a series of maneuvers in order to accommodate itself to the state of strain, maneuvers that may be radical in nature and that may result in gross alterations in behavior or lead to the development of symptoms"[p. 168]. A range of such maneuvers was portrayed by the subjects. Some of them dealt with traumatic images by utilizing massive repression which then generalized from the ideas and affects produced by the trauma to produce rigid, constricted characters. Others portrayed the "psychic helplessness" [Rangel, 1967] of the traumatic state in their sometimes profound feelings of vulnerability and depression. Some subjects attempted to dispel anxiety-laden fantasies with extensive study of the Holocaust. Still others dealt with the trauma by attempting to master it through repetitions in dreams and fantasies—the manifest content of which revolved around Holocaust imagery—and through repetitions by placing themselves in situations in which they felt threatened or exploited. Some of these situations, such as participating in political demonstrations in which there was a likelihood of police attack, were obvious. Others were less obvious. Among these are the perception of people around them with deep mistrust and the attribution of malevolent intent to their motives. Extreme intimidation by anyone in authority is another example. Still other subjects engaged in masochistic behavior which may be regarded as an attempt at seduction of the aggressor in order to neutralize the threat. And others, for whom the course of trauma was determined by their own sadistic aims, can be seen to have become moral masochists, exquisitely sensitive to the power and evil of the world around them. Still others, for example the subject who reported that she was "possessed," dealt with their trauma by immersing themselves in the ideas and affects produced by it. These can be seen as manifesting what Rangel (1967) called the "tertiary gain of symptoms." That is,

> The disabling and ego-alien symptom becomes incorporated and integrated into the self... and is tenaciously guarded with narcissistic libido and interest. The disease itself comes to serve multiple psychic functions and becomes a needed element in the total psychic life situation. [p. 71].

A final mode of adaptation was to integrate the trauma for the purpose of self-actualization. One manner by which this was achieved was by considering and gaining insight into the ways in which having been children of survivors had affected them.

None of these adaptations was mutually exclusive. Further, the specific features of each adaptation must be considered in the light of future developments in the lives of the subjects. However, it is important that the fact that there are almost as many responses to trauma among subjects as there were subjects not lead one to overlook the following: the fact that all subjects responded in some way to their trauma in itself constitutes a coherent, generalizable finding about the group as a whole.

In considering the process of adaptation, the reverberating nature of the influences has to be considered. That is, influences can be seen to combine and interact. Their effects in turn modify the original influences, leading to more new combination.

For example, in the past, after a pogrom, the community rebuilt itself (Dimont, 1971; Grayzel, 1968), and behind the suffering and lamentations the community ethos remained intact as the fundamental order of the universe continued to be affirmed. The Talmud as an ever-elaborating set of laws which prescribed even the smallest of everyday behaviors remained an invisible government-in-exile. Its importance was manifested by the fact that the highest value in the Jewish community was its study (Zborowski & Herzog, 1972). Where the Talmud was transplanted with its authority intact, the community was rebuilt as it had been in ages past—for example the Jewish community of Williamsburg (Poll, 1969). While no children of survivors from Williamsburg were interviewed, it is safe to guess that whatever other themes they may have shared with the sample, their way of life continued the Eastern European Hasidic tradition. For them, the traumatic imagery of the Holocaust had its impact in a cohesive community, the boundaries of which were rigid. In contrast, the children of survivors who were in the sample were forced to face the outside world with at least attenuated felt membership in a community. The relative lack of religious affiliation of subjects is evidence of their different adaptations. Even though the cycle of generations was also disrupted in the Williamsburg community (that is, there were comparatively few elderly persons in the family), the Talmud effectively assumed their role and the norms of family life were guided by the same religious convictions and cultural traditions which had prevailed for centuries (Poll, 1969). Without benefit of concrete observation, it may be speculated that at least some of the themes of family relationships in Williamsburg—for example, inhibition of separation and parental control—are quite similar to themes observed in the sample. However, it may be assumed that the adaptation among children of survivors in Williamsburg to these similar family patterns led to outcomes different from those observed in the subjects of this study.

A similar example of the differences produced by different combinations of influences is that children of survivors who visited Israel reported having been upset by characteristics of Israeli youth. The attributes which they reported simultaneously disliking and envying (but not sharing) included arrogance and self-assurance, forcefulness, and the repudiation of suffering as a value. These emerged in a nation which itself may be considered to have been a child of a survivor. Among the factors having shaped the influence of the Holocaust on Israel—which, according to Elon (1972), goes to the root of

Israeli life—are the availability of institutions which commemorate the Holocaust and thus provide cathartic relief, and the education of even the very young by providing a fully realistic picture of conditions in the concentration camps. Another influence is that the Arab-Israeli wars may provide an opportunity to master the trauma of the Holocaust by reliving it. Elon reported that in their courses on the Holocaust, "The incredulous reaction of some school children is to ask: 'Yes, but why didn't our army come to the rescue?'" [p. 272]. As a major difference between Israeli youth and the American-born children of survivors is that suspicions of cowardice and weakness in the victims and feelings of shame about the position of the victims exist openly in the former and tend to be repressed in the latter.

Another example of the reverberation of influences is that of the changes that took place as subjects in the present study attained separation from their families. It was the investigator's impression that increased separation led to increasing shifts away from the attitude that the family was the only safe haven in a world that was to be regarded as actively malevolent. It also led to attenuation of conflicts over anger and increasingly freed aggressive energy for creative initiative. Increased separation also seemed to lead to greater trust, evolving beliefs about the nature of the world and the meaning of the Holocaust; and it seemed that investment in certain beliefs, such as that the Holocaust was a unique event in history, declined. Finally, it was the investigator's impression that increased separation generally led to an increased capacity to empathize with the suffering of other groups based on the historical lessons of the Holocaust.

Finally, any given obervation may be a product of the convergence of influences; that is, any given outcome may be a result of many different influences, all of which are present. For example, mistrust may derive from inconsistencies in mothering during infancy, but may also derive from a transformation of anger which is experienced as a forbidden affect and which is then projected on the outside world. Mistrust may also be produced by images of an unstable world which are then reinforced by parents' warnings about the nature of the world. It may also be a product of inconsistencies in cultural values that are made more apparent as the child is caught between two cultures. Finally, as the child lives in a time defined by such manifestations of governmental deceit as Vietnam and Watergate, this trait may be cemented. Thus, mistrust observed in a subject may have derived from any or all of these influences. However, it is also necessary to note an error which is too easily made. That is, an observation may be interpreted from the point of view of one influence when, if fact, it belongs to another. For example, an excessive need to control, when observed in many American children, may be linked to the prevailing American value of subjugation of the environment. The same need to control, when observed in a child of a survivor, may be linked to a need to restore order to a world, which, in the words of one subject, went "whacky."

The Present Experiences through the Past

Although a number of outcomes have been defined, the outcome that is most central to this study's task of confronting the Holocaust as a psychohistorical event is that no subject, regardless of character organization or extent of conscious acknowledgment of the impact of the Holocaust on present identity, escaped the presence of Holocaust imagery as a means of constructing his experience.

The means by which subjects adopted the imagery of the Holocaust included using it as a source of instruction about the nature of the world, defining their status *vis-á-vis* others by defining themselves as children of survivors, and representing Holocaust images in dreams and daytime fantasies. In some subjects' descriptions of their thoughts about the Holocaust, they could be seen to be using the images from the past as symbols through which they expressed their own intrapsychic reality. For example, Nazis and Jews could be seen as becoming the unconscious symbols for their relationship to their parents. As other subjects described their thoughts and attitudes about present-day events, the imprint of the past could be perceived. For example, one subject compared his coming to regard cadavers without distress during the course of his medical studies to the German's increasing ability to commit the atrocities of the Holocaust. For other subjects, seemingly unrelated aspects of their lives were also seen to have a referent in the Holocaust. For example, for one subject the prospect of losing a job filled her with terror because it re-evoked the image of the tenuousness of her parents' past existence. For another subject, education became "something they can't take away from you."

Often behaviors in the subjects' own lives could be seen to be linked, sometimes out of the subjects' awareness, to events in their parents' lives. For example, one subject was an amateur musician; and although she was dissatisfied with any of the career choices that seemed open to her, she had foreclosed the possibility of seeking a vocation in music. Her understanding of her mother's experiences in the concentration camp was represented by one image. The first time her mother (who had also been a musician) realized the enormity of the horror that was to engulf her was when a guard who greeted her arrival to the camp took her one possession, a violin, and smashed it. The subject could be seen to have adopted a strategy for survival in her world based on magically undoing an image of the past by not becoming a musician. Other subjects could be seen to have adopted the very strategy for survival that they presumed enabled their parents to survive.

As certain subjects denied the role of the Holocaust in their lives, they could be seen to have maintained, in translated form, the psychic reality their parents had brought from the concentration camps. They revealed clear and compelling Holocaust imagery while describing their worst fantasies. As one subject denied the role of the Holocaust in his life, and insisted on his "distance" from it, he revealed that he had been drawn, as if by a magnet, to visit the site of a concentration camp.

For children of survivors, Holocaust imagery provided a vehicle, a series of metaphors, through which they could express their deepest conscious and unconscious concerns. But even more importantly, images synthesized from external history by internal processes and mediated through cultural experience, served to uniquely organize each individual's interaction with the world.

The Holocaust as a Problem or a Solution

Up to this point, the lives of children of survivors have been presented in the context of the problems posed to them by their common heritage. However, there is also evidence to support another point of view. That is, the historical past can be seen as providing a series of solutions to problems and needs deriving from other sources.

For example, the perception of parents' past sufferings can be seen as providing subjects with a basis for rationalizing their own inability to confront issues in their relationships with their parents. Thus, some subjects explained that they had never taken the developmental step of moving out of their parents' homes because they were loathe to cause further distress to their parents. By using the past in this way, they abdicated their own responsibility to confront their dependency needs and their own fearful hesitation to complete the task of individuation. Similarly, some subjects insisted that they had denied the press of their own interests as they consciously refrained from asking their parents about their experiences. They explained that they wanted to avoid re-evoking their parents' painful memories. However, with this explanation, they refused to confront their own fears of the painful knowledge they consciously desired to seek.

Subjects may also be seen to have utilized the Holocaust and their status as children of survivors as a technique for resolving their interpersonal difficulties. For example, one subject who condemned her peers because they failed to show the response of awe and horror to the Holocaust that she deemed appropriate can be seen as using her investment in the Holocaust as the means by which she justified and avoided confronting her isolation from and fear of others. Other subjects can be seen as using their affiliation with suffering in order to assert their moral superiority over others at the same time that they escaped any necessity of feeling moral obligation to others.

Perhaps the single most powerful solution offered by the Holocaust is that it fostered the use of projection as a mechanism of defense against ego-alien thoughts and feelings. That is, the process of the attribution of one's own most frightful thoughts and feelings to the outside world was bolstered by a reality in which thoughts became action.

Two Models of Psychohistory

In a review of Lifton's (1973) *Home from the War*, Liebert (1974) compared the approaches to psychohistory of Lifton and Freud. Liebert suggested that the model provided by *Oedipus the King* defined Freud's approach. In that play, Oedipus presumes to exert control over his fate. Because the future is preordained, his efforts lead inexorably to the crimes he commits, and to the blindness and exile which are his punishment. Thus, for Freud, the course of human life has already been prescribed by an individual's personal, biological, and historical past, and its tragic finale cannot be eluded.

Liebert suggested that the contrasting model provided by *Oedipus at Colonus* is closer to Lifton's views. In that play, after his years of wandering in exile, Oedipus at last arrives at Colonus. Perhaps because he has expiated his crimes, or perhaps because of his basic nobility, he is given sanctuary. In his death, he becomes the patron and preserver of Athens. Thus, for Lifton, not only can man be redeemed after his tragic fall, he may become triumphant.

The lives of the 20 psychohistorical figures on which this study was based, and in which broad historical events are seen to have been integrated into their intrapsychic, intrafamilial, and intracultural experiences, can be seen as providing evidence which confirms both models. Not only do different individuals appear to meet the criteria of each model, but particular features within their individual lives meet both models. The resolutions of these individuals of the problems of living in their present under the shadow of the past include: closing themselves off from the events of their world in what might be called a schizoid resolution; attempting to secure their lives by exploiting the environment, in what might be called a manipulative resolution; succumbing to personal suffering and feelings of helplessness, in what might be called a depressed resolution; withholding allegiance to any ideology beyond a generalized mistrusting stance, in what might be called a paranoid resolution; refighting the battles of the past by immersion into Jewish nationalism, in what might be called a militaristic resolution; engaging in acts which affirm the capacity of people to triumph over evil and injustice, in what might be called a heroic solution; and attempting to understand the meaning of the past for their present reality, in what might be called a contemplative resolution. Each of these resolutions has features which fit at least one and, in some cases, both models. Many influences form the choice of the resolution that any individual may adopt, but all individuals have attempted more than one.

In reviewing the characteristics of this group of children of survivors, one finds a number of confirmations of the model that *Oedipus the King* provides. These are apparent in that the heritage of the Holocaust directed psychological conflicts and potentiated impairment as subjects portrayed symbiotic ties to their parents, an extreme vulnerability to loss and the disruption of the capacity to form attachments, basic mistrust, and a pathological need to control.

However, one finds the model of *Oedipus at Colonus* tending to be confirmed in that individuals came to understand their parents and find meaning in their parents' experiences while they themselves maintained the right to their own separate existence. The *Oedipus at Colonus* model is confirmed again in that individuals became able to form ties with other people around them as they became increasingly able to trust, and discovered their capacity to master. Similarly, as aggression was too frightening to manage or became projected, and guilt activated the harsh oppression of the superego, the vision of *Oedipus the King* was sustained. But as aggression was freed without destructive consequences, and as it was transformed into initiative and—to use Lifton's (1973) term—guilt "animated" the individual to constructive action, the vision of *Oedipus at Colonus* was sustained. One also sees echoes of *Oedipus the King* in that individuals identified with either victim or aggressor. Consistent with *Oedipus at Colonus* individuals appreciated the complexity of human nature, the fact that people's capacity for evil coincides with their capacity for sacrifice and endurance, and, that each of these possibilities existed within themselves as well. As individuals had to numb themselves to the Holocaust, acted in the present as if they were living in a concentration camp, or brought from the past the justification for withholding fidelity to values and beliefs, and as they became rooted in a despairing vision of human life, they could be seen to reflect the universe of *Oedipus the King*. Alternatively, as they were able to open themselves up to the imagery of the Holocaust without being engulfed by it, as they drew into their lives a consciousness of the past without surrendering their present, as they brought from the past a richness of meaning from which their present values could emerge, and as their vision of life included hope, they reflected the universe of *Oedipus at Colonus*.

One final characterisic along which these 20 children of survivors supported one of the two models of psychohistory was their use of their relationship to the Holocaust as a boundary between themselves and others. For some, being children of survivors led to closing themselves off from further participation in the human community. For others, being children of survivors led to a feeling of shared experiences as they empathized with the suffering of others and, more importantly, used the self-awareness gained from studying themselves as children of survivors to perceive their essential kinship with others who also lived their lives in a world marked by the Holocaust.

Upon considering the dimension—defined on the one hand by the degree to which the Holocaust (by framing their existence) served to isolate children of survivors from others, and, on the other hand, the degree to which the Holocaust was an event that frames these times and thus unites people in their shared consciousness of it—the last question to be addressed in this study is raised. That is, to whom does the Holocaust belong? In his discussion of what he so eloquently called "the commanding voice of Auschwitz," the Jewish theologian Emile Frankenheim (1970) referred to the "affront" of suggestions that Jews "universalize the Holocaust, thus robbing the Jews of Auschwitz of their Jewish identity" [p. 85]. On the other hand, William Styron (1974), a Christian novelist, wrote, in reference to a symposium on Auschwitz held at the Cathedral of St. John the Divine in New York City:

> The holocaust is so incomprehensible and so awesomely central to our present-day consciousness—Jewish and gentile—that one almost physically shrinks with reticence from attempting to point out again what was barely touched upon in certain reports on the symposium: that at Auschwitz not only the Jews perished but at least one million souls who were not Jews [p. 37, cols. 3-4].

In considering Frankenheim's and Styron's views in the light of the *Oedipus* plays, one must conclude that where the impact of the Holocaust was felt because it was imposed, the model of *Oedipus the King* prevails. However, where people choose to listen to the Voice of Auschwitz, the model of *Oedipus at Colonus* prevails.

Appendix

Interview Schedule

How did you feel about coming here?
How old are you?
Any brothers or sisters? Ages?
Where were you born? Where did you grow up?

How old are your parents?
When did they come to this country? Where from?
What do they do for a living?

What kind of person is your mother? Your father?
Describe them, their general moods, interests,
   attitudes, likes, and dislikes? Have they
   changed much over the years?

How did they meet?
Describe their relationship with each other.
Relationship with friends, people they work with.
Relationship with extended family.

Can you tell me something about their socioeconomic status? Type of work, earnings,
   kind of community they live in, Americanization
   vs. European in America.

What is your relationship to your parents like?
What feelings and attitudes about you have you
   picked up? Have they changed as you've grown up?
Do you think they've had any expectations of you
   as you've been growing up? Now?
How do you think you've met these?
Were they satisfied?

While you were growing up, do you remember having
   talks with your parents? About what? Problems?

How often do you see them? Phone them?
Describe what goes on between you.
Describe a recent interaction.
Do they feel you see them enough? Do you?

Does any one thing they've told you stand
   out in your mind?
What about you are they most pleased with?
Most critical?

Which parent was in concentration camp? How long?
   What camps?
How much information would you say you had?
Do your parents ever talk about it: How do you feel then?
Do you ever ask? How do they respond?
When and how did you find out?

What was your parents' life like before the war?
Where were they from?
Family occupations? Economic status?

Do you know any specific experiences they had
   inside the camps?
Can you guess how it affected them, what they would
   be like today it they hadn't gone through it?

What did they do right after the war?
How did they happen to come to the U.S.A.?
Have you ever wanted to know more?

How do you think that your knowledge of what your
   parents' experiences were affects how you see,
   feel about them?
Affects how they react to you?

How does having been a child of a survivor
   affect who you are?

Conversation with friends, read books, gone to
   movies about the Holocaust?

As a child did you ever have any thought about
    camps or Nazis? Now?
Have you ever thought how you would have fared
    in a camp? Would you have survived?

What are your feelings about the camps as an
    event in history? Can you think of any events
    like them?
Could it happen again? To you? To Jews? To other groups?
What was the most destructive thing about the camps?
How were people able to survive?
How were survivors affected afterwards?

What were the people who perpetrated the crimes like?
What were their motives, what made them tick?
What about the Germans who later said they didn't know?
What might you have done in their place?
Do groups like church, refugee organizations do enough?
What do you think motivated the Nuremburg trials?
What's the first image of Nazis that comes to your mind?

Which of your parents do you most take after?
Did having been a survivor affect the way your parents see
    people, their view of the world?
Do you remember them ever attempting to teach you about the world?
How did you respond?
What impact do you think it had on the way you see things?

Do you ever think about the relatives your parents lost?
What thoughts cross your mind?
Are you named after anyone? Thoughts about it?
Would you tell your own children about your parents' experiences?

Earliest memory? Associations.
Did you ever have a favorite fairy tale? One your parents told?
Did you have daydreams, dreams, recurring dreams as a child? Now?
Ever have dreams or daydreams about Nazis?

Memories of going to kindergarten for first time?
Memories of first chum?
Memories of siblings, how do you get along with them?

Memories of first fight as a child?
What got you angry then? Now?
Ever at parents?
How do you typically express anger?

What was going to high school like? Were you happy?
    Have friends? Interests?
When was, what was it like, the first time you were away from home?

How did you choose college? Occupation?
Thoughts about marriage, starting family?

Do you have a steady boyfriend/girlfriend?
For how long? What's your relationship like?

Do you remember the first serious relationship you had with a boy/girl?
Describe. What was it like when you broke up?

Do you usually prefer being with a lot of people or a few people?
What kinds of people do you like? Dislike?
Think of someone important to you? How is that person important to you?
What's your relationship with that person like?
Do you tend to talk your problems over with friends? Parents? Anyone?
Do any characteristic issues, problems, conflicts come up between you
    and others—e.g., doing people favors and resenting it?

Would you ever consider psychoanalysis or psychotherapy?
What reasons?
Somatic complaints, headaches, depression, phobias?
Conflicts with others, major interpersonal difficulties?
Self-defeating behaviors?

Do you maintain Jewish traditions? Have you any Hebrew education?
Is family religious?
Do you believe in God? Kind of God? History of belief?

How interested are you in politics? Ever been involved in political
    affairs in school, community, attend demonstrations?
What issue in American political life is most important to you?
Feelings about blacks, minority groups?
Thoughts about atrocities that go on in other places in the world?

Thoughts about Arab-Israeli conflicts?
What do you think will happen to the state of Israel?
Thoughts during Six-Day War?
Thoughts about Arab raids? Israeli raids?

What kinds of things do you do with your spare time? Hobbies,
interests, education, group membership, participation in counterculture?

What do you think your life would have been like if brought up in
Europe? Have you ever thought about living in another country?

Catastrophe fantasies? Worst thing that could happen to you?
Who might you turn to for help?

Fantasies of the future? What will you be doing 10 years from now?
What factors will influence you?

What will the year 2000 be like?

What has this interview been like for you?

Bibliography

Aleksandrowiscz, D. "Children of Concentration Camp Survivors." *Yearbook of the International Association for Child Psychiatry and Allied Professions*, 1973, *2*, 385-94.

Barocas, H., and Barocas, C. "Manifestations of Concentration Camp Effects on the Second Generation." *American Journal of Psychiatry*, 1973, *130*, 820-21.

Bettleheim, B. "The Problem of Generations." In E. Erikson (Ed.), *The Challenge of Youth*. New York: Anchor, 1965.

Blos, P. "Report on Some Experiences in a Court Clinic." In: *Minutes of Discussion Group 7: Children of Social Catastrophe: Sequelae in Survivors and Children of Survivors*, at the December meeting of the American Psychoanalytic Association, New York, 1968. Cited by J. Kestenberg, "Psychoanalytic Contributions to the Problem of Children of Survivors of Nazi Persecution." *The Israel Annals of Psychiatry and Related Disciplines*, 1972, *10*, 311-25.

Devereaux, G. "Normal and Abnormal. The Key Concepts of Ethnopsychiatry." In W. Muensterberger (Ed.), *Man and His Culture*. New York: Taplinger, 1970.

Dimont, M. *The Indestructible Jews*. New York: Signet, 1971.

Eitinger, L. "A Follow-Up Study of the Norwegian Concentration Camp Survivor's Mortality and Morbidity." *The Israel Annals of Psychiatry and Related Disciplines*, 1973, *11*, 199-209.

Elon, A. *The Israelis: Founders and Sons*. New York: Bantam, 1972.

Erikson, E. *Childhood and Society*. New York: Norton, 1963.

———. *Insight and Responsibility: Lectures on the Ethical Implications of Psychoanalytic Insight*. New York: Norton, 1964.

———. "Youth: Fidelity and Diversity." In E. Erikson (Ed.), *The Challenge of Youth*. New York: Anchor, 1965.

———. *Gandhi's Truth: On the Origins of Militant Non-Violence*. New York, Norton, 1969.

———. "Autobiographical Notes on the Identity Crisis." *Daedalus*, 1970, *99*, 731-59.

Frankenheim, E. *History: Jewish Affirmations and Philosophical Reflections*. New York: New York University Press, 1970.

Freud, A. *Normality and Pathology in Childhood: Assessments of Development*. New York: International Universities Press, 1965.

Fromm, E. *Escape from Freedom*. New York: Avon, 1971.

Furman, E. "The Impact of Nazi Concentration Camps on the Children of Survivors." *Yearbook of the International Association for Child Psychiatry and Allied Professions*, 1973, *2*, 289-94.

Furst, S. (Ed.). *Psychic Trauma*. New York: Basic Books, 1967 (a).

———. "Psychic Trauma," A survey in S. Furst (Ed.), *Psychic Trauma*. New York: Basic Books, 1967 (b).

Grayzel, S. *A History of the Jews*. New York: Mentor, 1968.

Greenacre, P. "The Influence of Infantile Trauma on Genetic Patterns." In S. Furst (Ed.), *Psychic Trauma*. New York: Basic Books, 1967.

Handlin, O. *The Uprooted.* New York: Grosset & Dunlap, 1951.

Hoppe, K. "Re-Somatization of Affects in Survivors of Persecution." *International Journal of Psychoanalysis,* 1968, *49,* 324-26.

Jacobson, E. *The Self and Object World.* New York: International Universities Press, 1964.

Kazantzakis, N. *Report to Greco.* C. Bien (Trans.). New York: Bantam, 1968.

Keniston, K. *The Uncommitted: Alienated Youth in American Society.* New York: Delta, 1965.

_____. *Young Radicals: Notes on Committed Youth.* New York: Harvest, 1968.

Kestenberg, J. "Psychoanalytic contributions to the Problem of Children of Survivors from Nazi Persecution." *The Israel Annals of Psychiatry and Related Disciplines,* 1972, *10,* 311-25.

_____. "Introductory Remarks to Symposium: Children of the Holocaust." *Yearbook of the International Association for Child Psychiatry and Allied Professions,* 1973, *2,* 359-62.

Klein, H. "Families of Holocaust Survivors in the Kibbutz: Psychological Studies." *International Psychiatry Clinics,* 1971, *8,* 67-92.

_____. "Children of the Holocaust: Mourning and Bereavement." *International Yearbook of the Association for Child Psychiatry and Allied Professions,* 1973, *2,* 393-410.

Kogon, E. *The Theory and Practice of Hell.* H. Norden (Trans.) New York: Berkeley, 1971.

Kris, E. "Notes on the Development and on Some Current Problems in Psychoanalytic Child Psychology." *The Psychoanalytic Study of the Child,* 1950, *5,* 24-46.

Krystal, H. (Ed.) *Massive Psychic Trauma.* New York: International Universities Press, 1968.

_____. "Trauma: Considerations of Its Intensity and Chronicity." *International Psychiatry Clinics,* 1971, *8,* 11-27.

Laufer, M. "The Analysis of a Child of a Survivor." *Yearbook of the International Association for Child Psychiatry and Allied Professions,* 1973, *2,* 363-74.

Liebert, R. *Radical and Militant Youth.* New York: Praeger, 1971.

_____. Review of R. Lifton, *Home from the War. Journal of the American Academy of Psychoanalysis,* 1974, *2,* 171-73.

Lifton, R. *Death in Life: Survivors of Hiroshima.* New York: Vintage, 1969.

_____. "On Psychohistory." *Partisan Review,* Spring 1970, 11-32.

_____. *History and Human Survival: Essays on the Young and Old, Survivors and the Dead, Peace and War, and on Contemporary Psychohistory.* New York: Vintage, 1971.

_____. *Home from the War: Vietnam Veterans: Neither Victims nor Executioners.* New York: Simon and Schuster, 1973.

Lipkowitz, M. "The Child of Two Survivors: A Report of an Unsuccessful Therapy." *The Israel Annals of Psychiatry and Related Disciplines,* 1973, *11,* 141-55.

Luchterhand, E. "Sociological Approaches to Massive Stress in Natural and Man-Made Disasters." *International Psychiatry Clinics,* 1971, *8,* 29-52.

Mead, M. "Culture Change and Character Structure." In M. Stein, A. Vidich, & D. White (Eds.), *Identity and Anxiety.* New York: The Free Press, 1966.

_____. *Culture and Commitment: A Study of the Generation Gap.* Garden City, N.Y.: Doubleday, 1970.

Miller, A. *After the Fall.* New York: Bantam, 1968.

Niederland, W. "Introductory Notes on the Concept, Definition and Range of Psychic Trauma." *International Psychiatry Clinics,* 1971, *8,* 1-9.

Nyiszli, M. *Auschwitz: A Doctor's Eyewitness Account.* T. Kremer & R. Seaver (Trans.). New York: Fawcett, 1960.

Poll, S. *The Hasidic Community of Williamsburg: A Study in the Sociology of Religion.* New York: Schocken, 1969.

Proust, M. *The Past Recaptured.* F. Blossom (Trans.). New York: The Modern Library, 1959.

Rakoff, V., Sigal, J., & Epstein, N. "Children and Families of Concentration Camp Survivors." *Canada's Mental Health,* 1966, *14,* 24-26.

Rangel, L. "The Metapsychology of Psychic Trauma." In S. Furst (Ed.), *Psychic Trauma*. New York: Basic Books, 1967.

Rosenberger, L. "Children of Survivors." *Yearbook of the International Association for Child Psychiatry and Allied Professions*, 1973, *2*, 375-78.

Rustin, S. "Guilt, Hostility, and Jewish Identification among a Self-Selected Sample of Late-Adolescent Children of Jewish Concentration Camp Survivors." Unpublished doctoral dissertation, New York University, 1971.

————, & Lipsig, F. "Psychotherapy with Adolescent Children of Concentration Camp Survivors." *Journal of Contemporary Psychotherapy*, 1972, *4*, 87-94.

Sandler, J. "Trauma, Strain and Development." In S. Furst (Ed.), *Psychic Trauma*. New York: Basic Books, 1967.

Sigal, J. "Second Generation Effects of Massive Trauma." *International Psychiatry Clinics*, 1971, *8*, 55-65.

————. "Hypotheses and Methodology in the Study of Families of Holocaust Survivors." *Yearbook of the International Association for Child Psychiatry and Allied Professions*, 1973, *2*, 411-16.

————, and Rakoff, V. "Concentration Camp Survival: A Pilot Study of Effects on the Second Generation." *Canadian Psychiatric Association Journal*, 1971, *16*, 393-97.

————, Silver, D., Rakoff, V., & Ellin, B. "Some Second Generation Effects of Survival of the Nazi Persecution." *American Journal of Orthopsychiatry*, 1973, *43*, 320-27.

Singer, I.J. *The Family Carnowski*. J. Singer (Trans.). New York: Harrow, 1973.

Sonnenberg, S. "Workshop Report: Children of Survivors." Joint Workshop of the American Psychoanalytic Association and The Association for Child Psychoanalysis held at the fall meeting of the American Psychoanalytic Association, 1971. *Journal of the American Psychoanalytic Association*, 1974, *22*, 200-204.

Sophocles. *Oedipus at Colonus*. In D. Greene & R. Lattimore (Eds.), *Greek Tragedies*, Vol. 3. Chicago: University of Chicago Press, 1964.

Spiegel, J. *Transactions: The Interplay between Individual, Family and Society*. J. Papajohn (Ed.). New York: Science House, 1971.

Styron, W. "Auschwitz's Message." *The New York Times*, June 25, 1974, p. 37, cols. 3-4.

Trossman, B. "Adolescent Children of Concentration Camp Survivors." *Canadian Psychiatric Association Journal*, 1968, *13*, 121-23.

Tuteur, W. "One Hundred Concentration Camp Survivors Twenty Years Later." *The Israel Annals of Psychiatry and Related Disciplines*, 1966, *4*, 78-90.

Waelder, R. "Trauma and the Variety of Extraordinary Challenges." In S. Furst (Ed.), *Psychic Trauma*. New York: Basic Books, 1967.

Wiesel, E. *Souls on Fire: Portraits and Legends of the Hasidic Masters*. New York: Vintage, 1973.

Williams, M. Discussion of M. Laufer, "The Analysis of a Child of a Survivor." *Yearbook of International Association for Child Psychiatry and Allied Professions*, 1973, *2*, 367-71.

Winnik, H. "Contribution to Psychic Traumatization through Social Catastrophe." *International Journal of Psychoanalysis*, 1968, *49*, 298-301.

Wolferstein, M. *Disaster: A Psychological Essay*. Glencoe, Ill.: The Free Press, 1957.

Y Gasset, O. *What is Philosophy?* New York: Norton, 1960.

Zborowski, M., & Herzog, E. *Life is with People: The Culture of the Shtetl*. New York: Schocken, 1972.

Index

Also of interest from Other Press . . .

OTHER